intel

U.S. and CANADA LITERATURE ORDER FORM

NAME: ______________________________

COMPANY: ______________________________

ADDRESS: ______________________________

CITY: ______________________ STATE: __________ ZIP: __________

COUNTRY: ______________________________

PHONE NO.: (   ) ______________________________

ORDER NO.	TITLE	QTY.	PRICE	TOTAL
		____ ×	____ =	____
		____ ×	____ =	____
		____ ×	____ =	____
		____ ×	____ =	____
		____ ×	____ =	____
		____ ×	____ =	____
		____ ×	____ =	____
		____ ×	____ =	____
		____ ×	____ =	____
		____ ×	____ =	____

AF697248

Subtotal ____________

Must Add Your Local Sales Tax ____________

Postage: add 10% of subtotal → Postage ____________

Total ____________

Pay by check, money order, or include company purchase order with this form ($100 minimum). We also accept VISA, MasterCard or American Express. Make payment to Intel Literature Sales. Allow 2-4 weeks for delivery.

☐ VISA ☐ MasterCard ☐ American Express Expiration Date ____________

Account No. ______________________________

Signature ______________________________

Mail To: Intel Literature Sales
P.O. Box 7641
Mt. Prospect, Il 60056-7641

International Customers outside the U.S. and Canada should use the International order form or contact their local Sales Office or Distributor.

For phone orders in the U.S. and Canada
Call Toll Free: (800) 548-4725

Prices good until 12/31/90.

Source HB

intel

INTERNATIONAL LITERATURE ORDER FORM

NAME: ______________________________

COMPANY: ______________________________

ADDRESS: ______________________________

CITY: ______________________ STATE: __________ ZIP: __________

COUNTRY: ______________________________

PHONE NO.: (   ) ______________________

ORDER NO.	TITLE	QTY.	PRICE	TOTAL
		____ ×	____ =	____
		____ ×	____ =	____
		____ ×	____ =	____
		____ ×	____ =	____
		____ ×	____ =	____
		____ ×	____ =	____
		____ ×	____ =	____
		____ ×	____ =	____
		____ ×	____ =	____
		____ ×	____ =	____

Subtotal ________

Must Add Your Local Sales Tax ________

Total ________

PAYMENT

Cheques should be made payable to your local Intel Sales Office (see inside back cover.)

Other forms of payment may be available in your country. Please contact the Literature Coordinator at your local Intel Sales Office for details.

The completed form should be marked to the attention of the LITERATURE COORDINATOR and returned to your local Intel Sales Office.

CG/LOF2/100188

intel®

80186/188, 80C186/C188 HARDWARE REFERENCE MANUAL

1990

Intel Corporation makes no warranty for the use of its products and assumes no responsibility for any errors which may appear in this document nor does it make a commitment to update the information contained herein.

Intel retains the right to make changes to these specifications at any time, without notice.

Contact your local sales office to obtain the latest specifications before placing your order.

The following are trademarks of Intel Corporation and may only be used to identify Intel products:

376, 386, 387, 486, 4-SITE, Above, ACE51, ACE96, ACE186, ACE196, ACE960, BITBUS, COMMputer, CREDIT, Data Pipeline, DVI, ETOX, FaxBACK, Genius, i, $\overset{\Delta}{\imath}$, i486, i750, i860, ICE, iCEL, ICEVIEW, iCS, iDBP, iDIS, I²ICE, iLBX, iMDDX, iMMX, Inboard, Insite, Intel, int$_e$l, Intel386, int$_e$lBOS, Intel Certified, Intelevision, int$_e$ligent Identifier, int$_e$ligent Programming, Intellec, Intellink, iOSP, iPAT, iPDS, iPSC, iRMK, iRMX, iSBC, iSBX, iSDM, iSXM, Library Manager, MAPNET, MCS, Megachassis, MICROMAINFRAME, MULTIBUS, MULTICHANNEL, MULTIMODULE, MultiSERVER, ONCE, OpenNET, OTP, PRO750, PROMPT, Promware, QUEST, QueX, Quick-Erase, Quick-Pulse Programming, Ripplemode, RMX/80, RUPI, Seamless, SLD, SugarCube, ToolTALK, UPI, Visual Edge, VLSiCEL, and ZapCode, and the combination of ICE, iCS, iRMX, iSBC, iSBX, iSXM, MCS, or UPI and a numerical suffix.

MDS is an ordering code only and is not used as a product name or trademark. MDS® is a registered trademark of Mohawk Data Sciences Corporation.

MULTIBUS is a patented Intel bus.

CHMOS and HMOS are patented processes of Intel Corp.

Intel Corporation and Intel's FASTPATH are not affiliated with Kinetics, a division of Excelan, Inc. or its FASTPATH trademark or products.

Additional copies of this manual or other Intel literature may be obtained from:

Intel Corporation
Literature Sales
P.O. Box 7641
Mt. Prospect, IL 60056-7641

CG-101789

intel®

CUSTOMER SUPPORT

INTEL'S COMPLETE SUPPORT SOLUTION WORLDWIDE

Customer Support is Intel's complete support service that provides Intel customers with hardware support, software support, customer training, consulting services and network management services. For detailed information contact your local sales offices.

After a customer purchases any system hardware or software product, service and support become major factors in determining whether that product will continue to meet a customer's expectations. Such support requires an international support organization and a breadth of programs to meet a variety of customer needs. As you might expect, Intel's customer support is quite extensive. It can start with assistance during your development effort to network management. 100 Intel sales and service offices are located worldwide—in the U.S., Canada, Europe and the Far East. So wherever you're using Intel technology, our professional staff is within close reach.

HARDWARE SUPPORT SERVICES

Intel's hardware maintenance service, starting with complete on-site installation will boost your productivity from the start and keep you running at maximum efficiency. Support for system or board level products can be tailored to match your needs, from complete on-site repair and maintenance support to economical carry-in or mail-in factory service.

Intel can provide support service for not only Intel systems and emulators, but also support for equipment in your development lab or provide service on your product to your end-user/customer.

SOFTWARE SUPPORT SERVICES

Software products are supported by our Technical Information Service (TIPS) that has a special toll free number to provide you with direct, ready information on known, documented problems and deficiencies, as well as work-arounds, patches and other solutions.

Intel's software support consists of two levels of contracts. Standard support includes TIPS (Technical Information Phone Service), updates and subscription service (product-specific troubleshooting guides and; *COMMENTS Magazine*). Basic support consists of updates and the subscription service. Contracts are sold in environments which represent product groupings (e.g., iRMX® environment).

CONSULTING SERVICES

Intel provides field system engineering consulting services for any phase of your development or application effort. You can use our system engineers in a variety of ways ranging from assistance in using a new product, developing an application, personalizing training and customizing an Intel product to providing technical and management consulting. Systems Engineers are well versed in technical areas such as microcommunications, real-time applications, embedded microcontrollers, and network services. You know your application needs; we know our products. Working together we can help you get a successful product to market in the least possible time.

CUSTOMER TRAINING

Intel offers a wide range of instructional programs covering various aspects of system design and implementation. In just three to ten days a limited number of individuals learn more in a single workshop than in weeks of self-study. For optimum convenience, workshops are scheduled regularly at Training Centers worldwide or we can take our workshops to you for on-site instruction. Covering a wide variety of topics, Intel's major course categories include: architecture and assembly language, programming and operating systems, BITBUS™ and LAN applications.

NETWORK MANAGEMENT SERVICES

Today's networking products are powerful and extremely flexible. The return they can provide on your investment via increased productivity and reduced costs can be very substantial.

Intel offers complete network support, from definition of your network's physical and functional design, to implementation, installation and maintenance. Whether installing your first network or adding to an existing one, Intel's Networking Specialists can optimize network performance for you.

CG/CUSTSUPP/100389

Table of Contents

Table of Contents (continued)

Table of Contents (continued)

Table of Contents (continued)

Introduction 1

CHAPTER 1
INTRODUCTION

The 80186 microprocessor family holds the position of industry standard among high integration microprocessors. VLSI technology incorporates the most commonly used peripheral functions with a 16-bit CPU on the same silicon die to assure compatibility and high reliability. The 80186 family reputation for flexibility and uncomplicated programming makes it the first choice embedded microprocessor for such applications as local area network equipment, PC add-on cards, terminals, disk storage subsystems, avionics, and medical instrumentation. Figure 1 is a block diagram of the 80186 processor.

1.1 THE 80186 PRODUCT FAMILY

The 80186 family actually consists of four devices: the original 80186 and 80188, and the newer 80C186 and 80C188 microprocessors manufactured on Intel's CHMOS III process. The 80188 and 80C188 are 16-bit microprocessors but have 8-bit external data buses. The 80C186 and 80C188 offer the advantage of increased speed (up to 16 MHz) and important new features including a Refresh Control Unit, Power-Save logic, and ONCE™ Mode (see Figure 2).

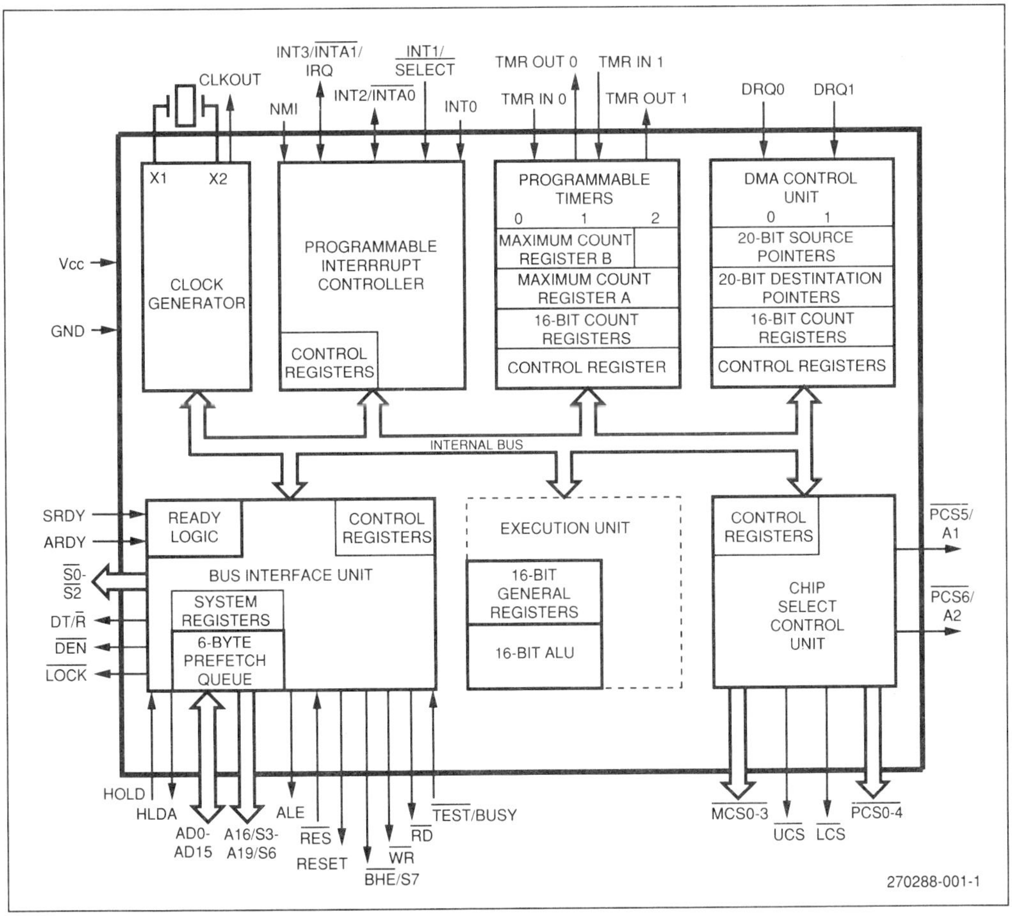

Figure 1. 80186 Block Diagram

All family members employ a 20-bit address bus for a one megabyte memory address space and a 64 kilobyte I/O address space. All processors use the same instruction format. Software written for one CPU will execute on the other CPUs without alteration (with the possible exception of floating-point code).

For simplicity, this Hardware Reference uses phrases like "80186 family processor" to refer to features and functions shared commonly by the 80186, 80188, 80C186, and 80C188. This manual refers to specific member or members of the product family directly by product number.

1.2 HOW TO USE THE HARDWARE REFERENCE

The purpose of this Hardware Reference is to explain the operation of 80186 family processors with a degree of detail not possible in the data sheet. The emphasis is on the integrated peripheral set, since that is the essence of the 80186 family. The designer with questions about the function of a particular peripheral is encouraged to turn directly to the specific sections suggested by the table of contents.

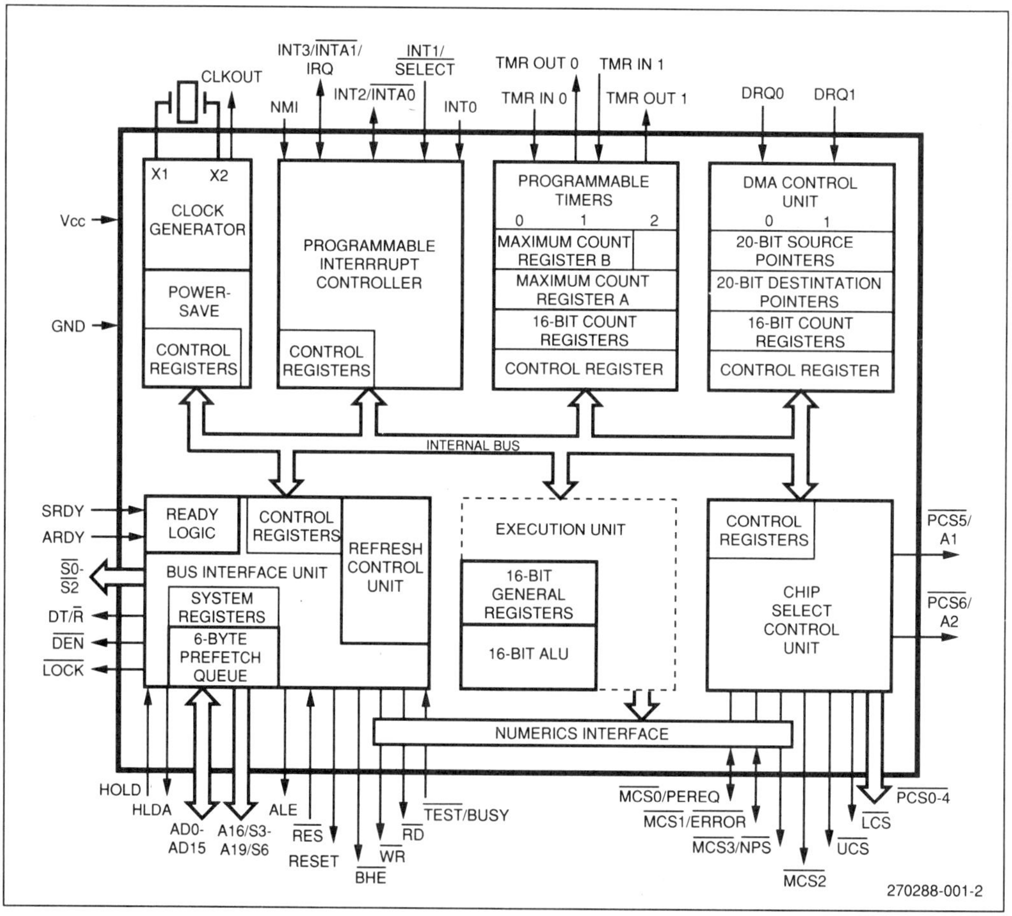

Figure 2. 80C186 Block Diagram

Overview of the 80186 Family 2

CHAPTER 2
OVERVIEW OF THE 80186 FAMILY

The 80186 processor shares a common base architecture with the 8086, 8088, 80286, 386TM, and 486TM processors. It is completely object code compatible with the well-known 8086/8088. However, most instructions require fewer clocks to execute on the 80186 family because of hardware enhancements in the Bus Interface Unit and the Execution Unit. In addition, there are a number of additional instructions which simplify programming and reduce code size (see Appendix A.7).

The 80186 family operates virtually the same as the 8086. The added benefits of the 80186 family are the on-chip DMA, Timer, Interrupt Control, Chip Select, and READY Generation Units. This concept of **high integration** greatly simplifies system design.

The 80186 family operates from a single +5 V supply. It is available in several standard package configurations. For a given product, the pinout is identical among any of the available 68-pin packages: Pin Grid Array (PGA), Leadless Chip Carrier (LCC), and Plastic Leaded Chip Carrier (PLCC). This means that sockets for any of the three package types may be mounted on a printed circuit board drilled with the same 68-pin pattern.

2.1 ARCHITECTURAL OVERVIEW

An 80186 family processor incorporates two separate processing units: an Execution Unit (EU) and a Bus Interface Unit (BIU). The EU is functionally identical among all family members. In the 80186/80C186 the BIU is configured for a 16-bit external data bus and in the 80188/80C188 the BIU is configured for an 8-bit external data bus. The two units are connected by an instruction prefetch queue.

The EU executes instructions and the BIU fetches instructions, reads operands, and writes results. Whenever the EU requires another opcode byte, it takes the byte out of the prefetch

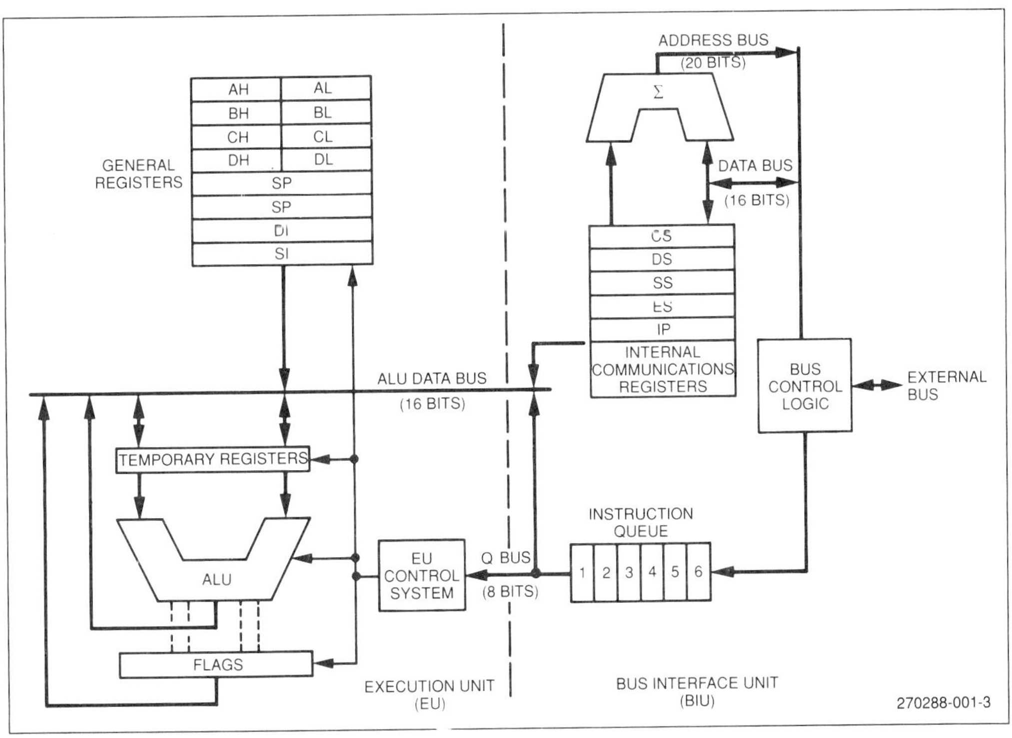

Figure 3. Simplied Functional Bock Diagram of 80186 Family CPU

queue. The two units can operate independently of one another and are able, under most circumstances, to extensively overlap instruction fetches and execution.

An 80186 family processor has a 16-bit Arithmetic Logic Unit (ALU) which performs 8-bit or 16-bit arithmetic and logical operations. It provides for data movement among registers, memory and I/O space. In addition, the CPU allows for high speed data transfer from one area of memory to another using string move instructions, and to or from an I/O port and memory using block I/O instructions. Finally, the CPU provides many conditional branch and control instructions.

This architecture features 14 basic registers which are grouped as general registers, segment registers, pointer registers, and status and control registers. The four 16-bit general purpose registers (AX, BX, CX, and DX) may be used as operands in most arithmetic operations in either 8- or 16-bit units. The four 16-bit pointer registers (SI, DI, BP, and SP) may be used both in arithmetic operations and in accessing memory-based variables. Four 16-bit segment registers (CS, DS, SS, and ES) allow simple memory partitioning to aid modular programming. The status and control registers consist of an instruction pointer (IP) and a status word register containing flag bits.

Figure 3 is a simplified CPU block diagram.

2.1.1 EXECUTION UNIT

The EU is responsible for the execution of all instructions, for providing data and addresses to the BIU, and for manipulating the general registers and the flag register. A 16-bit Arithmetic Logic Unit (ALU) in the EU maintains the CPU status and control flags, and manipulates the general registers and instruction operands. All registers and data paths in the EU are 16 bits wide for fast internal transfers.

The EU does not connect directly to the system bus. It obtains instructions from a queue maintained by the BIU. Likewise, when an instruction requires access to memory or to a peripheral device, the EU requests the BIU to obtain and store the data. All addresses manipulated by the EU are 16 bits wide. The BIU, however, performs an address calculation that gives the EU access to the full megabyte of memory space.

When the EU is ready to execute an instruction, it fetches the instruction object code byte from the BIU's instruction queue and then executes the instruction. If the queue is empty when the EU is ready to fetch an instruction byte, the EU waits for the instruction byte to be fetched. If a memory location or I/O port must be addressed during the execution of an instruction, the EU requests the BIU to perform the required bus cycle.

2.1.2 BUS INTERFACE UNIT

The 80186/80C186 and 80188/80C188 BIUs are functionally identical, but are implemented differently to match the structure and performance characteristics of their respective system buses. Data is transferred between the CPU and memory or peripheral devices upon demand from the EU. The BIU executes all external bus cycles. This unit consists of the segment registers, the instruction pointer, the instruction code queue, and several miscellaneous registers. The BIU transfers data to and from the EU on the ALU data bus.

The BIU generates 20-bit physical addresses in a dedicated adder. The adder shifts a 16-bit segment value left 4 bits and then adds an offset value derived from combinations of the pointer registers, the instruction pointer, and immediate values (see Figure 4). Any carry of this addition is ignored.

During periods when the EU is busy executing instructions, the BIU "looks ahead" and prefetches more instructions from

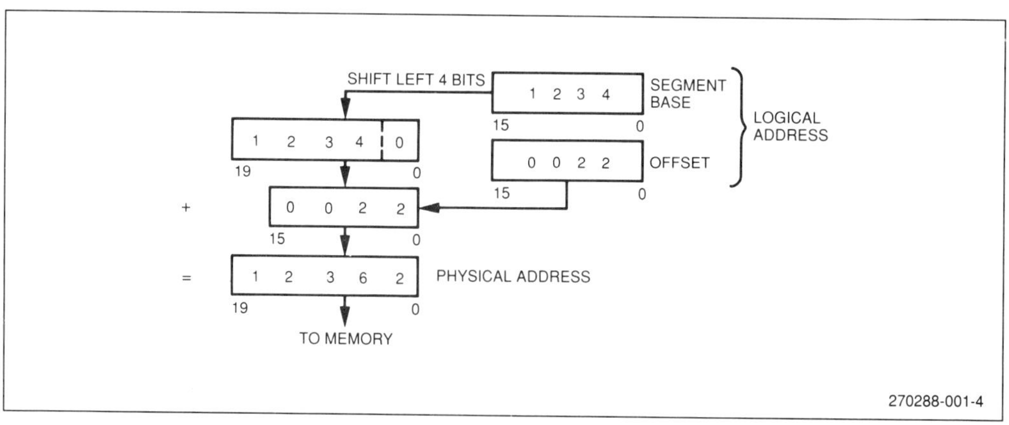

Figure 4. Physical Address Generation

memory. As long as the prefetch queue is partially full, the EU can quickly retrieve instructions upon demand.

2.1.3 GENERAL REGISTERS

80186 family CPUs have eight 16-bit general registers (see Figure 5). The general registers are subdivided into two sets of four registers each. These are the data registers (also called the H & L group for high and low), and the pointer and index registers (also called the P & I group).

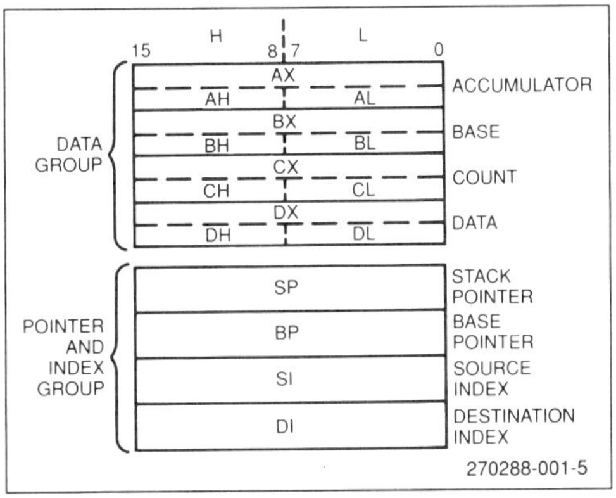

Figure 5. General Registers

The data registers are unique in that their upper and lower halves are separately addressable. This means that each data register can be used interchangeably as a 16-bit register or as two 8-bit registers. The other CPU registers are always accessed as 16-bit only. The CPU can use data registers without constraint in most arithmetic and logic operations. Most arithmetic and logic operations can also use the pointer and index registers. Additionally, some instructions use certain registers implicitly (see Table 1), therefore allowing compact yet powerful encoding.

Table 1. Implicit Use of General Registers

REGISTER	OPERATIONS
AX	Word Multiply, Word Divide, Word I/O
AL	Byte Multiply, Byte Divide, Byte I/O, Translate, Decimal Arithmetic
AH	Byte Multiply, Byte Divide
BX	Translate
CX	String Operations, Loops
CL	Variable Shift and Rotate
DX	Word Multiply, Word Divide, Indirect I/O
SP	Stack Operations
SI	String Operations
DI	String Operations

The state of any of the general registers is undefined at RESET.

2.1.4 SEGMENT REGISTERS

The 80186 family memory space (up to one megabyte) is divided into logical segments of up to 64 Kbytes each. The CPU has direct access to four segments at a time. The base addresses (starting locations) of these memory segments are contained in the segment registers (see Figure 6). The CS register points to the current code segment. Instructions are fetched from the CS segment. The SS register points to the current stack segment. Stack operations are performed on locations in the SS segment. The DS register points to the current data segment. The data segment generally contains program variables. The ES register points to the current extra segment, which also is typically used for data storage. The segment registers are accessible to programs and can be manipulated with several instructions.

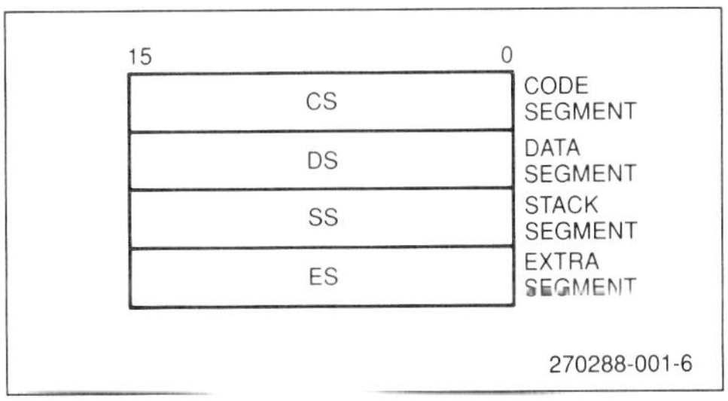

Figure 6. Segment Registers

Upon RESET, the CS register is initialized to 0FFFFH, and the DS, ES, and SS register are all initialized to zero.

2.1.5 INSTRUCTION POINTER

The BIU updates a 16-bit instruction pointer (IP) register so that it contains the offset (distance in bytes) of the next instruction from the beginning of the current code segment. In other words, the IP register points to the next instruction. During normal execution, the instruction pointer contains the offset of the next instruction to be **fetched** by the BIU. Whenever the IP register is saved on the stack, however, it is first automatically adjusted to point to the next instruction to be **executed**. Programs do not have direct access to the instruction pointer, but it may change, be saved, or be restored as a result of program execution.

RESET initializes the instruction pointer to 0000H. The concatenation of CS and IP values comprises a starting execution address of 0FFFF0H (see Section 2.1.8 for a description of address formation).

2.1.6 FLAGS

An 80186 family processor has six one-bit status flags (see Figure 7) that the EU posts as the result of an arithmetic or logic operation. Program branch instructions allow a program to alter its execution depending on conditions flagged by prior operation. Different instructions affect the status flags differently, generally reflecting the following states:

- If the auxiliary flag (AF) is set, there has been a carry out from the low nibble into the high nibble or a borrow from the high nibble into the low nibble of an 8-bit quantity (low-order byte of a 16-bit quantity). This flag is used by decimal arithmetic instructions.

- If the carry flag (CF) is set, there has been a carry out of, or a borrow into, the high-order bit of the instruction result (8- or 16-bit). The flag is used by instructions that add and subtract multibyte numbers. Rotate instructions can also isolate a bit in memory or a register by placing it in the carry flag.

- If the overflow flag (OF) is set, an arithmetic overflow has occurred; that is, a significant digit has been lost because the size of the result exceeded the capacity of its destination location. An Interrupt On Overflow instruction is available that will generate an interrupt in this situation.

- If the sign flag (SF) is set, the high-order bit of the result is a 1. Since negative binary numbers are represented in standard two's complement notation, SF indicates the sign of the result (0 = positive, 1 = negative).

- If the parity flag (PF) is set, the result has even parity, an even number of 1-bits. This flag can be used to check for data transmission errors.

- If the zero flag (ZF) is set, the result of the operation is 0.

The additional control flags (see Figure 7) can be set and cleared by programs to alter processor operations:

- Setting the direction flag (DF) causes string instructions to auto-decrement; that is, to process strings from the high address to the low address, or "right to left". Clearing DF causes string instructions to auto-increment, or process strings "left to right."

- Setting the interrupt-enable flag (IF) allows the CPU to recognize maskable external or internal interrupt requests. Clearing IF disables these interrupts. The interrupt-enable flag has no effect upon software interrupts or non-maskable externally generated interrupts.

- Setting the trap flag (TF) puts the processor into single-step mode for debugging. In this mode, the CPU automati-

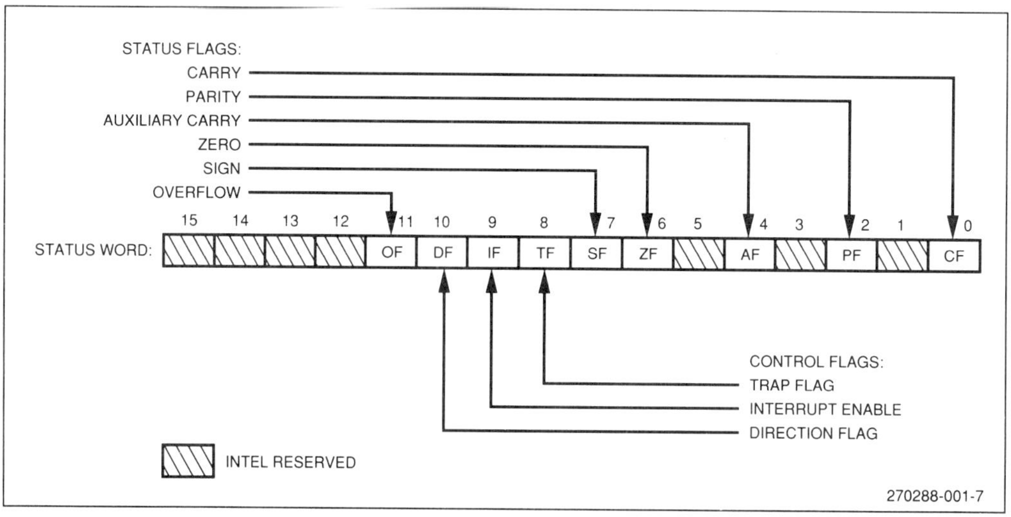

Figure 7. Status Word Format

cally generates an internal interrupt after each instruction, allowing a program to be inspected as it executes instruction by instruction.

Both the status and control flags are contained in a 16-bit status word (see Figure 7). The RESET condition of the status word is 0F000H.

2.1.7 MEMORY SEGMENTATION

Programs for the 80186 family view the one megabyte memory space as a group of segments that are user-defined according to application. A segment is a logical unit of memory that may be up to 64 Kbytes long. Each segment if made up of contiguous memory locations and is an independent, separately-addressable unit. Software assigns every segment a base address (starting location) in memory space. All segments begin on 16-bit memory boundaries. There are no other restrictions on segment locations. Segments may be adjacent, disjoint, partially overlapped, or fully overlapped (see Figure 8). A physical memory location may be mapped into (covered by) one or more logical segments.

The four segment registers point to four "currently addressable" segments (see Figure 9). The currently addressable segments provide a work space consisting of 64 Kbytes for code, a 64K stack, and 128K of data storage. Programs obtain access to code and data in other segments by changing the segment registers to point to the desired segments.

The segmented memory structure of the 80186 family is a hardware provision to encourage modular programming. Every program will use segmentation differently. Smaller applications tend to initialize the segment registers and then simply forget them. Larger applications give careful consideration to segment definition and use.

2.1.8 LOGICAL ADDRESSES

It is useful to think of every memory location as having two kinds of addresses, physical and logical. A physical address is a 20-bit value that identifies each unique byte location in the memory space. Physical addresses range from 0H to FFFFFH. All exchanges between the CPU and memory components use a physical address.

Programs deal with logical, rather than physical addresses. Program code can be developed without prior knowledge of where the code is to be located in memory; in larger applications, dynamic management of memory resources is a necessity. A logical address consists of a segment base value and an offset value. For any given memory location, the segment base value locates the first byte of the segment and the offset value is the distance, in bytes, of the target location from the beginning of the segment. Segment base and offset values are unsigned 16-bit quantities. Many different logical addresses can map to the same physical location. In the example (see Figure 10), physical memory location 2C3H is contained in two different overlapping segments, one beginning at 2B0H and the other at 2C0H.

If left alone, the processor automatically assigns segments based on the specific addressing needs of the program. The segment register to be selected is automatically chosen according to the rules in Table 2. All information in one segment type generally shares the same logical attributes (e.g., code or data), leading to programs which are shorter, faster, and better structured.

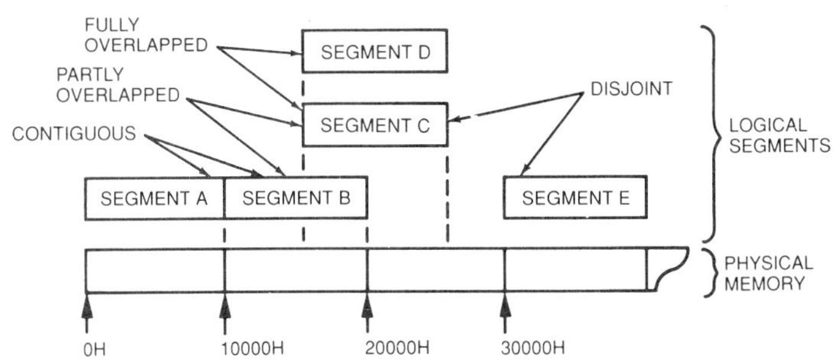

Figure 8. Segment Locations in Physical Memory

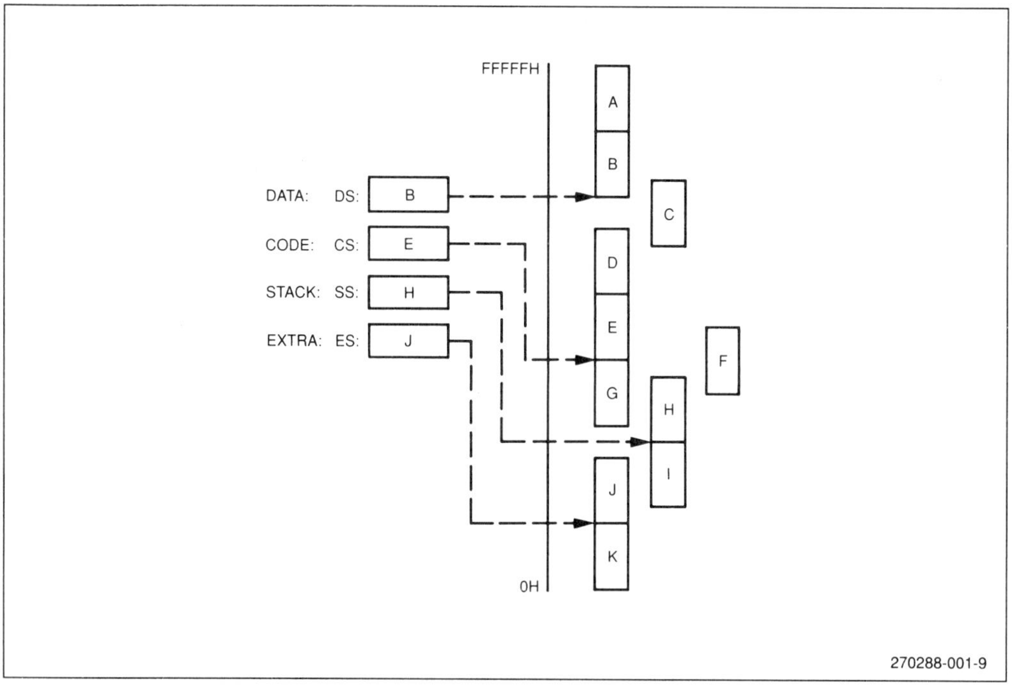

Figure 9. Currrently Addressable Segments

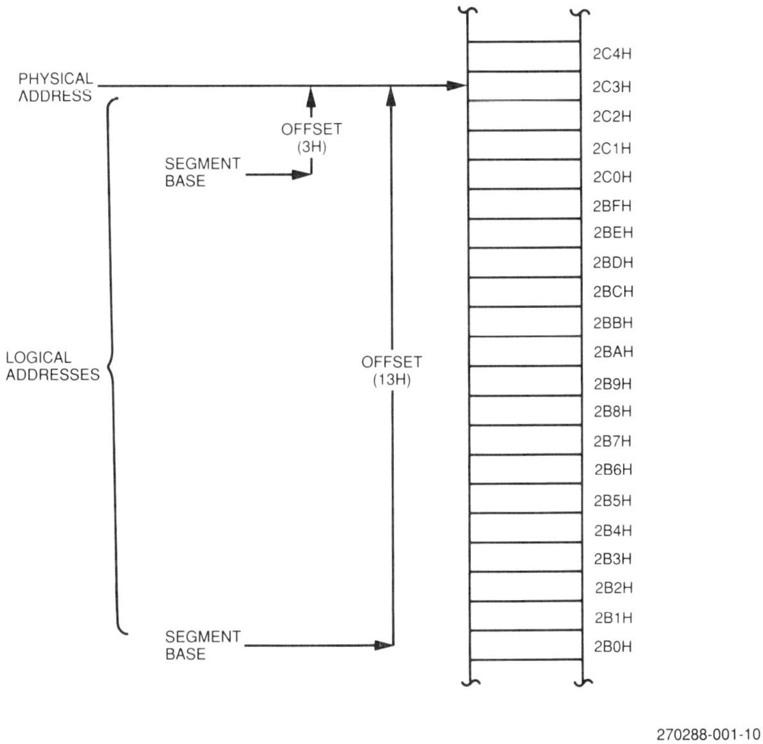

Figure 10. Logical and Physical Address

To generate a physical address, the BIU must first obtain the logical address. The logical address of a memory location can come from different sources, depending on the type of reference that is being made (see Table 2).

Segment base addresses are always held in the segment registers. The BIU conveniently assumes which segment register contains the base address according to the type of memory reference made. However, it is possible for a programmer to explicitly direct the BIU to access a variable in any of the currently addressable segments (except for the destination operand of a string instruction). In assembly language, this is done by preceding an instruction with a segment override prefix.

Table 2. Logical Address Sources

TYPE OF MEMORY REFERENCE	DEFAULT SEGMENT BASE	ALTERNATE SEGMENT BASE	OFFSET
Instruction Fetch	CS	NONE	IP
Stack Operation	SS	NONE	SP
Variable (except following)	DS	CS, ES, SS	Effective Address
String Source	DS	CS, ES, SS	SI
String Destination	ES	NONE	DI
BP Used As Base Register	SS	CS, DS, ES	Effective Address

Instructions are always fetched from the current code segment; the IP register contains the offset of the target instruction from the beginning of the segment. Stack instructions always operate on the current stack segment; the SP (stack pointer) register contains the offset of the top of the stack. Most variables (memory operands) are assumed to reside in the current data segment, but a program can instruct the BIU to override this assumption. Often, the offset of a memory variable is not directly available and must be calculated at execution time. This calculation is based on the addressing mode (see Section 2.2.2) specified in the instruction; the result is called the operand's effective address (EA).

Strings are addressed differently than other variables. The source operand of a string instruction is assumed to lie in the current data segment, but the program may use another currently addressable segment. The operand's offset is taken from the SI (source index) register. The destination operand of a string instruction always resides in the current extra segment; its offset is taken from the DI (destination index) register. The string instructions automatically adjust the SI and DI registers as they process the strings one byte or word at a time.

When register BP, the base pointer register, is designated as a base register in an instruction, the variable is assumed to reside in the current stack segment. Therefore, register BP provides a convenient way to address data on the stack. However, the BP register can also be used to access data in any of the other currently addressable segments.

2.1.9 DYNAMICALLY RELOCATABLE CODE

The segmented memory structure of the 80186 family makes it possible to write programs that are position-independent, or dynamically relocatable. Dynamic relocation allows a multiprogramming or multitasking system to make particularly

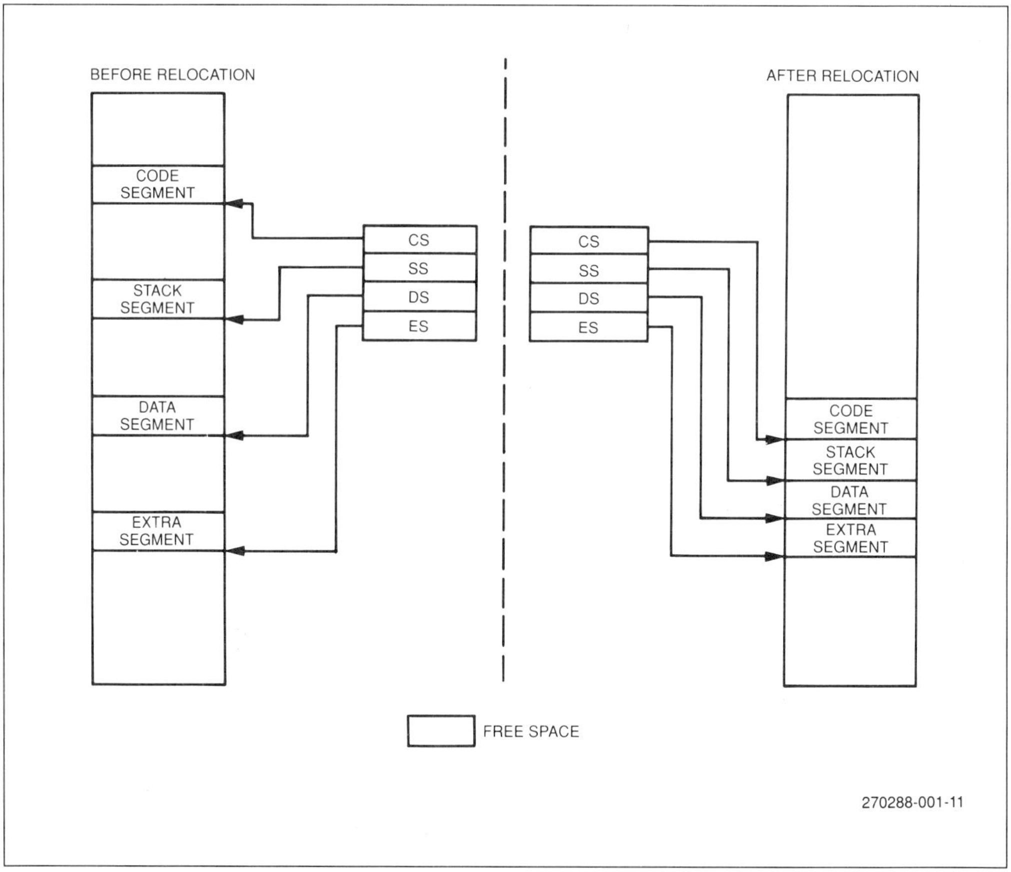

Figure 11. Dynamic Code Relocation

effective use of available memory. The processor can write inactive programs to a disk and reallocate the space they occupied to other programs. If a disk-resident program is needed later, it can be read back into any available memory location and restarted. Similarly, if a program needs a large contiguous block of storage, and the total amount is only available in non-adjacent fragments, other program segments can be compacted to free up a continuous space. This process is illustrated graphically in Figure 11.

To be dynamically relocatable, a program must not load or alter its segment registers and must not transfer directly to a location outside the current code segment. In other words, all offsets in the program must be relative to fixed values contained in the segment registers. This allows the program to be moved anywhere in memory as long as the segment registers are updated to point to the new base addresses.

2.1.10 STACK IMPLEMENTATION

Stacks in the 80186 family are implemented in memory and are located by the stack segment register (SS) and the stack pointer (SP). A system may have numerous stacks, and a stack may be up to 64 Kbytes long, the maximum length of a segment. An attempt to grow a stack beyond 64K overwrites the beginning of the segment. Only one stack is directly addressable at a time. The SS register contains the base address of the current stack; however, the base address is not the origination point of the stack. The SP register contains an offset which points to the top of stack (TOS).

Stacks are 16 bits wide; instructions that operate on a stack add and remove stack elements one word at a time. An element is pushed onto the stack (see Figure 12) by first **decrementing** the SP register by 2 and then writing the data word. An element is popped off the stack by copying it from TOS and then **incrementing** the SP register by 2. In other words, the stack goes **down** in memory toward its base address. Stack operations

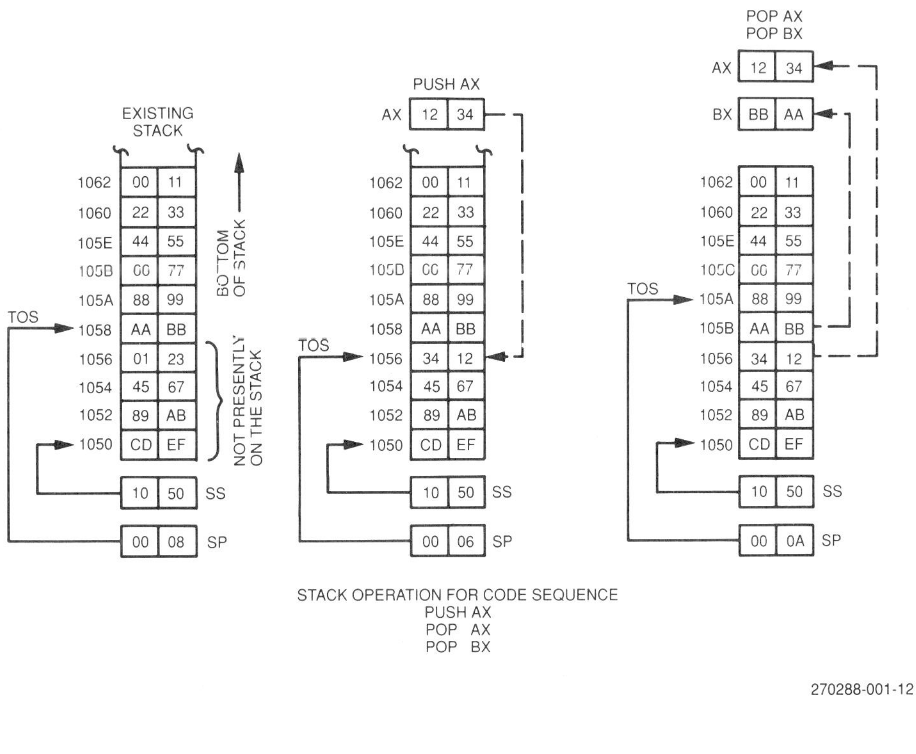

Figure 12. Stack Operation

never move elements on the stack, nor do they erase them. The top of the stack changes only as a result of updating the stack pointer.

2.1.11 RESERVED MEMORY AND I/O SPACE

Two specific areas in memory and one area in I/O space are reserved in the 80186 family.

- Locations 0H through 3FFH in low memory are reserved for interrupt vectors.
- Locations 0FFFF0H through 0FFFFFH in high memory are reserved for system reset code since the processor begins execution at 0FFFF0H.
- Locations 0F8H through 0FFH in I/O space are reserved for communication with other Intel hardware products. On the 80C186, these addresses are used as I/O ports for the 80C187 numerics processor extension.

The peripheral control block (see Section 5.0) may reside in memory or I/O space. All unused locations in the peripheral control block are also reserved.

2.2 SOFTWARE OVERVIEW

All 80186 family members execute exactly the same instructions. This instruction set includes all the 8086/8088 instructions plus several useful additions and enhancements. The following sections provide a description of the instructions by category and a detailed discussion of the various operand addressing modes.

Software for 80186 family systems does not need to be written in assembly language. The processor provides direct hardware support for programs written in the many high-level languages available. Most high-level languages store variables in memory; the symmetrical instruction set supports direct operation on memory operands, including operands on the stack. The hardware addressing modes provide efficient, straightforward implementations of based variables, arrays, arrays of structures and other high-level language data constructs. A powerful set of memory-to-memory string operations is available for efficient character data manipulation. Finally, routines with critical performance requirements that cannot be met with high-level languages may be written in assembly language and linked with high-level code.

2.2.1 INSTRUCTION SET

Instructions in the 80186 processor family treat different types of operands uniformly. Nearly every instruction can operate on either byte or word data. Register, memory and immediate operands may be specified interchangeably in most instructions. The exception to this is that immediate values serve as source and not destination operands. In particular, memory variables may be added to, subtracted from, shifted, compared, and so on, in place, without moving them in and out of registers. This saves instructions, registers, and execution time in assembly language programs. In high-level languages, where most variables are memory-based, compilers can produce faster and shorter object programs.

The 80186 family instruction set can be viewed as existing on two levels. One is the assembly level and the other is the machine level. To the assembly language programmer, the 80186 family appears to have a repertoire of about 100 instructions. One MOV (data move) instruction, for example, transfers a byte of a word from a register of a memory location or an immediate value to either a register or a memory location. The 80186 family CPUs, however, recognize 28 different machine versions of the MOV instruction.

The two levels of instruction set address two different requirements: efficiency and simplicity. The approximately 300 forms of machine-level instructions make very efficient use of storage. For example, the machine instruction that increments a memory operand is three or four bytes long because the address of the operand must be encoded in the instruction. To increment a register, however, does not require as much information, so the instruction can be shorter. The 80186 family has eight different machine-level instructions that increment a different 16-bit register. Each of these instructions is only one byte long.

The assembly level instructions simplify the programmer's view of the instruction set. The programmer writes one form of an INC (increment) instruction and the assembler examines the operand to determine which machine level instruction to generate. The following paragraphs provide a functional description of the assembly-level instructions.

2.2.1.1 DATA TRANSFER INSTRUCTIONS

The instruction set contains 14 data transfer instructions. These instructions move single bytes and words between memory and registers, and also move single bytes and words between the AL or AX registers and I/O ports. Table 3 lists the four types of data transfer instructions and their functions.

Data transfer instructions are categorized as general purpose, input/output, address object, and flag transfer. The stack manipulation instructions which are used for transferring flag contents, and the instructions for loading segment registers are also included in this group. Figure 13 shows the flag storage formats. The address object instructions manipulate the addresses of variables instead of the contents of values of the variables. This is useful for list processing, based variable, and string operations.

Table 3. Data Transfer Instructions

GENERAL PURPOSE	
MOV	Move byte or word
PUSH	Push word onto stack
POP	Pop word off stack
PUSHA	Push registers onto stack
POPA	Pop registers off stack
XCHG	Exchange byte or word
XLAT	Translate byte
INPUT/OUTPUT	
IN	Input byte or word
OUT	Output byte or word
ADDRESS OBJECT AND STACK FRAME	
LEA	Load effective address
LDS	Load pointer using DS
LES	Load pointer using ES
ENTER	Build stack frame
LEAVE	Tear down stack frame
FLAG TRANSFER	
LAHF	Load AH register from flags
SAHF	Store AH register in flags
PUSHF	Push flags onto stack
POPF	Pop flags off stack

2.2.1.2 ARITHMETIC INSTRUCTIONS

The arithmetic instructions (see Table 4) operate on four types of numbers:

1. Unsigned binary.
2. Signed binary (integers).
3. Unsigned packed decimal.
4. Unsigned unpacked decimal.

Table 5 shows the interpretations of various bit patterns according to each number type.

Binary numbers may be 8 or 16 bits long. Decimal numbers are stored in bytes, two digits per byte for packed decimal and one digit per byte for unpacked decimal. The processor always assumes that the operands specified in arithmetic instructions contain data that represent valid numbers for the instruction being performed. Invalid data may produce unpredictable results. The processor analyzes arithmetic results and posts certain characteristics of the operation to six flags.

2.2.1.3 BIT MANIPULATION INSTRUCTIONS

There are three groups of instructions for manipulating bits within both bytes and word. These three groups are logical, shifts and rotates. Table 6 lists these three groups of bit manipulation instructions with their functions.

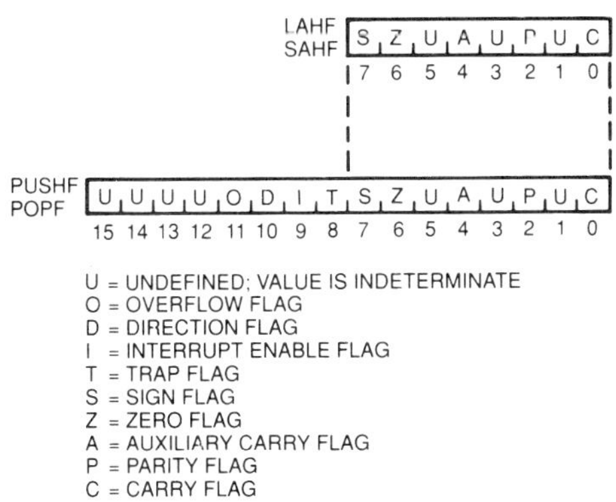

270288-001-13

Figure 13. Flag Storage Format

Table 4. Arithmetic Instructions

ADDITION	
ADD	Add byte or word
ADC	Add byte or word with carry
INC	Increment byte or word by 1
AAA	ASCII adjust for addition
DAA	Decimal adjust for addition
SUBTRACTION	
SUB	Subtract byte or word
SBB	Subtract byte or word with borrow
DEC	Decrement byte or word by 1
NEG	Negate byte or word
CMP	Compare byte or word
AAS	ASCII adjust for subtraction
DAS	Decimal adjust for subtraction
MULTIPLICATION	
MUL	Multiply byte or word unsigned
IMUL	Integer multiply byte or word
AAM	ASCII adjust for multiply
DIVISION	
DIV	Divide byte or word unsigned
IDIV	Integer divide byte or word
AAD	ASCII adjust for division
CBW	Convert byte to word
CWD	Convert word to doubleword

Table 6. Bit Manipulation Instructions

LOGICALS	
NOT	"Not" byte or word
AND	"And" byte or word
OR	"Inclusive or" byte or word
XOR	"Exclusive or" byte or word
TEST	"Test" byte or word
SHIFTS	
SHL/SAL	Shift logical/arithmetic left byte or word
SHR	Shift logical right byte or word
SAR	Shift arithmetic right byte or word
ROTATES	
ROL	Rotate left byte or word
ROR	Rotate right byte or word
RCL	Rotate through carry left byte or word
RCR	Rotate through carry right byte or word

Table 5. Arithmetic Interpretation of 8-Bit Numbers

HEX	BIT PATTERN	UNSIGNED BINARY	SIGNED BINARY	UNPACKED DECIMAL	PACKED DECIMAL
07	0 0 0 0 0 1 1 1	7	+7	7	7
89	1 0 0 0 1 0 0 1	137	-119	invalid	89
C5	1 1 0 0 0 1 0 1	197	-59	invalid	invalid

The logical instructions include the Boolean operators NOT, AND, inclusive OR, and exclusive OR (XOR). A TEST instruction that sets the flags as a result of a Boolean AND operation, but does not alter either of its operands, is also included.

The bits in bytes and words may be shifted arithmetically or logically. Up to 255 shifts may be performed, according to the value of the count operand coded in the instruction. The count may be specified as an immediate value or as a variable in the CL register, allowing the shift count to be a variable supplied at execution time. Arithmetic shifts may be used to multiply and divide binary numbers by powers of two. Logical shifts can be used to isolate bits in bytes or words.

Bits in bytes and words can also be rotated. The processor does not discard the bits rotated out of an operand; the bits circles back to the other end of the operand. As in the shift instructions, the number of bits to be rotated is taken from the count operand, which may specify either an immediate value, or the

CL register. The carry flag may act as an extension of the operand in two of the rotate instructions, allowing a bit to be isolated in CF and then tested by a JC (jump if carry) or JNC (jump if not carry) instruction.

2.2.1.4 STRING INSTRUCTIONS

Five basic string operations allow strings of bytes or words to be operated on, one element (byte or word) at a time. Strings of up to 64 Kbytes may be manipulated with these instructions. Instructions are available to move, compare and scan for a value, as well as moving string elements to and from the accumulator. Table 7 lists the string instructions. These basic operations may be preceded by a special one-byte prefix that causes the instruction to be repeated by the hardware, allowing long strings to be processed much faster than would be possible with a software loop. The repetitions can be terminated by a variety of conditions, and repeated operations may be interrupted and resumed.

Table 7. String Instructions

REP	Repeat
REPE/REPZ	Repeat while equal/zero
REPNE/REPNZ	Repeat while not equal/not zero
MOVS	Move byte or word string
MOVSB/MOVSW	Move byte or word string
INS	Input byte or word string
OUTS	Output byte or word string
CMPS	Compare byte or word string
SCAS	Scan byte or word string
LODS	Load byte or word string
STOS	Store byte or word string

The string instructions operate similarly in many respects (refer to Table 8). A string instruction may have a source operand, a destination operand, or both. The hardware assumes that a source string resides in the current data segment. A segment prefix may be used to override this assumption. A destination string must be in the current extra segment. The assembler checks the attributes of the operands to determine if the elements of the strings are bytes or words. However, the assembler does not use the operand names to address strings. Instead, the contents of register SI (source index) are used as an offset to address the current element of the source string. Also, the contents of register DI (destination index) are taken as the offset of the current destination string element. These registers must be initialized to point to the source/destination strings before executing the string instructions. The LDS, LES and LEA instructions are useful in performing this function.

Table 8. String Instruction Register and Flag Use

SI	Index (offset) for source string
DI	Index (offset) for destination string
CX	Repetition counter
AL/AX	Scan value Destination for LODS Source for STOS
DF	0 = auto-increment SI, DI 1 = auto-decrement SI, DI
ZF	Scan/compare terminator

String instructions automatically update the SI or DI register or both prior to processing the next string element. Setting the direction flag (DF) determines whether the index registers are auto-incremented (DF = 0) or auto-decremented (DF = 1). The processor adjusts the DI or SI register or both by one if byte strings are being processed. The adjustment is two for word strings.

If a repeat prefix has been coded, then register CX (the count register) is decremented by one after each repetition of the string instruction. The CX register must be initialized to the number of repetitions desired before the string instruction is executed. If the CX register is 0, the string instruction is not executed and control goes to the following instruction.

2.2.1.5 PROGRAM TRANSFER INSTRUCTIONS

The sequence in which instructions are executed in the 80186 family is determined by the contents of the CS and IP registers. The CS register contains the base address of the current code segment. The IP register points to the memory locations from which the next instruction is to be fetched. In most operating conditions, the next instruction to be executed will have already been fetched and is waiting in the CPU instruction queue. The program transfer instructions operate on the instruction pointer and on the CS register; changing the content of these causes normal sequential operation to be altered. When a program transfer occurs, the queue no longer contains the correct instruction. When the BIU obtains the next instruction from memory using the new IP and CS values, it passes the instruction directly to the EU and begins refilling the queue from the new location.

Four groups of program transfers are available with the 80186 family processors. See Table 9. These are unconditional transfers, conditional transfers, iteration control instructions, and interrupt-related instructions.

Table 9. Program Transfer Instructions

UNCONDITIONAL TRANSFERS	
CALL	Call procedure
RET	Return from procedure
JMP	Jump
CONDITIONAL TRANSFERS	
JA/JNBE	Jump if above/not below nor equal
JAE/JNB	Jump if above or equal/ not below
JB/JNAE	Jump if below/not above nor equal
JBE/JNA	Jump if below or equal/ not above
JC	Jump if carry
JE/JZ	Jump if equal/zero
JG/JNLE	Jump if greater/not less nor equal
JGE/JNL	Jump if greater or equal/ not less
JL/JNGE	Jump if less/not greater nor equal
JLE/JNG	Jump if less or equal/ not greater
JNC	Jump if not carry
JNE/JNZ	Jump if not equal/not zero
JNO	Jump if not overflow
JNP/JPO	Jump if not parity/parity odd
JNS	Jump if not sign
JO	Jump if overflow
JP/JPE	Jump if parity/parity even
JS	Jump if sign
ITERATION CONTROLS	
LOOP	Loop
LOOPE/LOOPZ	Loop if equal/zero
LOOPNE/LOOPNZ	Loop if not equal/not zero
JCXZ	Jump if register CX=0
INTERRUPTS	
INT	Interrupt
INTO	Interrupt if overflow
BOUND	Interrupt if out of array bounds
IRET	Interrupt return

The unconditional transfer instructions may transfer control to a target instruction within the current code segment (intrasegment transfer) or to a different code segment (intersegment transfer). The assembler terms an intrasegment transfer SHORT or NEAR and an intersegment transfer FAR. The transfer is made unconditionally any time the instruction is executed.

The conditional transfer instructions are jumps that may or may not transfer control depending on the state of the CPU flags at the time the instruction is executed. These 18 instructions (see Table 10) each test a different combination of flags for a condition. If the condition is logically TRUE then control is transferred to the target specified in the instruction. If the condition is FALSE then control passes to the instruction that follows the conditional jump. All conditional jumps are SHORT, that is, the target must be in the current code segment and within -128 to +127 bytes of the first byte of the next instruction. For example, JMP 00H causes a jump to the first byte of the next instruction. Since jumps are made by adding the relative displacement of the target to the instruction pointer, all conditional jumps are self-relative and are appropriate for position-independent routines.

The iteration control instructions can be used to regulate the repetition of software loops. These instructions use the CX register as a counter. Like the conditional transfers, the iteration control instructions are self-relative and may only transfer to targets that are within -128 to +127 bytes of themselves, i.e., they are SHORT transfers.

The interrupt instructions allow interrupt service routines to be activated by programs as well as by external hardware devices. The effect of software interrupts is similar to hardware-initiated interrupts. However, the processor cannot execute an interrupt acknowledge bus cycle if the interrupt originates in software or with an NMI (Non-Maskable Interrupt).

2.2.1.6 PROCESSOR CONTROL INSTRUCTIONS

The processor control instructions (see Table 11) allow programs to control various CPU functions. One group of instructions updates flags, and another group is used primarily for synchronizing the microprocessor to external events. A final instruction causes the CPU to do nothing. Except for the flag operations, none of the processor control instructions affects the flags.

2.2.2 ADDRESSING MODES

An 80186 family member accesses instruction operands in many different ways. Operands may be contained in registers, within the instruction itself, in memory, or at I/O ports. Also, the addresses of memory and I/O port operands can be calculated in several different ways. These addressing modes greatly

Table 10. Interpretation of Conditional Transfers

MNEMONIC	CONDITION TESTED	"JUMP IF ..."
JA/JNBE	(CF or ZF)=0	above/not below nor equal
JAE/JNB	CF=0	above or equal/not below
JB/JNAE	CF=1	below/not above nor equal
JBE/JNA	(CF or ZF)=1	below or equal/not above
JC	CF=1	carry
JE/JZ	ZF=1	equal/zero
JG/JNLE	((SF xor OF) or ZF) = 0	greater/not less nor equal
JGE/JNL	(SF xor OF)=0	greater or equal/not less
JL/JNGE	(SF xor OF)=1	less/not greater nor equal
JLE/JNG	((SF xor OF) or ZF)=1	less or equal/not greater
JNC	CF=0	not carry
JNE/JNZ	ZF=0	not equal/not zero
JNO	OF=0	not overflow
JNP/JPO	PF=0	not parity/parity odd
JNS	SF=0	not sign
JO	OF=1	overflow
JP/JPE	PF=1	parity/parity equal
JS	SF=1	sign

Note: "above" and "below" refer to the relationship of two unsigned values;
"greater" and "less" refer to the relationship of two signed values.

Table 11. Processor Control Instructions

FLAG OPERATIONS	
STC	Set carry flag
CLC	Clear carry flag
CMC	Complement carry flag
STD	Set direction flag
CLD	Clear direction flag
STI	Set interrupt enable flag
CLI	Clear interrupt enable flag
EXTERNAL SYNCHRONIZATION	
HLT	Halt until interrupt or reset
WAIT	Wait for $\overline{\text{TEST}}$ pin active
ESC	Escape to external processor
LOCK	Lock bus during next instruction
NO OPERATION	
NOP	No operation

extend the flexibility and convenience of the instruction set. The following paragraphs briefly describe the register and immediate modes of operand addressing, and then provide a detailed description of the memory and I/O addressing modes.

2.2.2.1 REGISTER AND IMMEDIATE OPERAND ADDRESSING MODES

Instructions that specify only register operands are usually the most compact and fastest executing of the operand addressing forms. This is because the register operand addresses are encoded in instructions in just a few bits, and because these operands are performed entirely within the CPU (no bus cycles are run). Registers may serve as source operands, destination operands, or both.

Immediate operands are constant data contained in an instruction. The data may be either 8 or 16 bits in length. Immediate operands can be accessed quickly because they are available directly from the instruction queue. Like the register operand, no bus cycles need to be run to get an immediate operand. The limitations on immediate operands are that they may only serve as source operands and that they are constant in value.

2.2.2.2 MEMORY ADDRESSING MODES

Although the EU has direct access to register and immediate operands, memory operands must be transferred to and from the CPU over the bus. When the EU needs to read or write a memory operand, it must pass an offset value to the BIU. The BIU adds the offset to the shifted contents of a segment register producing a 20-bit physical address and then executes the bus cycle or cycles needed to access the operand.

The offset that the EU calculates for memory operand is called the operand's effective address or EA. This address is an unsigned 16-bit number that expresses the operand's distance in bytes from the beginning of the segment in which it resides. The EU can calculate the effective address in several ways. Information encoded in the second byte of the instruction tells the EU how to calculate the effective address of each memory operand. A compiler or assembler derives this information from the statement or instruction written by the programmer. Assembly language programmers have access to all addressing modes.

The EU calculates the EA by summing a displacement, the content of a base register and the content of an index register (see Figure 14). Any combination of these three components may be present in a given instruction. This allows a variety of memory addressing modes.

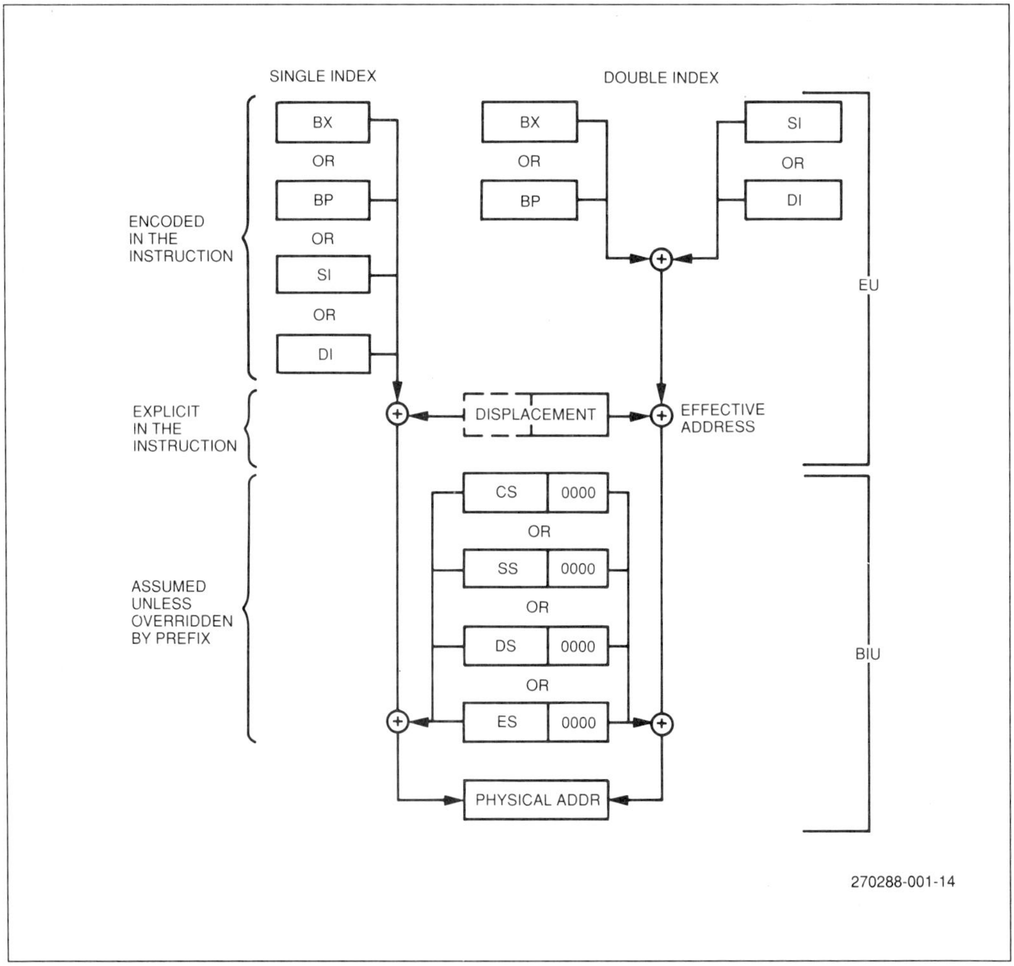

Figure 14. Memory Address Computation

The displacement element is an 8-bit or 16-bit number that is contained in the instruction. The displacement generally is derived from the position of the operand name (a variable or label) in the program. The programmer can also modify this value or explicitly specify the displacement.

A programmer may specify that either the BX or BP register is to serve as a base register whose content is to be used in the EA computation.

Similarly, either the SI or DI register may be specified as the index register. The displacement value is a constant. The contents of the base and index registers may change during execution. This allows one instruction to access different memory locations as determined by the current values in the base or base and index registers. Effective address calculations with the BP register are made using the SS register, by default, although either the DS or the ES register may be specified instead.

Direct addressing is the simplest memory addressing mode (see Figure 15). No registers are involved and the EA is taken directly from the displacement of the instruction. The programmer typically uses direct addressing to access scaler variables.

With register indirect addressing, the effective address of a memory operand may be taken directly from one of the base or index registers (see Figure 16). One instruction can operate on many different memory locations if the value in the base or index register is updated appropriately. Any 16-bit general register may be used for register indirect addressing with the JMP or CALL instructions.

In based addressing (see Figure 17), the effective address is the sum of a displacement value and the content of register BX or BP. Specifying register BP as a base register directs the BIU to obtain the operand from the current stack segment (unless a segment override prefix is present). This makes based addressing with the BP register a very convenient way to access stack data.

Based addressing also provides a simple way to address data structures which may be located at different places in memory

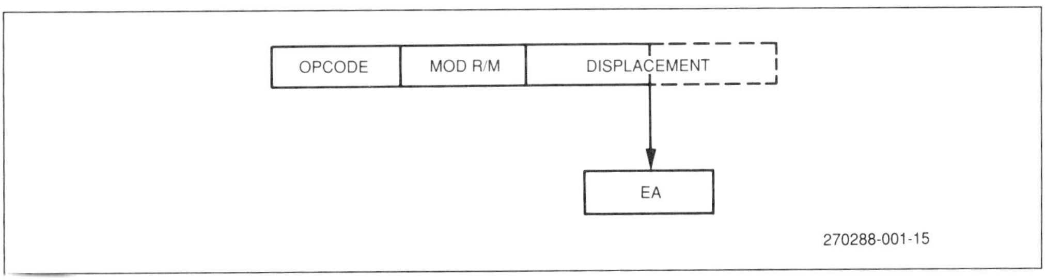

Figure 15. Direct Addressing

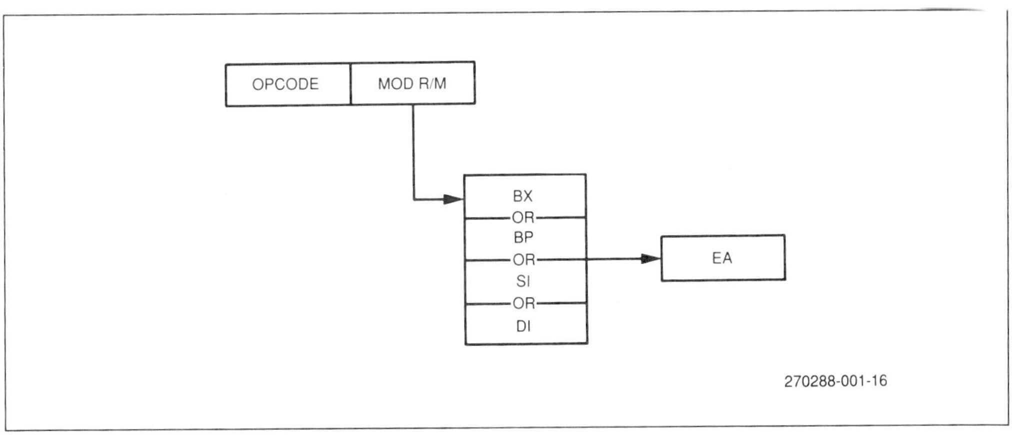

Figure 16. Register Indirect Addressing

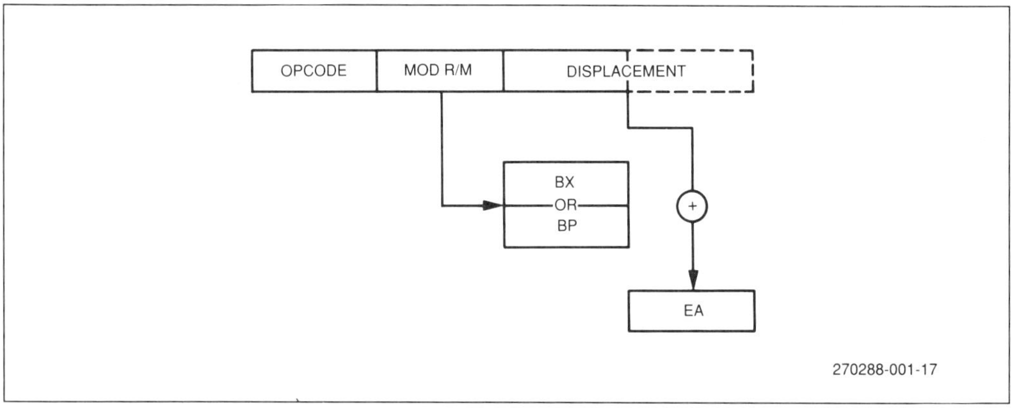

Figure 17. Based Addressing

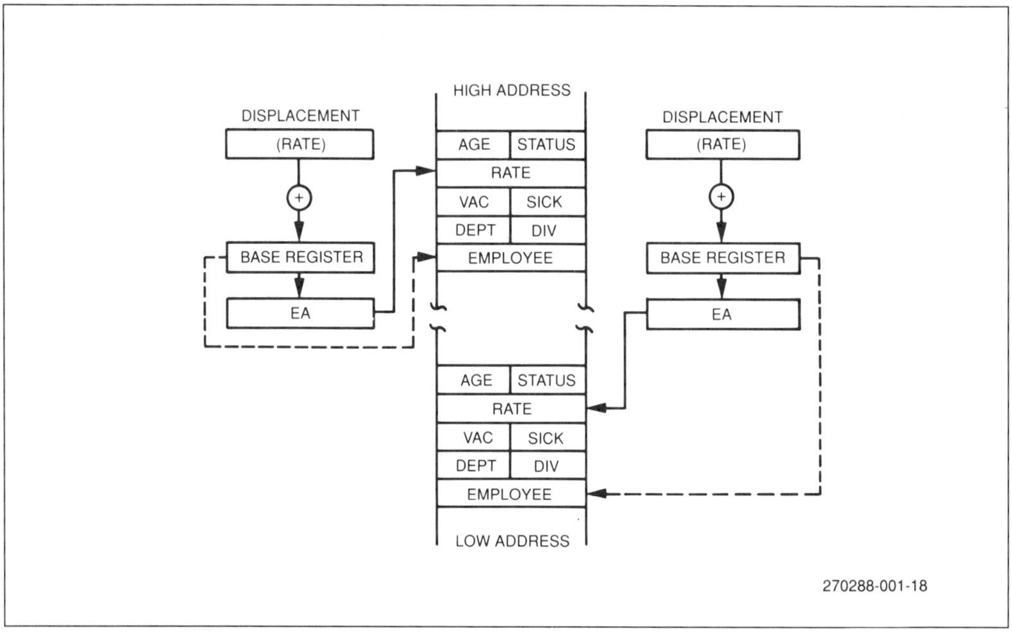

Figure 18. Accessing a Structure with Based Addressing

(see Figure 18). A base register can be pointed at the structure and elements of the structure can be addressed by their displacement. Different copies of the same structure can be accessed by simply changing the base register.

With indexed addressing, the effective address is calculated from the sum of a displacement plus the content of an index register (SI or DI). See Figure 19. Indexed addressing is often used to access elements in an array (see Figure 20). The displacement locates the beginning of the array, and the value of the index register selects one element. If the index register contains 0000H, the processor selects the first element. Since all array elements are the same length, simple arithmetic on the register may select any element.

Based index addressing generates an effective address that is the sum of a base register, an index register, and a displacement (see Figure 21). This mode of addressing is very flexible because the values of two address components can be determined at execution time.

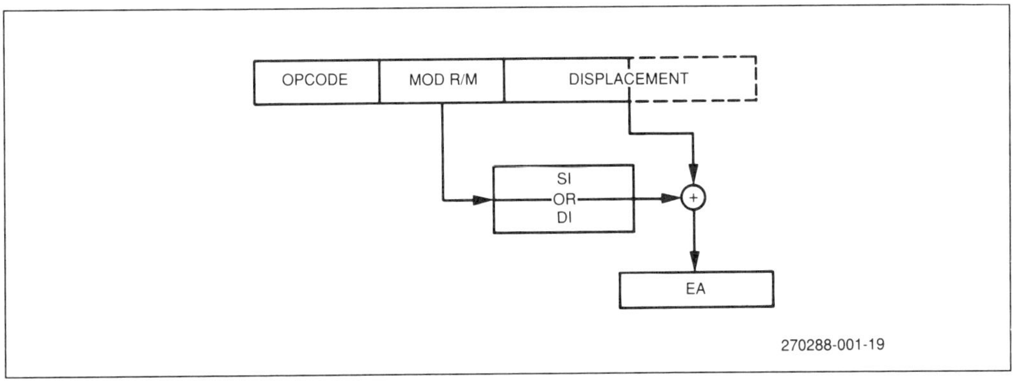

Figure 19. Indexed Addressing

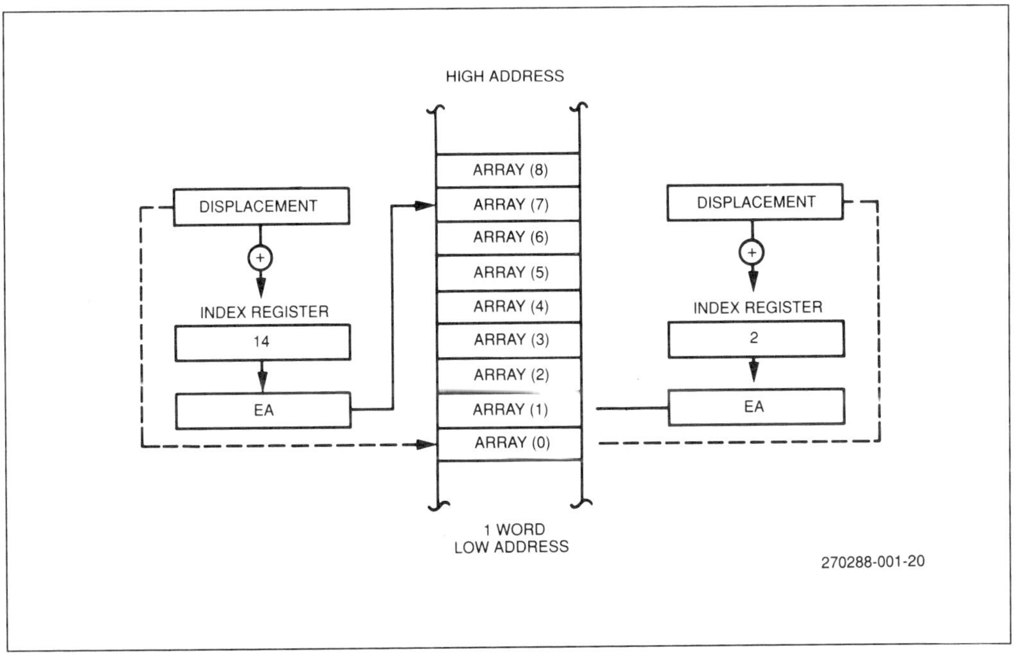

Figure 20. Accessing an Array with Indexed Addressing

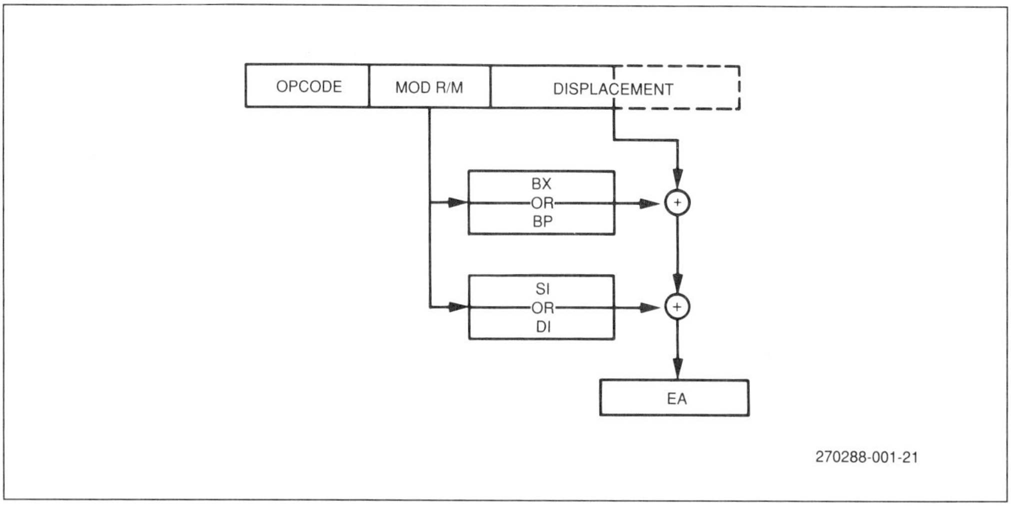

Figure 21. Based Index Addressing

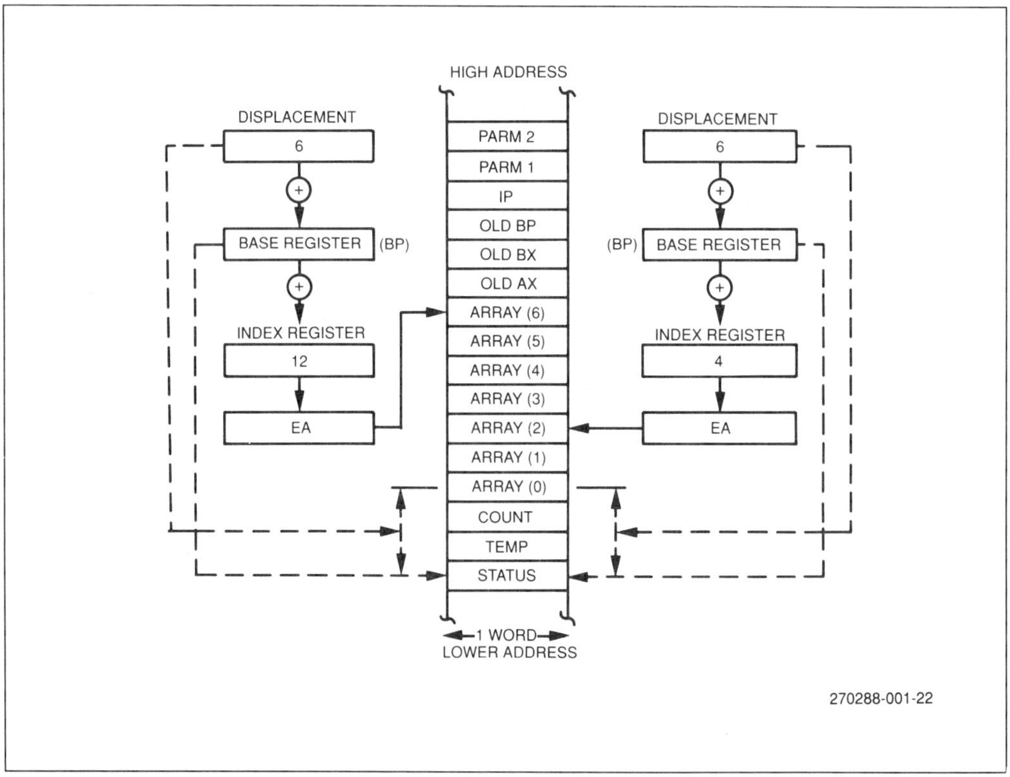

Figure 22. Accessing a Stacked Array with Based Index Addressing

Based index addressing provides a convenient way for a procedure to address an array allocated on a stack (see Figure 22). Register BP can contain the offset of a reference point on the stack, typically the top of the stack after the procedure has saved registers and allocated local storage. The offset of the beginning of the array from the reference point can be expressed by a displacement value, and the index register can be used to access individual array elements. Arrays contained in structures and matrices (two-dimensional arrays) can also be accessed with based indexed addressing.

String instructions do not use the normal memory addressing modes to access operands. Instead, the index registers are used implicitly (see Figure 23). When a string instruction is executed, the SI register is assumed to point to the first byte or word of the source string. The DI register is assumed to point to the first byte or word of the destination string. In a repeated string operation, the CPU will automatically adjust the SI and DI registers to obtain subsequent bytes or words. Note that for string instructions the DS register is the default segment register for the SI register and the ES register is the default segment register for the DI register . This allows string instructions to easily operate on data located anywhere within the one megabyte address space.

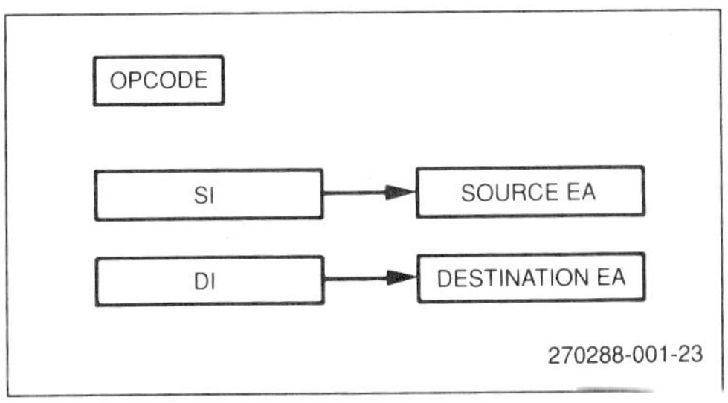

Figure 23. String Operand

2.2.2.3 I/O PORT ADDRESSING

Any of the memory operand addressing modes may be used to access an I/O port if the port is memory-mapped. String instructions can also be used to transfer data to memory-mapped ports with an appropriate hardware interface.

Two different address modes can be used to access ports located in the I/O space (see Figure 24). The port number is an 8-bit immediate operand for direct addressing. This allows fixed access to ports numbered 0-255. Indirect I/O port addressing is similar to register indirect addressing of memory operands. The port number is taken from register DX and can range from 0 to 65,535. By previously adjusting the content of register DX, one instruction can access any port in the I/O space. A group of adjacent ports can be accessed using a simple software loop that adjusts the value of the DX register.

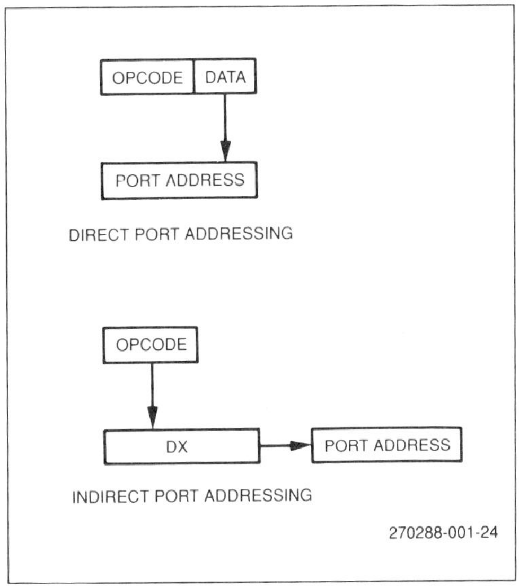

Figure 24. I/O Port Addressing

2.2.3 DATA TYPES USED IN THE 80186 FAMILY

The 80186 family supports the following data types:

- Integer - A signed binary numeric value contained in an 8-bit byte or a 16-bit word. All operations assume a 2's complement representation. Signed 32-and 64-bit integers are directly supported with the addition of an 8087 Numeric Coprocessor to an 80186/80188 system or by the addition of an 80C187 Numerics Processor Extension to an 80C186 system.
- Ordinal - An unsigned binary numeric value contained in an 8-bit byte or a 16-bit word.
- Pointer - A 16- or 32-bit quantity, composed of a 16-bit offset component or a 16-bit segment base component in addition to a 16-bit offset component.
- String - A contiguous sequence of bytes of words. A string may contain from one byte to 64 Kbytes.
- ASCII - A byte representation of alphanumeric and control characters using the ASCII standard.
- BCD - A byte (unpacked) representation of the decimal digits 0-9.

- Packed BCD - A byte (packed) representation of two decimal digits (0-9). One digit is stored in each nibble (4 bits) of the byte.

- Floating Point - A signed 32-, 64-, or 80-bit real number representation. Floating point operands are directly supported with the addition of an 8087 Numerics Coprocessor to an 80186/80188 system or by addition of an 80C187 Numerics Processor Extension to an 80C186 system.

In general, individual data elements must fit within defined segment limits. Figure 25 graphically represents the data types supported by the 80186 family.

2.3 DMA CONTROL UNIT

The 80186 processor family includes a DMA Control Unit which provides two flexible DMA channels. The DMA Unit will perform transfers to or from any combination of I/O space and memory space in either byte or word units. Every DMA cycle requires two to four bus cycles, one or two to fetch the data and one or two to deposit the data. This allows word data to be located on odd boundaries, or byte data to be moved from odd locations to even locations.

Each DMA channel maintains independent 20-bit source and destination pointers. Each of these pointers may independently address either I/O or memory space. After each DMA cycle, the processor can increment, decrement, or retain the pointer values. Each DMA channel also maintains a transfer count which can terminate a series of DMA transfers after a programmed number of transfers.

2.4 TIMERS

The Timer Unit contains three independent 16-bit timer/counters. Two of them can count external events, provide waveforms based on either the CPU clock or an external clock, or interrupt the CPU after a specified count. The third timer/counter counts only CPU clocks. After a programmable interval, it can interrupt the CPU, provide a clock pulse to either or both of the other timer/counters, or initiate a DMA request to the integrated DMA Control Unit.

2.5 INTERRUPT CONTROL UNIT

The integrated Interrupt Controller arbitrates interrupt requests between all internal and external sources. It can be directly cascaded as the master to an external 8259A or 82C59A Interrupt Controller. In addition, it can be configured as a slave controller to an external master.

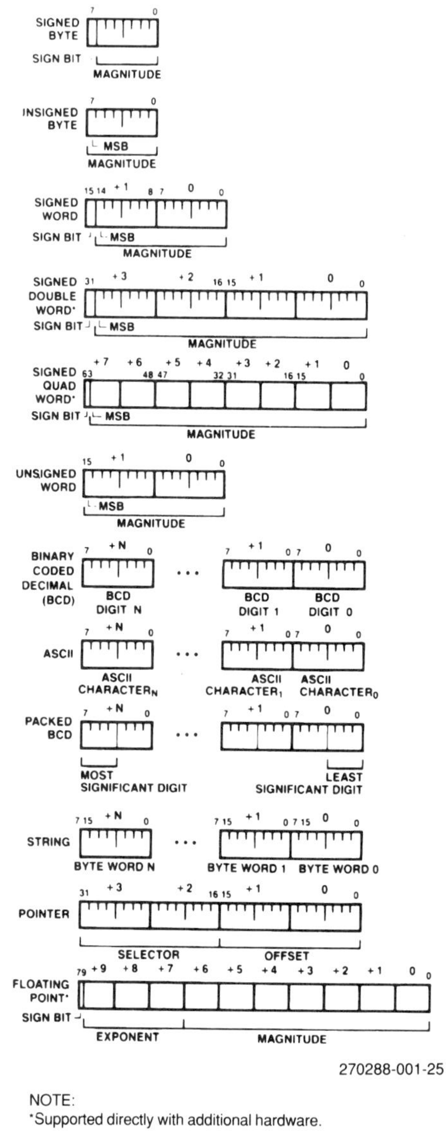

NOTE:
*Supported directly with additional hardware.

Figure 25. 80186 Family Supported Data Types

2.6 CLOCK GENERATOR

The on-board crystal oscillator can be used with a parallel resonant crystal at twice the desired CPU clock frequency (e.g., 25 MHz for a 12.5 MHz 80C186), or with an external oscillator also at twice the CPU clock. The output of oscillator is internally divided by two to provide a 50 percent duty cycle CPU clock from which all system timing is derived. The CPU clock is externally available, and most timing parameters are referenced to it.

2.7 CHIP SELECT AND READY GENERATION UNIT

The 80186 family includes integrated chip select logic which can be used to enable memory or peripheral devices. Six output lines are used for memory addressing and seven output lines are used for peripheral addressing.

The six memory chip select lines are split into 3 groups for separately addressing the major memory areas in a typical 80186-based system: upper memory for boot ROM, lower memory for interrupt vectors, and mid-range memory for program memory. The size of each of these regions is user-programmable. The starting location and ending location of lower memory and upper memory are fixed at 00000H and FFFFFH respectively; the starting location of the mid-range memory is user-programmable.

Each of the seven peripheral select lines addresses one of seven contiguous 128 byte blocks above a programmable base address. This base address can be located in either memory or I/O space so that peripheral devices may be I/O-mapped or memory-mapped.

Each of the programmed chip select areas has associated with it a set of programmable READY bits. These bits allow a programmable number of wait states (0 to 3) to be automatically inserted whenever an access is made to the area of memory associated with the chip select. One of the READY bits determines whether the external READY signals (ARDY and SRDY) will be used, or whether they will be ignored (i.e., a bus cycle will end even though READY is not returned on the external pins). There are five sets of READY bits which allow independent READY generation for each of upper memory, lower memory, mid-range memory, peripheral devices 0-3 and peripheral devices 4-6.

2.8 DRAM REFRESH CONTROL UNIT (80C186/80C188 ONLY)

The most important functional improvement of the 80C186/80C188 over the 80186/80188 is the DRAM Refresh Control Unit (RCU). The RCU consists of a timer and an address counter which work with the Bus Interface Unit and chip select logic to provide DRAM refresh bus cycles at timed intervals. These bus cycles are the same as ordinary read cycles except that control signals are specially coded. An external DRAM controller circuit can use the 80C186/80C188 control signals to generate other necessary signals such as address strobes RAS and CAS.

2.9 POWER-SAVE UNIT (80C186/80C188 ONLY)

The 80C186/80C188 also contains a programmable clock divisor circuit. This Power-Save Unit provides for greatly reduced operating currents by dividing the processor clock frequency by 1, 4, 8, or 16 (to as low as CLKOUT = 0.5 MHz). Power-save operation is under complete programmer control. Applications which spend most of the time in idle operation can also exit power-save operation at any time upon receipt of a hardware interrupt.

2.10 ACCESS TO INTEGRATED PERIPHERALS

The integrated 80186 family peripherals operate semi-autonomously from the CPU. Access to them is via peripheral control registers located within a 256 byte block of either memory or I/O space. These registers are all 16-bit, most are read/write, and are accessed exactly as if they were external devices. Therefore, standard input, output, or memory instructions may be used.

80186 Bus Interface Unit 3

CHAPTER 3
BUS INTERFACE UNIT

The 80186 is a true 16-bit microprocessor family with 16-bit internal data paths, one megabyte (220) of memory address space, and a separate 64 Kbyte (216) I/O address space. The CPU communicates with its external environment via a twenty-bit time-multiplexed address and data bus. There also exists a command and status bus (see Table 12). This communication is managed by the Bus Interface Unit. To understand the operation of the address/data bus requires an understanding of the BIU's bus cycles.

3.1 T-STATES

To transfer data, fetch instructions, or run DMA cycles, the CPU executes a bus cycle. A bus cycle consists of a minimum of four CPU clock cycles or T-states plus any number of wait states necessary to accommodate the access time limitations of external memory or peripheral devices. T-states are numbered sequentially T_1, T_2, T_3, T_4, and T_W. Additional idleT-states (T_i) can occur between T_4 and T_1 when the processor requires no bus activity. The beginning of a T-state is signaled by a HIGH-to-LOW transition of the CPU clock. Each T-state is divided into two phases, phase 1 (the LOW phase) and phase 2 (the HIGH phase). Figure 26 illustrates an 80186 family clock cycle.

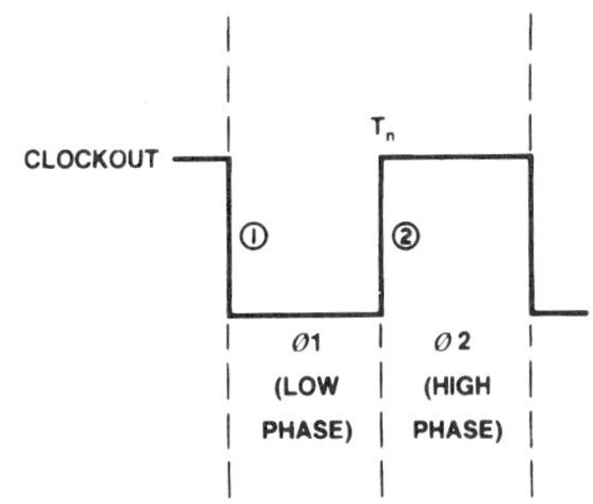

NOTES:
1. Falling edge of T_n.
2. Rising edge of T_n.

Figure 26. T-State in a 80186 Family Processor

Table 12. 80186 Family Bus Signals

Function	Single Name (with Alternates)
address/data	AD0-AD15 (Varies)
address/status	A16/S3-A19-S6, $\overline{\text{BHE}}$/S7 ($\overline{\text{BHE}}$, S7, $\overline{\text{RFSH}}$)
coprocessor control	$\overline{\text{TEST}}$ ($\overline{\text{TEST}}$/BUSY), PEREQ, $\overline{\text{ERROR}}$)
local bus arbitration	HOLD, HLDA
local bus control	ALE, $\overline{\text{RD}}$, $\overline{\text{WR}}$, DT/$\overline{\text{R}}$, $\overline{\text{DEN}}$
multi-master bus	$\overline{\text{LOCK}}$
ready (wait) interface	SRDY, ARDY
status information	$\overline{\text{S0}}$-$\overline{\text{S2}}$

Different types of bus activity occur for all of the T-states (see Figure 27). Address generation information occurs during T_1, and data generation occurs during T_2, T_3, T_W and T_4. The beginning of a bus cycle is signaled by the status lines of the processor going from a passive state (all HIGH) to an active state in the middle of the T-state immediately before T_1 (either a T_4 or a Ti). Information concerning an impending bus cycle appears during the T-state immediately before the first T-state of the cycle itself. Two different types of T_4 and T_i can be generated, one where the T-state is immediately followed by a bus cycle, and one where the T-state is immediately followed by an idle T-state.

During the first type of T_4 or T_i, the processor generates status information concerning the impending bus cycle. This information will be available no later than T_{CHSV} after the LOW-to-HIGH transition of the processor's CLKOUT in the middle of the T-state. During the second type of T_4 or T_i, the status outputs remain inactive because no bus cycle will follow. The decision on which type T_4 or T_i state to present is made at the beginning of the T-state preceding the T_4 or T_i state (see Figure 28). This determination has an effect on bus latency (see Section 3.8.2).

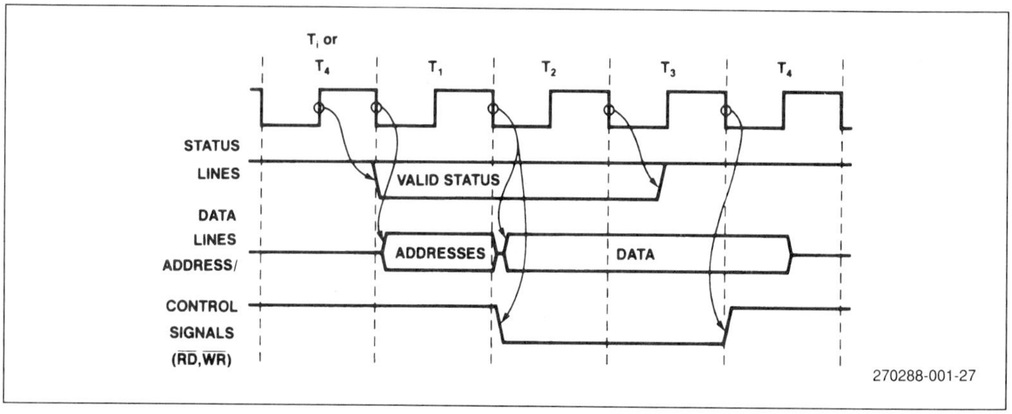

Figure 27. Example Bus Cycle of the 80186

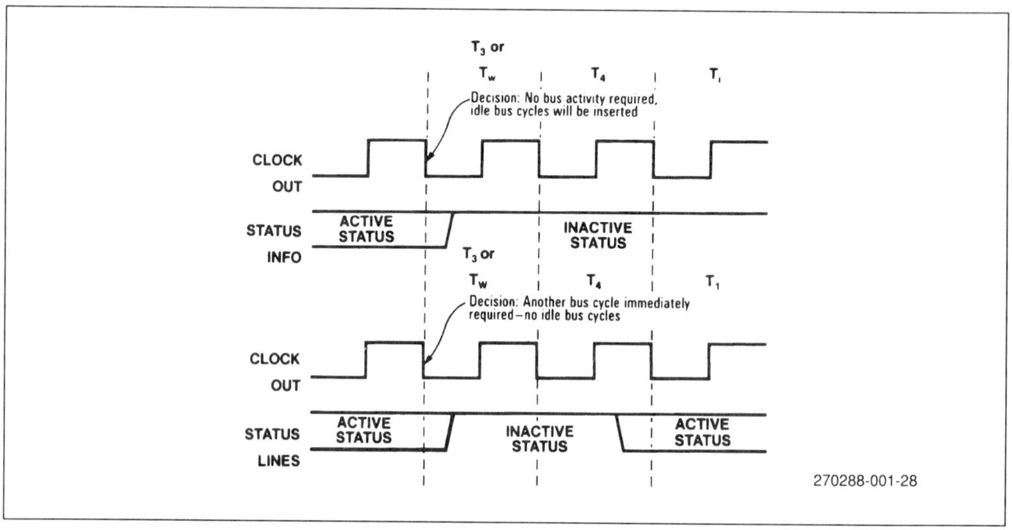

Figure 28. Active-Inactive Status Transitions in 80186 Family Processor

The READY signals control the number of wait states (T_W) inserted in each bus cycle. The maximum number of wait states is unbounded.

The bus may remain idle for several T-states (T_i) between accesses initiated by an 80186 family processor. This situation occurs under the following diverse conditions:

- When the prefetch queue is full.
- When the processor is running a type of bus cycle which always includes idle states (interrupt acknowledge, for example).
- When an instruction forces idle states (LOCK, for example).
- When the DMA Control Unit forces idle states in destination-synchronized mode.

During idle states, the processor may not necessarily float the bus; however, if the processor does drive the bus, no control strobes are active.

3.2 PHYSICAL ADDRESS GENERATION

Physical addresses are generated by 80186 family processors during T_1 of a bus cycle. Since the address and data lines are multiplexed, addresses must be latched during T_1 if they are required to remain stable for the duration of the bus cycle. To facilitate latching of the physical address, 80186 family processors generate an active-HIGH ALE (Address Latch Enable) signal which can be directly connected to the strobe input of a transparent latch. ALE is active for all bus cycles and never floats (except during ONCE Mode for system testing).

Figure 29 illustrates the physical address generation parameters. Addresses are valid no later than T_{CLAV} after the beginning of T_1, and remain valid at least T_{CLAX} after the end of T_1. The ALE signal is driven HIGH in the middle of the T-state (either T_4 or T_i) immediately preceding T_1 and is driven LOW in the middle of T_1, no sooner than T_{AVLL} after address becomes valid. T_{AVLL} satisfies the address latch set-up times of address valid to strobe inactive. Addresses remain stable on the address/data bus at least T_{LLAX} after ALE goes inactive to satisfy address latch hold times.

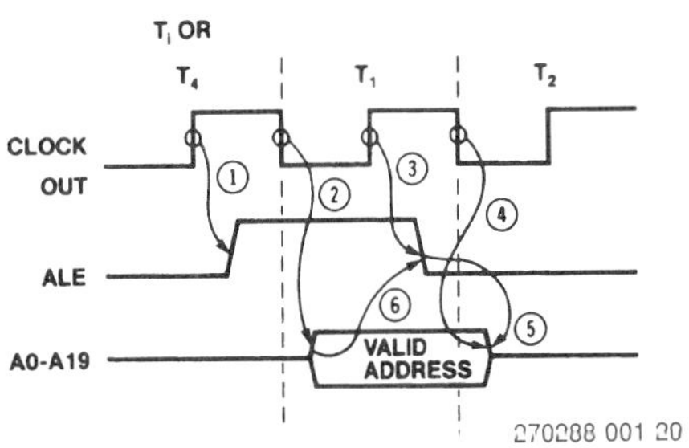

NOTES:
1. T_{CHLH}: Clock high to ALE high.
2. T_{CLAV}: Clock high to address valid.
3. T_{CHLL}: Clock high to ALE low.
4. T_{CLAX}: Clock low to address invalid (address hold from clock low).
5. T_{LLAX}: ALe low t address invalid (address hold from ALE).
6. T_{AVLL}: Address valid to ALE low (address setup to ALE).

Figure 29. Address Generation Timing

Because ALE goes HIGH before addresses become valid, the delay through the address latches will be the propagation delay through the latch rather than the delay from the latch strobe.

A typical circuit for latching physical addresses is shown in Figure 30. This circuit uses 3 transparent non-inverting latches to demultiplex the 20 address bits provided on all 80186 family microprocessors. Typically, the upper 4 address bits only select among various memory components or subsystems, so when the integrated chip selects (see Chapter 7) are used, these upper bits need not be latched. The worst case address generation time from the beginning of T1 (including address latch propagation) time for the circuit is:

$$T_{CLAV} + T_{PD}$$

Some memory and peripheral devices do not require addresses to remain stable throughout a data transfer. If a system is constructed wholly with these types of devices, addresses need not be latched. In addition, two of the peripheral chip select outputs may be configured to provide latched A1 and A2 outputs for peripheral register selects in a system which does not demultiplex the address/data bus.

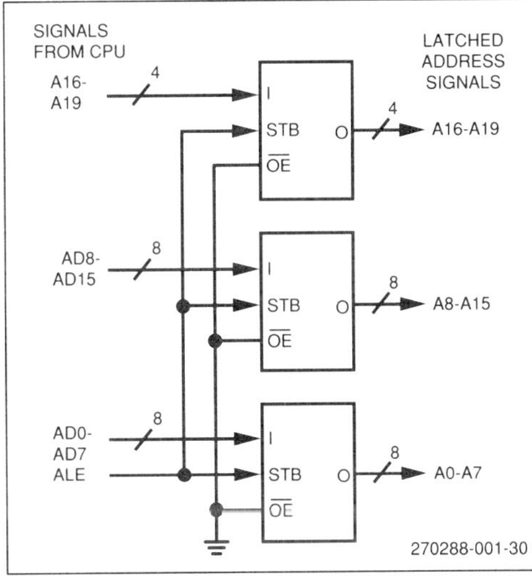

Figure 30. Demultiplexing the Address Bus of an 80186 Family Processor Using Transparent Latches

The 80186/80C186 generates one more signal, $\overline{BHE}$ (Bus High Enable), to address memory. $\overline{BHE}$ and A0 are used to enable data transfers on either or both halves of the 16-bit bus. Since A0 only enables devices onto the lower half of the data bus, systems commonly drive address inputs with address bits A1-A19. This provides 512K unique word addresses, or 1M unique byte addresses. $\overline{BHE}$ does not need to be latched. On the 80188/80C188, $\overline{BHE}$ is absent; all data transfers take place across a single byte-wide data bus.

On 80186 family processors, effective (physical) address calculations take place in dedicated hardware. An effective address (EA) calculation may be either fully-pipelined or non-pipelined. The BIU gives no indication when a fully-pipelined address calculation occurs.

Non-pipelined EA calculations are required anytime an instruction has MOD and R/M bits in its opcode. These bits often denote addressing modes which take longer to calculate the EA, such as register-offset or two-register addressing. Here are some assembly code examples which cause non-pipelined EA calculations:

```
MOV     AX, ES:[DI]           ; Uses indirect
                                addressing.
AND     AX, [DI] + 5          ; Uses register-offset
                                addressing.
XCHG    mem_variable, DX      ; Direct offset but has
                                MOD and R/M bits.
```

A non-pipelined EA calculation takes four clocks, and occurs during T_3(or T_W)-T_4-T_i-T_i, T_4(or T_i)-T_i-T_i-T_i, or DMA deposit bus cycle sequences. In addition to inserting any necessary idle T-states, a non-pipelined EA calculation alters the usual bus cycle priority scheme. Data cycles (reads or writes) associated with the instruction temporarily take the highest bus priority possible, higher than even 80C186/80C188 DRAM refresh cycles. The altered priority scheme is a mechanism to better utilize the Execution Unit.

3.3 DATA BUS

Many small systems do not require buffering because 80186 family devices have adequate bus drive capabilities. If data buffers are not used, care should be taken not to allow bus contention between the processor and the devices directly connected to the data bus. Since the processor floats the address/data bus before activating any command lines, the only requirement on a directly connected device is that it float its output drivers after a read before the processor begins to drive address information for the next bus cycle. The parameter of interest here is the minimum time from RD inactive until addresses go active for the next bus cycle (T_{RHAV}). If the memory or peripheral device cannot disable its output drivers in this time, data buffers will be required to prevent both the processor and the device from driving these lines simultaneously. This parameter is unaffected by the addition of wait states. Data buffers solve this problem because their output float times are typically much faster than the required minimum.

3.3.1 80186/80C186 DATA BUS OPERATION

Throughout T_2, T_3, T_W and T_4 of a bus cycle the multiplexed address/data bus becomes a 16-bit data bus. Data transfers on this bus may be either bytes or words. All memory is byte addressable (see Figure 31).

All bytes with even addresses (A0 = 0) reside on the lower 8 bits of the data bus, while all bytes with odd addresses (A0 = 1) reside on the upper 8 bits of the data bus. Whenever an access is made to only the even byte, A0 is driven LOW, BHE is driven HIGH, and the data transfer occurs on D0-D7 of the data bus. Whenever an access is made to only the odd byte, $\overline{BHE}$ is driven LOW, A0 is driven HIGH, and the data transfer occurs on D8-D15 of the data bus. Finally, if a word access is performed to an even address, both A0 and $\overline{BHE}$ are driven LOW and the data transfer occurs on D0-D15 of the data bus.

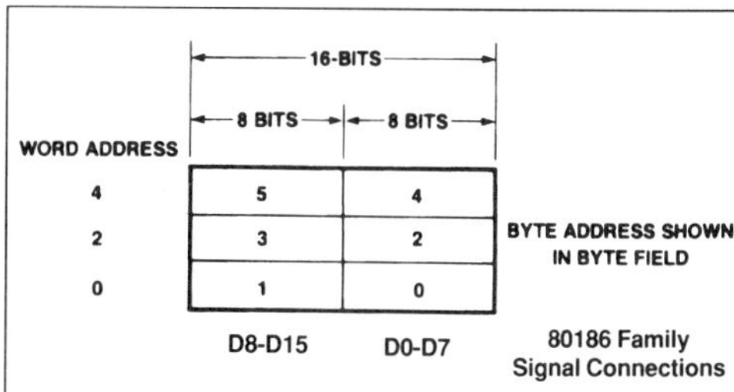

80186 Family Signal Connections

270288-001-31

Figure 31. Physical Memory Byte/Word Addressing in 80186 Family Microprocessors

Word accesses are made to the addressed byte and to the next higher numbered byte. If a word access is performed to an odd address, two byte accesses must be performed, the first to access the odd byte at the first word address on D8-D15, the second to access the even byte at the next sequential word address on D0-D7. For example, in Figure 31, byte 0 and byte 1 can be individually accessed in two separate bus cycles to byte address 0 and 1 at word address 0. They may also be accessed together in a single bus cycle to word address 0. However, if a word access is made to address 1, two bus cycles will be required, the first to access byte 1 at word address 0 (byte 0 will not be accessed), and the second to access byte 2 at word address 2 (byte 3 will not be accessed). This is why all word data should be located at even addresses to increase processor performance.

When byte reads are made, the data returned on the unused half of the data bus is ignored. When byte writes are made, the data driven on the unused half of the data bus is indeterminate.

The 80186/80C186 always fetches the instruction stream in words from even addresses except that the first fetch after a program transfer to an odd address obtains a byte. The processor disassembles the instruction stream inside the processor; so instruction alignment will not materially affect the performance of most systems.

3.3.2 80188/80C188 DATA BUS OPERATION

Because the 80188 and 80C188 externally have only 8-bit data buses, the above discussion about upper and lower bytes of the data bus does not apply. No performance improvement will occur if word data is placed on even boundaries in memory space. All word accesses require two bus cycles, the first to access the lower byte of the word and the second to access the upper byte of the word.

Any 80188/80C188 access to the integrated peripherals is performed 16 bits at a time, whether byte or word addressing is used. If a byte operation is used, the external bus indicates only a single byte transfer even though the word access takes place. See Section 5.2 for more information on peripheral control block registers.

3.3.3 PERIPHERAL INTERFACE

The 80186 family can interface with peripheral devices using either I/O instructions or memory instructions (memory-mapped I/O). The I/O instructions allow the peripheral devices to reside in a separate I/O address space while memory-mapped I/O allows the full power of the instruction set to be used for peripheral operations. Up to 64 Kbytes of I/O address space may be defined for system peripherals. To the programmer, the separate I/O address space is only accessible with IN and OUT commands, which transfer data between peripheral devices and the AX register (or AL for 8-bit data). The first 256 bytes of I/O space (0 to 255) are directly addressable while the entire 64K is only accessible via register indirect addressing through the DX register. The latter technique is particularly desirable for service procedures that handle more than one peripheral by allowing the desired device address to be passed to the procedure as a parameter. Peripherals may be connected to the local CPU bus or a buffered system bus.

On the 80186/80C186, 8-bit peripherals may be connected to either the upper or lower half of the data bus. Assigning an equal number of devices to the upper and lower halves of the bus will distribute the bus loading. If a device is connected to the upper half of the data bus, all I/O addresses assigned to the device must be odd (A0 = 1). If the device is on the lower half of the bus, its addresses must be even (A0 = 0). The address assignment directs the 8-bit transfer to the upper (odd) or lower (even) half of the 16-bit data bus. Since A0 will always be a one or zero for a specific device, A0 cannot be used as an address input to select registers within a specific device. If a device on the upper half of the bus and one on the lower half are assigned addresses that differ only in A0 (adjacent odd and even address), A0 and $\overline{BHE}$ must be conditions of chip select decode to prevent a write to one device from erroneously performing a write to the other.

16-bit peripheral devices should be assigned even addresses for reasons of efficient bus utilization and simplicity of device selection. To guarantee the device is selected only for word operations, A0 and $\overline{BHE}$ should be conditions of chip select decode.

3.4 BUS CONTROL SIGNALS

80186 family processors directly provide the control signals $\overline{RD}$, $\overline{WR}$, $\overline{LOCK}$, and $\overline{TEST}$. In addition, the processors provide the status signals $\overline{S0}$-$\overline{S2}$ and S6 from which other required bus control signals can be generated.

3.4.1 $\overline{RD}$ AND $\overline{WR}$

The $\overline{RD}$ and $\overline{WR}$ signals strobe data from or to memory or I/O space.

The $\overline{RD}$ signal is driven LOW at the beginning of T_2 during all memory and I/O reads (see Figure 32). $\overline{RD}$ will not become active until the microprocessor ceases driving address information on the address/data bus. Data is sampled into the processor at the beginning of T_4. $\overline{RD}$ will not go inactive until the processor's data hold time has been satisfied.

Note that 80186 family processors do not provide separate I/O and memory $\overline{RD}$ signals. If separate I/O read and memory read signals are required, they can be synthesized using the $\overline{S2}$ signal (LOW for I/O operations and HIGH for memory operations) and the $\overline{RD}$ signal (see Figure 33). If this approach is used, the $\overline{S2}$ signal will require latching, since the $\overline{S2}$ signal (like $\overline{S0}$ and $\overline{S1}$) goes to an inactive state well before the beginning of T_4 (where $\overline{RD}$ goes inactive). If $\overline{S2}$ was directly used for this purpose, the type of read command (I/O or memory) could change just before T_4 as $\overline{S2}$ goes to the inactive state (HIGH). The status signals may be latched using ALE.

Often the lack of separate I/O and memory $\overline{RD}$ signals is not important in a system. Each chip select signal will respond to accesses exclusively in memory or I/O space. Thus, when a chip select is used, the external device is enabled only during accesses to the proper address in the proper space.

The $\overline{WR}$ signal is also driven LOW at the beginning of T_2 and driven HIGH at the beginning of T_4 (see Figure 34). The $\overline{WR}$ signal is active for all memory and I/O writes, similar to the $\overline{RD}$ signal. Again, separate memory and I/O control lines may be generated using the latched $\overline{S2}$ signal along with $\overline{WR}$. More important, however, is the role of the active-going edge of $\overline{WR}$. At the time $\overline{WR}$ makes its HIGH-to-LOW transition, valid write data is not present on the data bus. This has consequences when using $\overline{WR}$ to generate signals such as column address strobe ($\overline{CAS}$) for DRAMs where data is required to be stable on the falling edge. In DRAM applications, the problem is solved by a DRAM controller. For other applications which require valid data before the $\overline{WR}$ transition, place cross-coupled NAND gates between the CPU and the device on the $\overline{WR}$ line (see Figure 35). The added gates delay the active-going edge of $\overline{WR}$ to the device by one clock phase, at which time valid data is driven on the bus by the microprocessor.

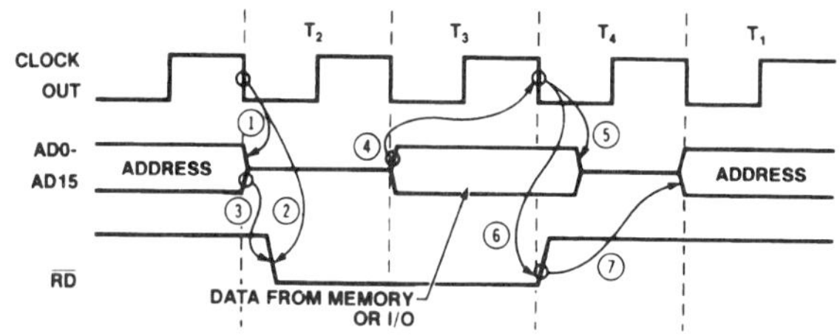

270288-001-32

NOTES:

1. T_{CLAZ}: Clock low unit address float.
2. T_{CRL}: Clock low unit $\overline{RD}$ active.
3. T_{AZRL}: Address float until $\overline{RD}$ active.
4. T_{DVCL}: Data valid until clock low (data input set-up time).
5. T_{CLDX}: Clock low until data invalid (data input hold time).
6. T_{CLRH}: Clock low until $\overline{RD}$ high.
7. T_{RHAVE}: RD high until addresses valid.

Figure 32. Read Cycle Timing of 80186 Family Microprocessors

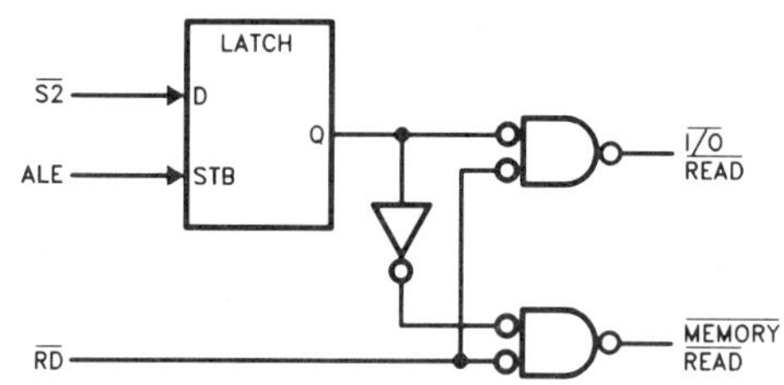

270288-001-33

Figure 33. Generating I/O and Memory Read Signals

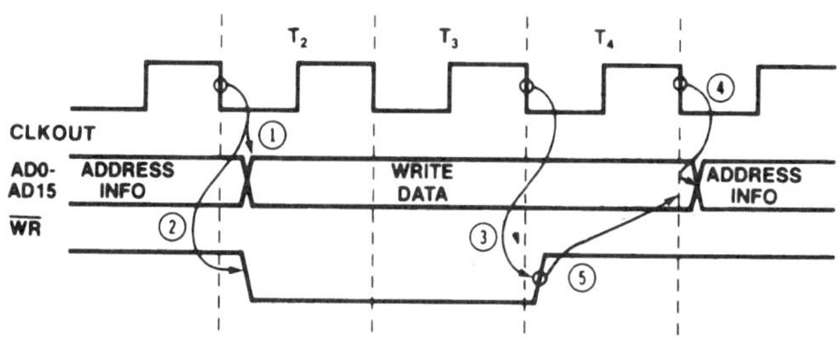

270288-001-34

NOTES:

1. T_{CLDV}: Clock low until data valid.
2. T_{CVTV}: Clock low until $\overline{WR}$ active.
3. T_{CVCTX}: Clock low until $\overline{WR}$ inactive.
4. T_{CLDOX}: Clock high until data valid.
5. T_{WHDX}: $\overline{WR}$ inactive until data invalid.

Figure 34. Family Write Cycle Timing

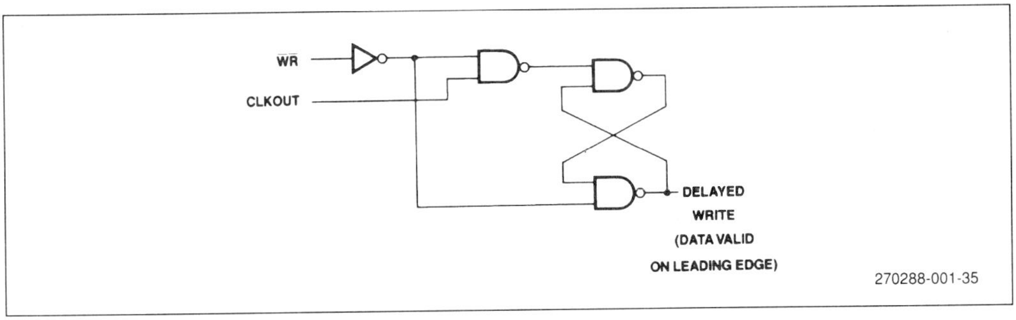

Figure 35. Synthesizing a Delayed Write Signal

3.4.2 QUEUE STATUS SIGNALS

If the $\overline{\text{RD}}$ line is externally grounded during RESET and remains grounded during processor operation, the processor enters Queue Status Mode. When in this mode, the $\overline{\text{WR}}$ and ALE signals become queue status outputs, reflecting the status of the internal prefetch queue during each clock cycle. These signals are provided to allow a coprocessor (such as the Intel 8087) to track execution of instructions within the microprocessor. The interpretation of QS0 (ALE) and QS1 ($\overline{\text{WR}}$) is given in Table 13. Note that since Execution Unit operation is independent of Bus Interface Unit operation, queue status lines may change in any T-state.

Table 13. Queue Status Encoding

QS1	QS0	Interpretation
0	0	no operation
0	1	first byte of instruction taken from queue
1	0	queue was reinitialized
1	1	subsequent byte of instruction taken from queue

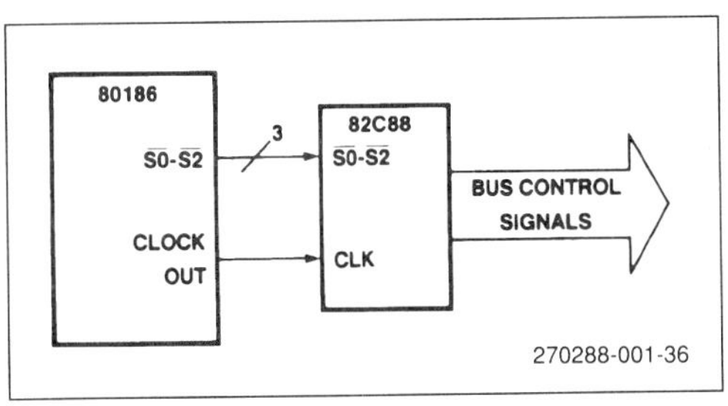

Figure 36. 80186/82C88 Bus Controller Inteconnection

ALE, $\overline{\text{RD}}$, and $\overline{\text{WR}}$ signals are not directly available from an 80186 family processor when it is configured in Queue Status Mode. These signals must be derived from the status lines $\overline{\text{S0}}$-$\overline{\text{S2}}$ using an external 82C88 or 82188 Bus Controller (see Figure 36). To prevent the microprocessor from accidentally entering Queue Status Mode during RESET, the $\overline{\text{RD}}$ line is internally provided with a weak pullup device.

3.4.3 STATUS LINES

An 80186 family processor provides three status outputs which indicate the type of bus cycle in progress. These signals go from an inactive state (all HIGH) to one of seven possible active states during the T-state immediately preceding T_1 of a bus cycle (see Figure 28). The possible status line encodings are given in Table 14. The status lines are driven inactive in the T3 or TW state immediately preceding T_4 of the current bus cycle.

Table 14. Status Line Interpretation

S2	S1	S0	Operation
0	0	0	interrupt acknowledge
0	0	1	read I/O
0	1	0	write I/O
0	1	1	halt
1	0	0	instruction fetch
1	0	1	read memory
1	1	0	write memory
1	1	1	passive

The status lines may be directly connected to an 82C88 Bus Controller, which provides local bus control signals or MULTIBUS™ control signals (see Figure 36). Use of the 82C88 Bus Controller does not preclude the use of the CPU-generated $\overline{\text{RD}}$, $\overline{\text{WR}}$ and ALE signals, however. The processor-generated signals can provide local bus control signals, while an 82C88 can provide MULTIBUS control signals.

Two additional status signals are provided by 80186 family members. S6 provides information concerning the unit generating the bus cycle. It is multiplexed with A19 and available during T_2, T_3, T_4 and T_W. The processor drives this line LOW whenever the bus cycle is generated by the CPU, but drives it HIGH when the bus cycle is generated by the integrated DMA Unit.

S7 is logically equivalent to $\overline{\text{BHE}}$ and is provided by the 80186. This pin is always HIGH on the 80188 and 80C188 (except during 80C188 DRAM refresh cycles) which signifies the presence of an 8-bit data bus.

3.4.4 SOFTWARE-INITIATED BUS CONTROL

The programmer may control the progress of 80186 family execution-related bus activity by using the WAIT (or FWAIT), LOCK, and HLT instructions.

3.4.4.1 $\overline{\text{TEST}}$ INPUT AND $\overline{\text{LOCK}}$ OUTPUT

The 80186 family processor provides a $\overline{\text{TEST}}$ input ($\overline{\text{TEST}}$/BUSY on the 80C186) and a $\overline{\text{LOCK}}$ output for coordinating instruction execution and bus activity.

The $\overline{\text{TEST}}$ input is used in conjunction with the processor WAIT instruction, typically in a system containing a coprocessor. If the input is HIGH when WAIT executes, instruction execution suspends. $\overline{\text{TEST}}$ will be resampled every five clocks until it goes LOW, resuming execution. Any enabled interrupts will be serviced while the processor waits for $\overline{\text{TEST}}$. This input must also be driven at RESET to configure an 80C186/80C188 for Enhanced Mode (see Appendix C.2).

The $\overline{\text{LOCK}}$ output is driven LOW whenever the data cycles of a LOCKed instruction are executed. A LOCKed instruction is generated whenever the LOCK prefix occurs immediately before an instruction. The LOCK prefix is active for the single instruction immediately following the LOCK prefix. The $\overline{\text{LOCK}}$ signal indicates to a bus arbiter (e.g., the 8289) that an atomic (uninterruptible) bus operation is occurring. The bus arbiter should under no circumstances release the bus while LOCKed transfers are occurring. An 80186 family processor will not recognize a bus HOLD, nor will it allow DMA cycles to be run by the integrated DMA Controller during LOCKed operations. LOCKed transfers are typically used in multiprocessor systems to access memory-based semaphore variables which control access to shared system resources.

On 80186 family devices, the $\overline{\text{LOCK}}$ signal will go active during T1 of the first data cycle of the LOCKed transfer. It is driven inactive at the end of T4 of the last data cycle of the LOCKed transfers independent of the number of wait states.

On the 80186 or the 80188, back-to-back LOCKed instructions are not allowed. Insert at least six bytes of code between the end of the first LOCKed instruction and the beginning of the second LOCKed instruction. This restriction does not apply to the 80C186/80C188.

The $\overline{\text{LOCK}}$ output is also driven LOW during interrupt acknowledge cycles when the integrated Interrupt Controller operates in Cascade or Slave Modes (see Sections 9.5.2.2 and 9.6). In these modes, the operation of the $\overline{\text{LOCK}}$ pin may be altered when an interrupt occurs during execution of a LOCKed instruction. See Section 9.5.4.2 for a circuit necessary to block DMA and HOLD requests under such circumstances.

80186 family processors drive $\overline{\text{LOCK}}$ HIGH for one clock during RESET. Then, the pin floats until the start of the first bus cycle. $\overline{\text{LOCK}}$ also floats during HOLD.

3.4.4.2 PROCESSOR HALT

A HALT bus cycle signifies that the CPU has executed the HLT (HALT) instruction. It differs from a regular bus cycle in two ways.

The first way a HALT bus cycle differs is that neither $\overline{\text{RD}}$ nor $\overline{\text{WR}}$ will be driven active. Address and data information will not be driven by the processor. The second way a HALT bus cycle differs is that the $\overline{\text{S0}}$-$\overline{\text{S2}}$ status lines go to their inactive state (all HIGH) during T_2 of the bus cycle, well before they go to their inactive state during a regular bus cycle.

Like a normal bus cycle, however, ALE is driven active. Since no valid address information is present, the information strobed into the address latches should be ignored. This ALE pulse can be used, however, to latch the HALT status from the $\overline{\text{S0}}$-$\overline{\text{S2}}$ status lines. READY is ignored during HALT cycles.

The HALTed state of the processor does not interfere with the operation of any of the 80186 family integrated peripheral units. This means that if a DMA transfer is pending while the processor is HALTed, the bus cycles associated with the transfer will run. In fact, DMA latency time will improve while the processor is HALTed because the DMA Unit will not be contending with the processor for access to the bus (see Section 8.5.1). After the processor HALTs, a HOLD input can elicit HLDA and release of the bus by the processor as usual.

Activation of $\overline{\text{RES}}$, an NMI request, or a non-masked interrupt request from the integrated Interrupt Controller forces the processor out of the HALT state.

3.5 TRANSCEIVER CONTROL SIGNALS

If data buffers are required, the 80186 family processor provides $\overline{DEN}$ (Data ENable) and DT/$\overline{R}$ (Data Transmit/Receive) signals to simplify buffer interfacing. The $\overline{DEN}$ and DT/$\overline{R}$ signals are activated during all bus cycles, including transfers between the 80C186 and 80C187.

The $\overline{DEN}$ signal is driven LOW whenever the processor is either ready to receive data (during a read) or when the processor is ready to send data (during a write). In other words, $\overline{DEN}$ is LOW during any active bus cycle when address information is not being generated on the address/data pins. In most systems, the $\overline{DEN}$ signal should not be directly connected to the $\overline{OE}$ inputs of a buffer, since unbuffered devices (or other buffers) may be directly connected to the processors's address/data pins. If $\overline{DEN}$ were directly connected to several buffers, contention would occur during read cycles, as many devices attempt to drive the processor bus. Rather, it should be a factor along with the chip selects in generating the output enable. $\overline{DEN}$ is HIGH whenever DT/$\overline{R}$ changes state.

The DT/$\overline{R}$ signal determines the direction of data through the bi-directional buffers. It is HIGH whenever data is being written from the processor, and is LOW whenever data is being read into the processor. DT/$\overline{R}$ does not change states between sequential reads or sequential writes. Unlike the $\overline{DEN}$ signal, it may be directly connected to bus buffers, since this signal does not usually enable the output drivers of the buffer. Figure 37 shows an example data bus subsystem supporting both buffered and unbuffered devices. Note that the A side of the buffer is connected to the 80186 family device, the B side to the external device. The DT/$\overline{R}$ signal can directly drive the T (transmit) signal of a typical buffer since it has the correct polarity.

The processor drives the DT/$\overline{R}$ and $\overline{DEN}$ pins HIGH for one clock during RESET. Then the pins float until the first bus cycle.

3.6 READY INTERFACING

80186 family devices provide two READY lines, a synchronous (SRDY) line and an asynchronous (ARDY) line. These lines signal the Bus Interface Unit to insert wait states (T_W) into a CPU bus cycle, allowing slower devices to respond to bus activity. Wait states will only be inserted when both ARDY and SRDY are LOW, i.e., only one of the lines needs to be active to terminate a bus cycle. Figure 38 depicts the logical ORing of the ARDY and SRDY functions. Any number of wait states may be inserted into a bus cycle. The processor will ignore the READY inputs during any accesses to the integrated peripheral registers and to any area where the chip select READY bits indicate that the external READY should be ignored. The timings required by the SRDY and ARDY lines are different.

Only the ARDY line can be fully synchronized (see Appendix B) by the CPU before presentation to the rest of the bus control logic. As shown in Figure 38, the first flip-flop is used to resolve the asynchronous transition of the ARDY line. It will achieve a definite HIGH or LOW level before its output is latched into the second flip-flop. When latched HIGH, it passes along the level present on the ARDY line; when latched LOW, it forces Not READY to be passed along to the rest of the circuit. With this design, note that only the rising edge of ARDY is fully synchronized; the falling edge of ARDY must be externally synchronized to the processor clock. Any asynchronous transition on the ARDY line when the processor is not sampling the input does not matter.

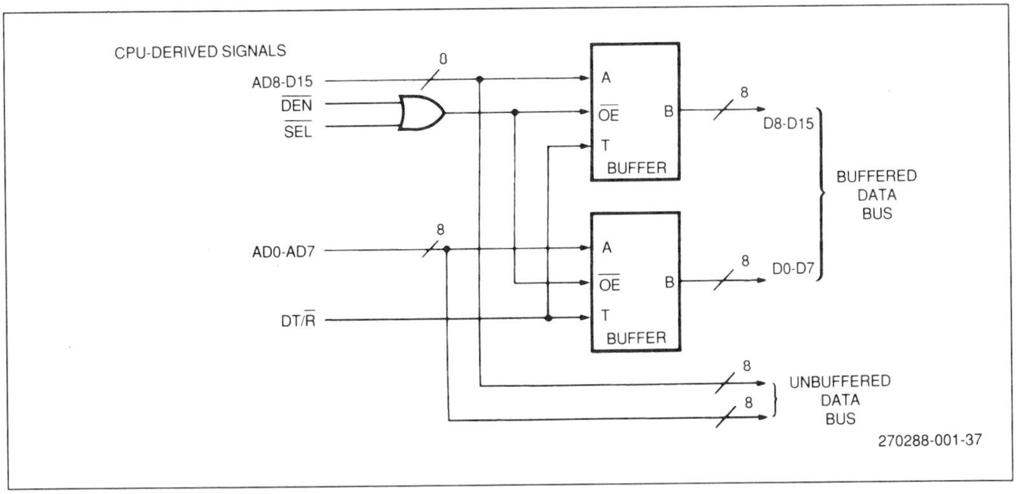

Figure 37. Example Buffered/Unbuffered Data Bus

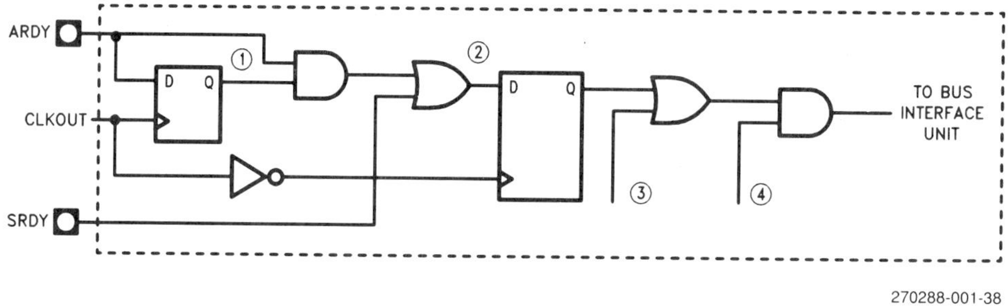

NOTES:
1. Asynchronous Resolution Flip-Flop.
2. Ready Latch Flip-Flop.
3. R2 Bit in Chip Select Registers (Selects Internal Only (1) or External (0).
4. Internally Generated Unit States Controlled by R0 and R1 Bits in Chip Select Registers.

Figure 38. 80186 READY Circuitry

Figure 39 depicts activity for Normally-READY and Normally-Not-READY configurations of external logic. Remember that for ARDY to force wait states, SRDY must be LOW as well.

In a Normally-Not-READY implementation the setup and hold times of both the resolution flip-flop and the READY latch must be satisfied. The ARDY pin must go active at least T_{ARYHCH} (also denoted T_{ARYCH}) before the rising edge of T_2, T_3 or T_W, and stay active until T_{CLARX} after the falling edge of T_3 or T_W to stop generation of wait states and terminate the bus cycle. If ARDY goes active after the falling edge of T_3 there will be no wait state inserted.

In a Normally-READY implementation the setup and hold times of either the resolution flip-flop or the READY latch must be met. If the external hardware does not meet this requirement, the CPU will not function properly. Wait states will be generated if ARDY goes inactive T_{ARYHCH} (also denoted T_{ARYCH}) before the rising edge of T_2 and stays inactive a minimum of T_{ARYCH} before the rising edge of T_2 and stays inactive a minimum of T_{ARYCHL} after the edge, or if ARDY goes inactive at least T_{ARYLCL} before the falling edge of T_3 and stays inactive a minimum of T_{CLARX} after the edge. The READY circuitry performs this way to allow a slow device the maximum amount of time to respond with a Not READY after it has been selected.

The synchronous READY (SRDY) line requires that all transitions during T_2, T_3, or T_W satisfy setup and hold times (T_{SRYCL} and T_{CLSRY} respectively). If the external hardware does not meet this requirement, the CPU will not function properly. Valid transitions on this line and subsequent wait state insertion is shown in Figure 40. The Bus Interface Unit samples SRDY at the beginning of each T_3 and T_W. If the line is sampled active at the beginning of either of these two cycles, that cycle will be immediately followed by T_4. If the line is sampled inactive at the beginning of either T-state, that cycle will be followed by a T_W. An asynchronous transition on the SRDY line occurring at any time the processor is not sampling the input will not cause CPU malfunction.

3.7 EXECUTION UNIT/BUS INTERFACE UNIT RELATIONSHIP

The 80186 family employs a pipelined architecture that allows instructions to be prefetched during spare bus cycles. The Bus Interface Unit (BIU) fetches instructions from memory and loads them into a prefetch queue. The Execution Unit (EU) executes instructions from the prefetch queue while other instructions are prefetched. The process of fetching new instructions while executing the current instruction is invisible to the user.

3.7.1 PREFETCH QUEUE AND BUS PERFORMANCE

The prefetch queue is six bytes long on the 80186/80C186. When two or more bytes are empty and the EU does not require the BIU to perform a bus cycle, the BIU executes instruction fetch cycles to refill the queue. Figure 41 shows how instruction fetches are interleaved with EU-initiated bus cycles. The chosen queue size allows the BIU to keep the EU supplied with prefetched instructions under most conditions without monopolizing the system bus. Recall that the 80186/80C186 BIU normally accesses two bytes (one word) of opcode per

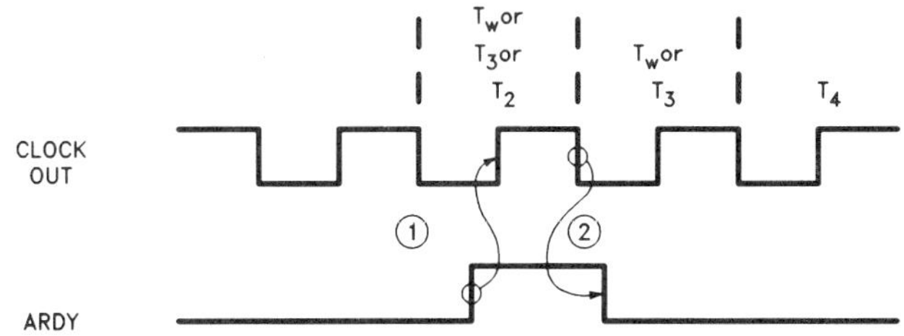

270288-001-39

In a Normally-Not-READY system, wait states will be inserted unless:
1. T_{ARYCH} (also denoted T_{ARYCH}): ARDY active to clock high (ARDY resolution setup time).
2. T_{CLARX}: Clock low to ARDY inactive (ARDY active hold time).

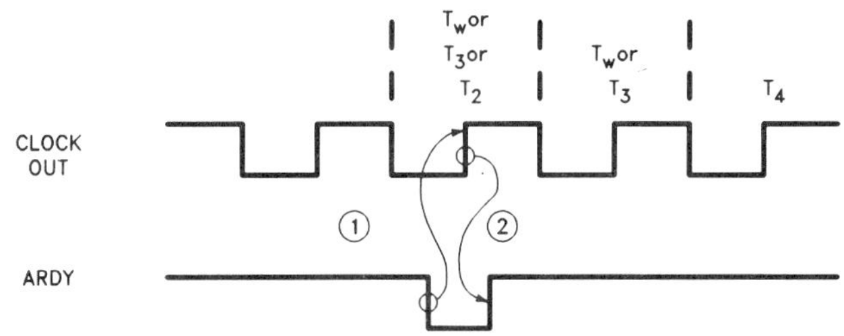

270288-001-40

In a Normally-READY system, wait states will be inserted if:
1. T_{ARYHCH} (also denoted T_{ARYCH}): ARDY low to clock high (ARDY resolution setup time).
2. T_{ARYCHL}: (Clock high to ARDY high (ARDY inactive hold time).

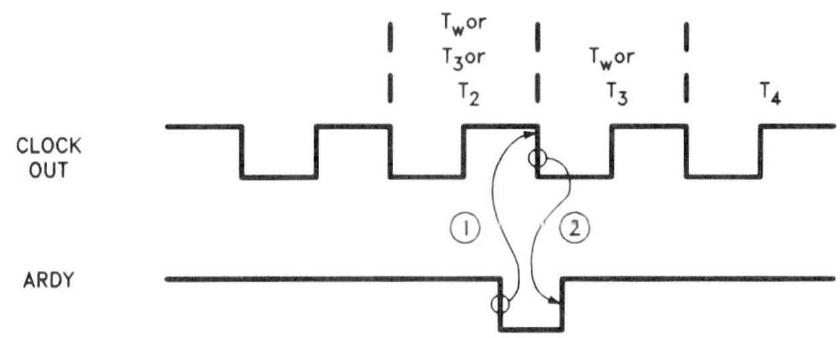

270288-001-41

Alternatively, in a Normally-READY system, wait states will be inserted if:
1. T_{ARYCL}: ARDY low to clock low (ARDY setup time).
2. T_{CLARX}: Clock low to ARDY high (ARDY active time).
ARDY must meet T_{ARYLCL} and T_{CLARX} or undesired CPU operation will result.

Figure 39. ARDY Transitions

bus cycle. If a program transfer forces fetching from an odd address, the 80186/80C186 automatically reads one byte from the odd address and then resumes fetching words from the subsequent even addresses.

The prefetch queue is four bytes long on the 80188/80C188. When one or more bytes are empty, the processor attempts to refill the queue. With an 8-bit data bus, the 80188/80C188 BIU accesses one byte of opcode per bus cycle.

In most circumstances the queues contain at least one byte of the instruction stream and the EU does not have to wait for instructions to be fetched. The queue holds instructions from memory locations just above the source of the current instruction. That is, they are the next logical instructions so long as execution proceeds serially. If the EU executes an instruction that transfers control to another location, the BIU resets the queue, fetches the instruction from the new address, passes it immediately to the EU, and then begins refilling the queue

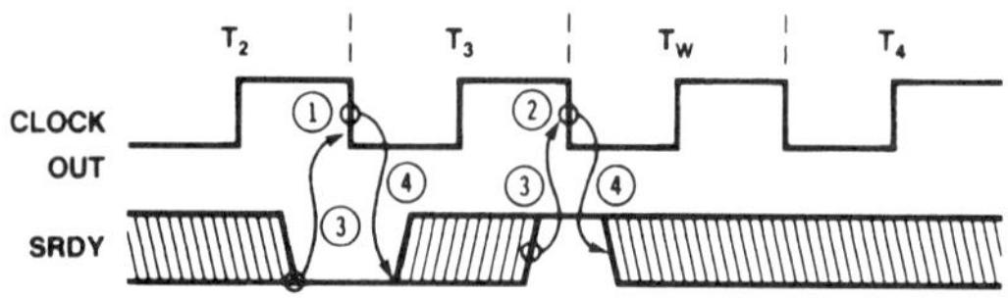

270288-001-42

NOTES:
1. Decision: Not READY, T-State will be followed by a wait state.
2. Decision: READY, T-State will not be follwed by a wait state.
3. T_{SRYCL}: Synchronous Ready stable until clock low (SRDY set-up time).
4. T_{CLSRY}: Clow low until Synchronous Ready transition (SRDY hold time).

Figure 40. Valid SRDY Transitions

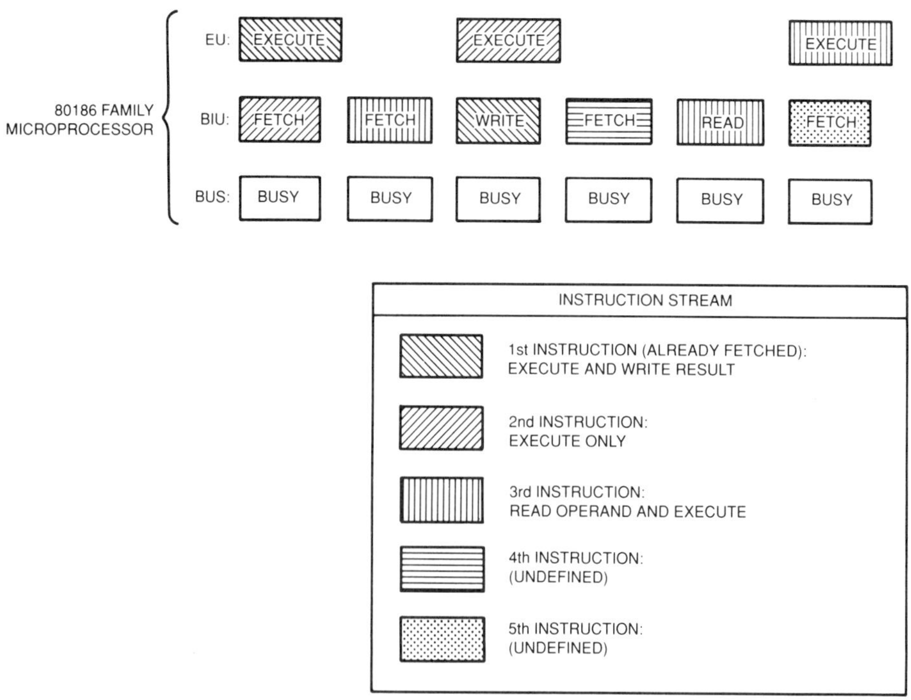

270288-001-43

Figure 41. Overlapped Instruction Fetch and Execution

from the new location. In addition, the BIU suspends instruction fetching whenever the EU requests a memory or I/O read or write, except for a fetch already in progress.

Bus cycles occur sequentially, but do not necessarily follow immediately one after another. Since the CPU prefetches up to six bytes of the instruction stream for storage and execution from an internal instruction queue, the relationship between prefetching and instruction execution may be skewed in time and separated by additional instruction fetch bus cycles. In general, if the BIU fetches an instruction into the processor's internal instruction queue, it may also fetch several additional instructions before the EU removes the instruction from the queue and executes it. If the EU executes a jump or other control transfer instruction from the queue, it ignores any instructions remaining in the queue; the CPU discards these instructions with no effect on operation. The bus activity observed during execution of a specific instruction depends on the preceding instructions; the activity, however, may always be determined within a specific sequence.

3.7.2 BUS PERFORMANCE AND CPU PERFORMANCE

Overall performance of a system based on an 80186 family member system depends on both the bus bandwidth and execution rate.

The number of clock cycles required to execute an instruction varies from two clocks for a register to register move to 67 clocks for an integer divide. If a program contains many long instructions, program execution will be CPU-limited, i.e., the prefetch queue will be full most of the time. If a program contains mainly short instructions or data move instructions, execution will be bus-limited. Here the processor will be required to wait often for an instruction to be fetched before it continues its operation.

With their 8-bit data buses, the 80188 and 80C188 provide an opportunity for significant system cost savings over their 16-bit counterparts, the 80186 and 80C186. In applications which manipulate only 8-bit quantities, the performance of the processors with 8-bit buses can approach that of the processors with 16-bit buses. The same is true for applications that are highly CPU-intensive (but not memory-intensive) since all 80186 family CPUs are internally 16-bit.

Typical 80186 family applications are more data-intensive than computation-intensive. The processor with an 8-bit bus must not only move data around eight bits at a time but also fetch instructions eight bits at a time. A sufficient number of prefetched bytes may not reside in the prefetch queue much of the time. In many cases, the performance degradation of an 8-bit bus will be significant.

Adding up instruction clock counts given in 80186 family data sheets and reference manuals yields only a rough approximation of execution time. Published clock counts assume that all the necessary opcode bytes reside in the prefetch queue, frequently not the case in the 80188/80C188. A conservative rule of thumb for the 80188/80C188 is to add 100 per cent to the calculated clock count. The correction for the 80186/80C186 is typically about five to seven per cent. If there is any doubt of the performance capabilities of either the 80186/80C186 or the 80188/80C188, Intel suggests the use of a performance analyzer on critical code sections early in the design process.

3.7.3 WAIT STATES AND CPU PERFORMANCE

Because an 80186 family processor contains separate Bus Interface and Execution Units, the actual performance of the processor will not degrade at a constant rate as wait states are added to the memory cycle time from the processor. Shown below are two disparate 80186 assembly language routines, and the actual execution time for the two procedures as wait states are added to the memory system of the processor (CLKOUT = 8 MHz). The percentage degradation from each wait state level to the following wait state level is also indicated. The actual rate of performance degradation is not as important as the conclusion that wait state degradation will depend on the type and mix of instructions encountered in the user's program.

Table 15. Performance Degradation vs. Wait States

# of Wait States	Program 1		Program 2	
	Exec Time (µsec)	Perf Degr	Exec Time (µsec)	Perf Degr
0	505		294	
1	595	18%	311	6%
2	669	12%	337	8%
3	752	12%	347	3%

Procedure Bench_1 is very bus intensive. It performs many memory operations using elaborate addressing modes which also require more opcode bytes. As a result, the Execution Unit must constantly wait for the Bus Interface Unit to fetch and perform the memory cycles to allow it to continue. Thus, the execution time of this type of routine will grow quickly as wait states are added, since the execution time depends mainly on the speed at which the processor can run bus cycles.

```
$mod186
name                    example_wait_state_performance
;
; This file contains two programs which demonstrate the 80186 family processor
;       performance degradation as wait states are inserted. Procedure Bench1
;       performs a transformation between two types of characters sets, then
;       copies the transformed characters back to the original buffer (which is
;       64 bytes long. Procedure Bench2 performs the same type of
;       transformation, however instead of performing a table lookup, it
;       multiplies each number in the original 32 word buffer by a constant 3
;       (note the use of the integer immediate multiply instruction). Program
;       nothing_ is used to measure the call and the return times from the
;       driver program only.
;
cgroup              group   code
dgroup              group   data
data                segment public_data_

t_table             db      256 dup(?)
t_string            db      64 dup(?)
m_array             dw      32 dup(?)
data                ends

code                segment public'code'
                    assume  CS:cgroup,DS:dgroup
                    public  bench_1,bench_2,nothing_,wait state_,set_timer_
bench_1             proc    near
                    push    SI                      ; save registers used
                    push    CX
                    push    BX
                    push    AX

                    mov     CX,64                   ; translate 64 bytes
                    mov     SI,0
                    mov     BH,0

loop_back:
                    mov     BL,t_string[SI]         ; get the byte
                    mov     AL,t_table[BX]          ; translate byte
                    mov     t_string[SI],AL         ; and store it
                    inc     SI                      ; increment index
                    loop    loop_back               ; do the next byte

                    pop     AX
                    pop     BX
                    pop     CX
                    pop     SI
bench_1             endp

bench_2             proc    near
                    push    AX                      ; save registers used
                    push    SI
                    push    CX

                    mov     CX,32                   ; multiply 32 numbers
                    mov     SI,offset m_array

loop_back_2:
                    imul    AX,word ptr [SI],3       ; immediate multiply
                    mov     word ptr [SI],AX
                    inc     SI
                    inc     SI
                    loop    loop_back_2

                    pop     CX
                    pop     SI
                    pop     AX
                    ret
bench_2             endp
```

Figure 42. Assembly Language Program for Wait State Evaluation

```
nothing_                proc    near
                        ret
nothing_                endp
;
;  Wait_state(n) sets the 80186 family processor LMCS register to the number of
;         wait states (0 to 3) indicated by the parameter n (which is passed on
;         the stack). No other bits of the LMCS register are modified.
;
wait_state_             proc    near
                        enter   0,0                     ; set up stack frame
                        push    AX                      ; save registers used
                        push    BX
                        push    DX

                        mov     BX,word ptr [BP +4]     ; get argument
                        mov     DX,0FFA2h               ; get current LMCS register
                                                        ; contents
                        in      AX,DX

                        and     AX,0FFCh                ; and off existing ready bits
                        and     BX,3                    ; insure ws count is good
                        or      AX,BX                   ; adjust the ready bits
                        out     DX,AX                   ; and write to LMCS
                        pop     DX
                        pop     BX
                        pop     AX
                        leave                           ; tear downstack frame
wait_state_             endp
;

;  Set_timer() initializes the 80186 family processor timers to count
;         microseconds. Timer 2 is set up as a prescaler to timer 0, the
;         microsecond count can be read directly out of the timer 0 count
;         register at location FF50H in I/O space.
;
set_timer_              proc    near
                        push    AX
                        push    DX

                        mov     DX,0ff66h               ; stop timer 2
                        mov     AX,4000h
                        out     DX,AX

                        mov     DX,0ff50h               ; clear timer 0 count
                        mov     AX,0
                        out     DX,AX

                        mov     DX,0ff52h               ; timer 0 counts up to 65535
                        mov     AX,0
                        out     DX,AX

                        mov     DX,0ff56h               ; enable timer 0
                        mov     AX,0c009h
                        out     DX,AX

                        mov     DX,0ff60h               ; clear timer 2 count
                        mov     AX,0
                        out     DX,AX

                        mov     DX,0ff62h               ; set maximum count of timer 2
                        mov     AX,2
                        out     DX,AX

                        mov     DX,0ff66h               ; re-enable timer 2
                        mov     AX,0c001h
                        out     DX,AX
```

Figure 42. Assembly Language Program for Wait State Evaluation (continued)

```
                    pop     DX
                    pop     AX
                    ret
set_timer_          endp
code                ends
                    end
```

270288-001-44

Figure 42. Assembly Language Program for Wait State Evaluation (continued)

Note also that the program execution time calculated by merely summing up the number of clock cycles given in the data sheet will typically be less than the number of clock cycles actually required to run the program. This is true because the numbers quoted in the data sheet assume that the opcode bytes have been prefetched and reside in the prefetch queue for immediate access by the execution unit. If the Execution Unit cannot access the opcode bytes immediately upon request, dead clock cycles will be inserted in which the Execution Unit will remain idle, thus increasing the number of clock cycles required to complete execution of the program.

On the other hand, procedure Bench_2 is more CPU intensive. The Bus Interface Unit can fill up the instruction prefetch queue in parallel with the Execution Unit performing integer multiplies. In this program, the Bus Interface Unit can perform bus operations faster than the Execution Unit actually requires them to be run. The performance degradation is much less as wait states are added to the memory interface. The execution time of this program is close to the number calculated by adding the number of cycles per instruction because the Execution Unit does not have to wait for the Bus Interface Unit to place an opcode byte in the prefetch queue as often. Fewer clock cycles are wasted by the Execution Unit lying idle for want of instructions.

3.8 HOLD/HLDA INTERFACE

The 80186 family employs a HOLD/HLDA bus exchange protocol. This protocol allows other asynchronous bus masters (i.e., ones which drive address, data, and control information on the bus) to gain control.

3.8.1 RESPONSE TO HOLD

In the HOLD/HLDA protocol, a device requiring bus control (e.g., a token-ring communications controller) raises the HOLD line. In response to this HOLD request, the processor will raise its HLDA line after it has finished its current bus activity. When the external device is finished with the bus, it drops its bus HOLD request. The processor responds by dropping its HLDA line and resuming bus operation.

When the processor recognizes a bus HOLD by driving HLDA HIGH, it will float many of its signals (see Figure 43). AD0-AD14 and $\overline{\text{DEN}}$ are floated within T_{CLAZ} after the clock edge when HLDA is driven active. A16-A19, $\overline{\text{RD}}$, $\overline{\text{WR}}$, $\overline{\text{BHE}}$, DT/R, and $\overline{\text{S0-S2}}$ are floated within TCHCZ after the clock edge on which HLDA becomes active.

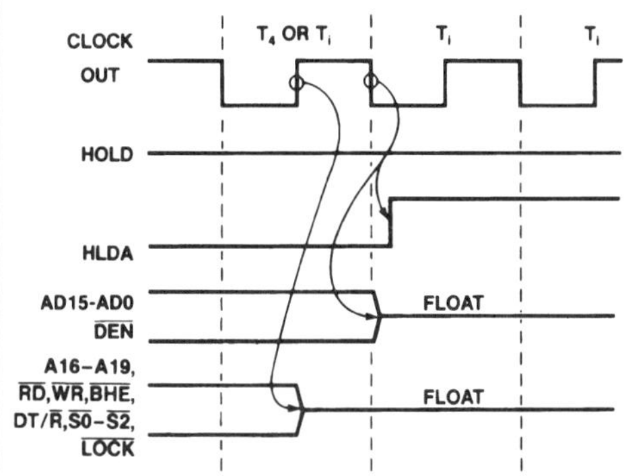

270288-001-45

Figure 43. Signal Float/HLDA Timing of 80186 Processor

Only the above mentioned signals are floated during bus HOLD. Of the signals not floated by the processor, some have to do with peripheral functionality (e.g., timer outputs). Many others either directly or indirectly control bus devices. These signals are ALE and all chip select lines ($\overline{\text{UCS}}$, $\overline{\text{LCS}}$, $\overline{\text{MCS0-3}}$, and $\overline{\text{PCS0-6}}$). If Latched A1 or Latched A2 is selected instead of $\overline{\text{PCS5}}$ or $\overline{\text{PCS6}}$, the programmed pin retains its latched value during HOLD.

3.8.2 HOLD/HLDA TIMING AND BUS LATENCY

The time required between HOLD going active and the microprocessor driving HLDA active is known as bus latency. Many factors affect bus latency, including synchronization delays, bus cycle times, LOCKed transfer times, interrupt acknowledge cycles, and DRAM refresh cycles.

The HOLD request line is internally synchronized by the 80186 family processor, and may therefore be an asynchronous input. To guarantee recognition on a particular falling clock edge, it must satisfy setup and hold times. A full CPU clock cycle is required for synchronization (see Appendix B). If the bus is idle, HLDA will follow HOLD by two CPU clock cycles plus setup and propagation delay time. The first clock cycle synchronizes the input; the second signals the internal circuitry to initiate a bus HOLD (see Figure 44).

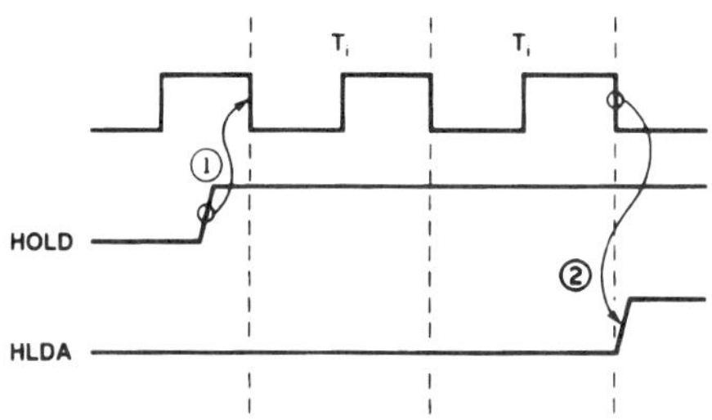

NOTES:
1. T_{HVCL}: Hold valid until clock low.
2. T_{CLHAV}: Clock low until HLDA active.

Figure 44. Idle Bus Hold/HLDA Timing

Many factors make bus latency longer than the best case described above. Perhaps the most important factor is that the processor will not relinquish the local bus until the bus is idle. The bus can become idle only at the end of a bus cycle. The processor will normally insert no Ti states between T_4 and T_1 of the next bus cycle if it requires any bus activity (e.g., instruction fetches or I/O reads). However, the processor may not have an immediate need for the bus after a bus cycle, and will insert Ti states independent of the HOLD input (see Section 3.1).

When the HOLD request is active, the 80186 family BIU will proceed from T_4 to T_i to relinquish the bus. HOLD must go active two T-states before the end of a bus cycle to force the BIU to insert idle T-states after T4. One T-state is spent synchronizing the request and one T-state is spent signaling the processor that T4 of the bus cycle will be followed by idle T-states (see Section 3.1). After the bus cycle has ended, the HOLD will be immediately acknowledged. If, however, the processor has already determined that an idle T-state will follow T_4 of the current bus cycle, HOLD needs to go active only two T-states before the end of the bus cycle to force the microprocessor to relinquish the bus. Figure 45 shows these processes.

Also, if HOLD is asserted during RESET, the processor releases the bus prior to the first fetch.

An external HOLD has higher priority than both the CPU or integrated DMA Unit. However, an external HOLD will not separate the two cycles needed to perform a word access when the word accessed is located at an odd location (see Section 3.3.1). In addition, an external HOLD will not separate the two to four bus cycles required for the integrated DMA Unit to perform a complete transfer. Each of these factors will add to the bus latency of the 80186 family processor.

Another factor influencing bus latency time is LOCKed transfers. Whenever a LOCKed transfer is occurring, the processor will not recognize external HOLDs. Also, the processor will not recognize requests from the DMA Control Unit for DMA cycles. LOCKed transfers are programmed by preceding an instruction with the LOCK prefix. String instructions may be LOCKed. Since string transfers may require thousands of bus cycles, bus latency time will suffer if they are LOCKed.

The final factor affecting bus latency time is interrupt acknowledge cycles. When an external interrupt controller is used (Cascade or Slave Modes) the CPU will run two interrupt acknowledge cycles back-to-back (Sections 9.5.4.2 and 9.6.4). These cycles are automatically LOCKed and will never be separated by bus HOLD.

3.8.3 LEAVING HOLD

When the HOLD input goes inactive, the processor lowers its HLDA line in a single clock as shown in Figure 46. If there is pending bus activity, only two T_i states will be inserted after HLDA goes inactive. Status information will go active during the last idle state concerning the bus cycle about to be run (see Section 3.1). If there are no bus cycles to be run by the CPU, it will continue to float all lines until the last T_i before it begins its first bus cycle after the HOLD.

A special mechanism exists on the 80C186/80C188 to provide for DRAM refreshing while the bus is in HOLD. See Section 10.4 for details.

3.9 PRIORITY OF BUS CYCLE TYPES

The 80186 family Bus Interface Unit arbitrates requests for bus cycles originating in the integrated peripherals as well as the Execution Unit. Here is a summary of the overall priority for all bus cycle types (highest to lowest):

1. Instruction execution reads or writes following a non-pipelined effective address calculation.

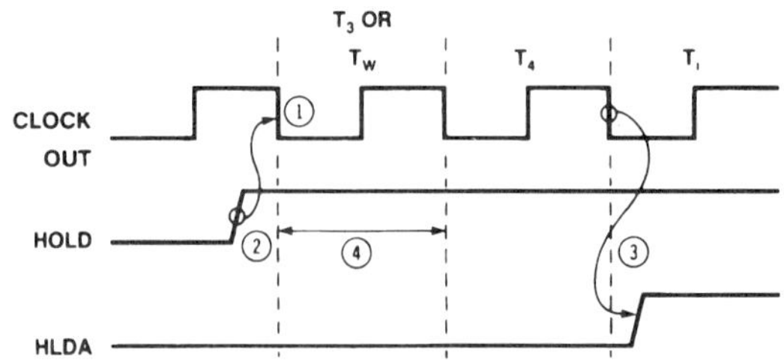

270288-001-47

NOTES:
1. Decision: No addtional internal bus cycles required, idle T-States will be inserted after T4.
2. Greater than T_{HVCL}.
3. Less than T_{CHLAV}.
4. HOLD request internally synchronized.

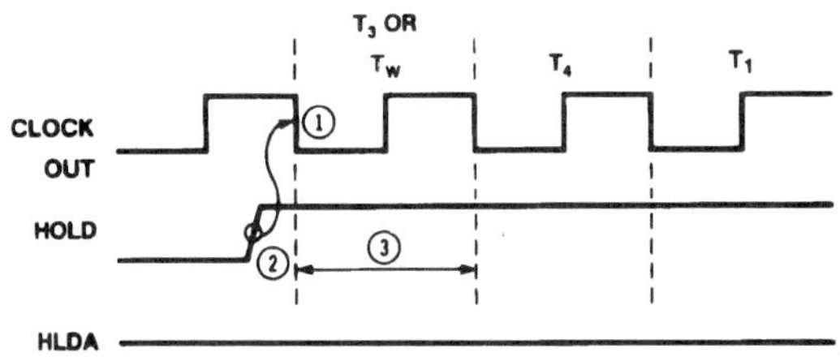

270288-001-48

NOTES:
1. Decision: Addtional internal bus cycles required, no idle T-States will be inserted, HOLD not active soon enough to force idle T-States.
2. Greater than T_{HVCL}: not required since it will not get recognized anyway.
3. HOLD request internally synchronized.

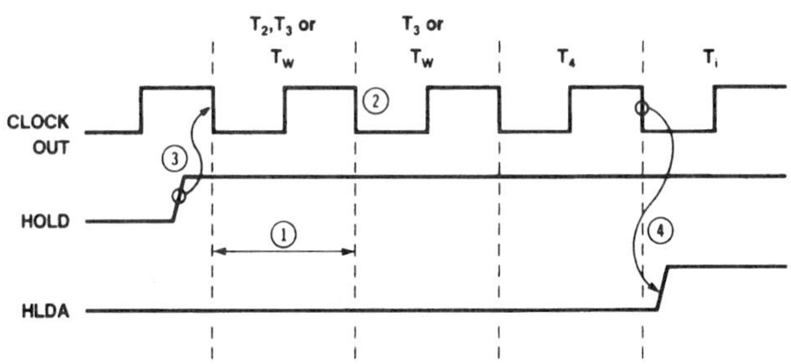

270288-001-49

NOTES:
1. HOLD request internally synchronized.
2. Decision: HOLD request active, idle T-States will be inserted at end of current bus cycle.
3. Greater than T_{HVCL}.
4. Less than T_{CLHAV}.

Figure 45. HOLD/HLDA Timing in the 80186 Family

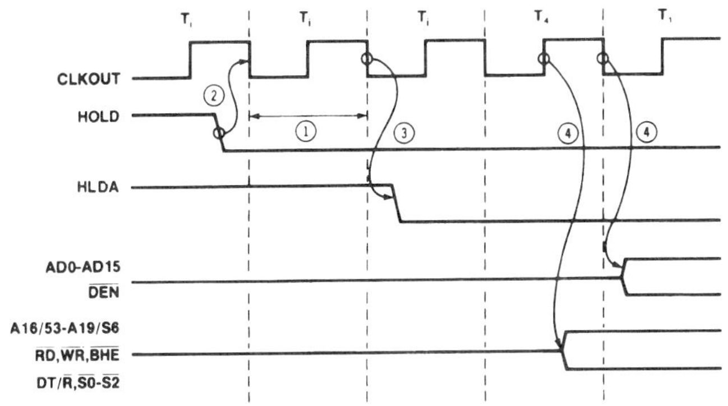

NOTES:
1. HOLD internally synchronized.
2. Greater than T_{HVCL}.
3. Less than T_{CLHAV}.
4. Lines come out of float only if a bus cycle is pending.

Figure 46. 80186 Coming Out of Hold

2. DRAM refresh cycles (80C186/80C188 only).

3. Bus cycles run by an external bus master during HOLD. The 80C186/80C188 signals its need to use the bus for a DRAM refresh cycle by lowering HLDA.

4. Vectoring sequence for the single step interrupt.

5. Vectoring sequence for the NMI interrupt.

6. Vectoring sequence for divide error, breakpoint, overflow, array bounds, unused opcode, and ESCape trap interrupts, according to priority resolution.

7. Vectoring sequence for hardware interrupts from the timers, DMA Control Unit, and external pins. Interrupts on pins INT0-3 can cause 80C186/80C187 numerics instructions to be aborted even when masked.

8. Vectoring sequence for 80C187 Numerics Coprocessor Extension errors. Such exceptions are sampled on the 80C186 ERROR pin during numerics code execution.

9. DMA cycles. DMA cycles can be interspersed with the bus cycles necessary for an interrupt vectoring sequence. The DMA fetch and deposit phases (up to four bus cycles total) are inseparable.

10. General instruction execution. This category includes reads or writes following a fully-pipelined effective address calculation, vectoring sequences for user-designated software interrupts, and numerics code execution. The following points are applicable to sequences of related execution cycles:

    - The second read/write cycle of an 80186/80C186 odd-addressed word operation is inseparable from the first bus cycle.
    - On the 80188/80C188, the two bus cycles associated with any word operation are inseparable.
    - The second read/write cycle of an instruction with both load and store accesses (e.g., XCHG) may be separated from the first cycle by other bus cycles.
    - Successive execution cycles of string instructions (e.g., MOVS) may be separated by other bus cycles.
    - When a LOCKed instruction begins, its execution cycles are elevated to the highest priority level, making LOCKed cycles inseparable even to DRAM refresh cycles. String operations and 80C186/80C187 execution may be LOCKed like any other instructions.

11. Fetches necessary to fill the prefetch queue with opcodes and operands.

Clock Generator 4

CHAPTER 4
CLOCK GENERATOR

The clock generator provides the main clock signal for all integrated components, and all CPU synchronous devices in a system based on the 80186 family. This clock generator includes a crystal oscillator, divide-by-two counter, RESET circuitry, and READY generation logic. A block diagram of the clock generator is shown in Figure 47.

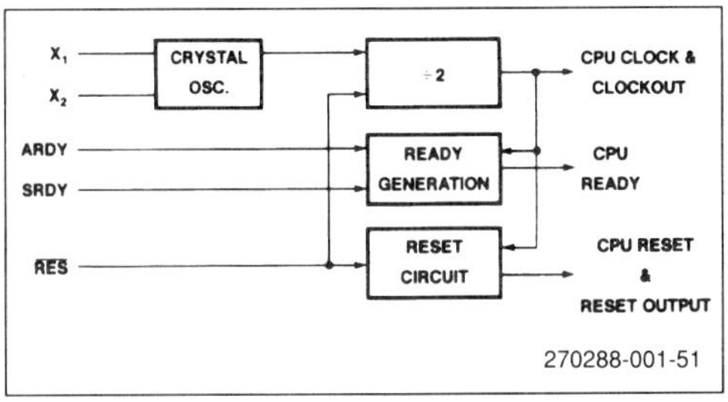

Figure 47. 80186 Family Clock Generator Block Diagram

4.1 CRYSTAL OSCILLATOR

All 80186 family microprocessors use a parallel resonant Pierce oscillator. For all NMOS 80186/80188 applications and lower frequency 80C186/80C188 applications, a fundamental mode crystal is appropriate. At higher frequencies, the diminishing thickness of fundamental mode crystals makes a third overtone crystal the appropriate choice. The addition of external capacitors at X1 and X2 is always required, and a third overtone crystal also requires an RC tank circuit to select the third overtone frequency over the fundamental frequency (see Figure 48).

The recommendations given in 80186 family data sheets for the values of the external components should be taken only as rough guidelines, since there are situations which alter typical oscillator characteristics. One example would be the case in which the circuit layout introduces significant stray capacitance to the X1 and X2 pins. Another example is at low frequencies (CLKOUT less than 6 MHz) where slightly larger capacitors are desirable. Finally, it is also possible to use ceramic resonators in place of crystals for low cost when precise frequencies are not required.

For assistance in selecting the external oscillator components for unusual circumstances, the best resource is the crystal manufacturer. In general, almost any microprocessor grade crystal will work satisfactorily with any member of the 80186 family. The foremost circuit consideration is that the oscillator start correctly over the entire voltage and temperature ranges expected in operation.

4.2 USING AN EXTERNAL OSCILLATOR

An external oscillator may be used with the 80186 family. The external frequency input (EFI) signal is connected directly to the X1 input of the oscillator. X2 must be left unconnected. This oscillator input drives an internal divide-by-two counter to generate the CPU clock signal. Thus the external frequency input can be of practically any duty cycle, so long as the minimum HIGH and LOW times for the signal (as stated in the data sheet) are met.

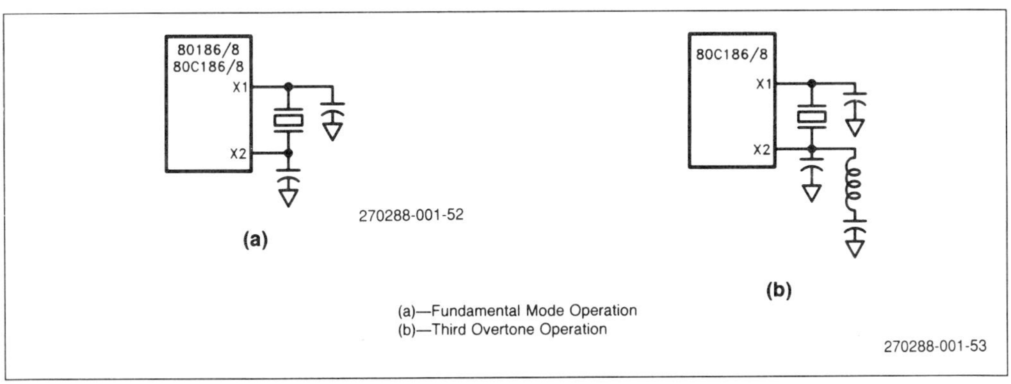

Figure 48. 80186 Family Crystal Connections

4.3 OUTPUT FROM CLOCK GENERATOR

The output of the crystal oscillator (or the external frequency input) drives a divide-by-two circuit which generates a 50 percent duty cycle clock for the 80186 family processor system. All processor timing is referenced to this clock, available externally at the CLKOUT pin. CLKOUT changes state on the HIGH-to-LOW transition of the EFI signal, and is active during RESET and bus HOLD.

4.4 RESET

The 80186 family clock generator also provides a synchronized RESET signal for the system. This signal is generated from the $\overline{RES}$ input to the device. The clock generator synchronizes this signal to the CLKOUT signal.

A Schmitt trigger in the $\overline{RES}$ input circuit ensures that a voltage difference separates the switch points for logic states 0 and 1. This hysteresis measures approximately 200-500 mV. An 80186 family processor must remain in RESET a minimum of four CLKOUT cycles after VCC and CLKOUT stabilize. The hysteresis allows the $\overline{RES}$ input to be driven with a simple RC circuit as shown in Figure 49. Typical applications can use an RC time constant of approximately 100 ms. $\overline{RES}$ must be held LOW upon power-up for correct processor initialization.

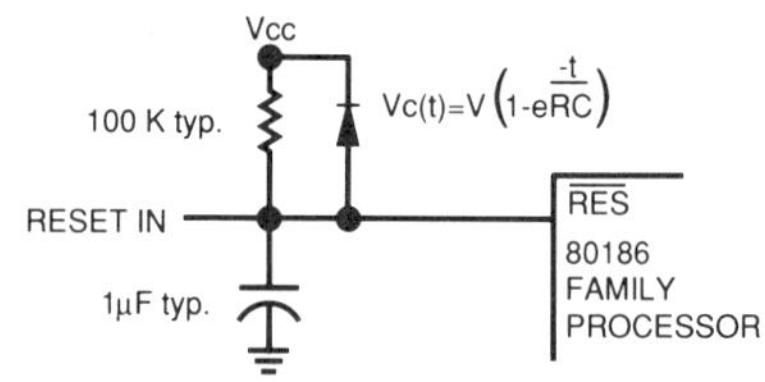

Figure 49. Simple RC Circuit for Powerup RESET

The $\overline{RES}$ input also resets the divide-by-two clock counter. A one clock internal clear pulse is generated when the $\overline{RES}$ input goes active. This clear pulse goes active beginning on the first LOW-to-HIGH transition of the X1 input after $\overline{RES}$ goes active, and goes inactive on the next LOW-to-HIGH X1 transition.

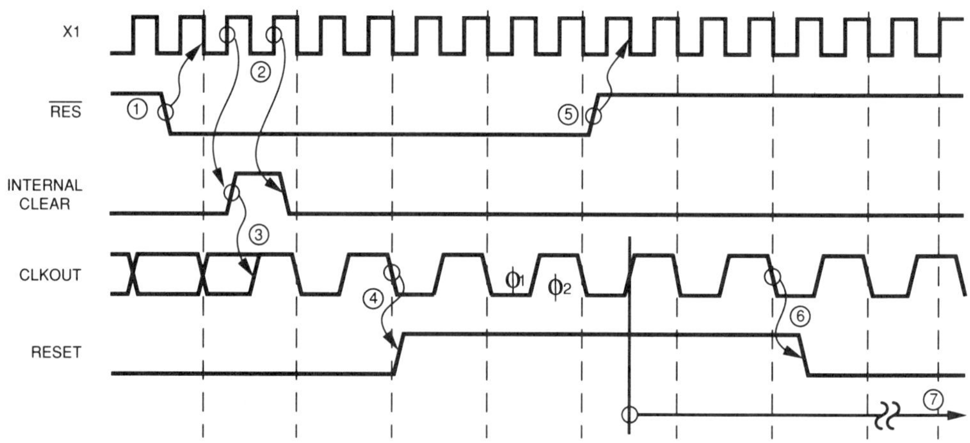

NOTES:
1. $\overline{RES}$ sampled on rising edge of oscillator input signal (X1).
2. Internal clear pulse generated.
3. Internal clear pulse drives CLKOUT high, resynchronizing the clock generator.
4. RESET output goes active (T_{CLRO}).
5. $\overline{RES}$ allowed to go inactive after minimum 4 CLKOUT cycles.
6. RESET output goes inactive 1-1/2 CLKOUT cycles plus T_{CLRO} after rising CLKOUT corresponding to recognition of $\overline{RES}$ inactive.
7. First instruction prefetch occurs 6-1/2 CLKOUT cycles after rising CLKOUT corresponding to recognition of $\overline{RES}$ inactive.

Figure 50. 80186 Reset

To ensure that the clear pulse is generated on the next oscillator cycle, the $\overline{RES}$ input signal must satisfy a setup time to the HIGH-to-LOW oscillator input signal (see Figure 50). During the clear pulse, CLKOUT will be HIGH. On the next HIGH-to-LOW transition of X1, CLKOUT will go LOW, and will change state on every subsequent HIGH-to-LOW X1 transition.

The internal RESET signal is presented to the rest of the 80186 family processor. The signal present on the RESET output pin of the processor is synchronized by the HIGH-to-LOW transition of the processor's CLKOUT signal. This signal remains active an integer number of clocks corresponding to the length of the $\overline{RES}$ input. RESET goes inactive two CLKOUT periods after the $\overline{RES}$ input goes inactive. After the $\overline{RES}$ input goes inactive, the processor will start the fetch of its first instruction (at memory location 0FFFF0H) after 6 1/2 CPU clock cycles.

Peripheral Control Block 5

CHAPTER 5
PERIPHERAL CONTROL BLOCK

All the integrated peripherals with an 80186 family microprocessor are controlled by sets of registers contained within an integrated peripheral control block. The registers are physically located with the peripheral devices they control, but are addressed as a single block of registers. This set of registers encompasses 256 contiguous bytes and can be located on any 256 byte boundary of the memory or I/O space. Maps of these registers are shown in Figure 51 for the 80186/80188 and in Figure 52 for the 80C186/80C188. Any unused locations are reserved.

5.1 SETTING THE BASE LOCATION

In addition to the control registers for each of the integrated peripheral devices, the peripheral control block contains the peripheral control block relocation register. This register allows the peripheral control clock to be relocated on any 256 byte boundary within the processor's memory or I/O space. Figure 53 shows the layout of this register.

The relocation register is located at offset 0FEH within the peripheral control block. Since it is contained within the peripheral control block, any time the peripheral control block is moved, the relocation register will also move.

In addition to the peripheral control block relocation information, the relocation register contains two additional bits. One is used to set the Interrupt Control Unit into Slave Mode. The other is used to force the processor to trap whenever an EScape (coprocessor) instruction is encountered.

The relocation register contains the value 20FFH upon RESET. This means that the peripheral control block will be located at the very top (0FF00H to 0FFFFH) of I/O space.

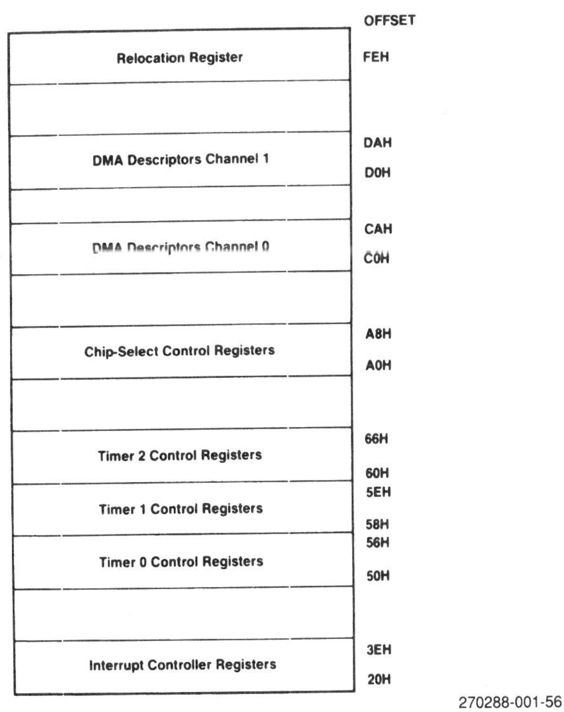

Figure 51. 80186/80188 integrated Peripheral Control Block

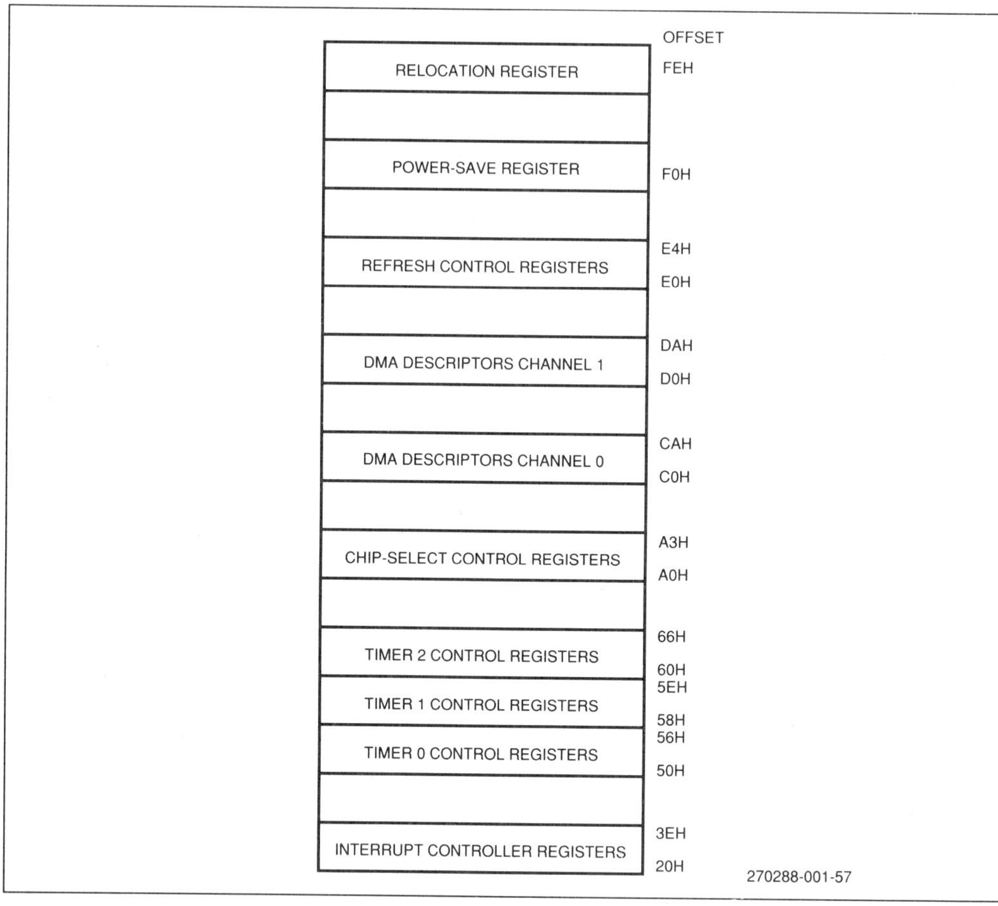

Figure 52. 80C186/80C188 Integrated Peripheral Control Block

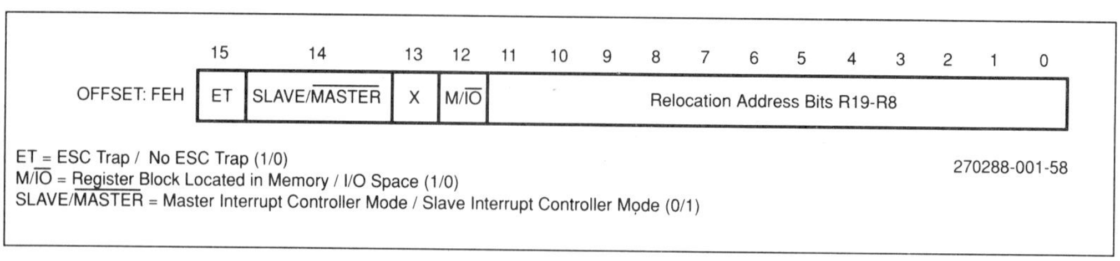

Figure 53. 80186 Family Relocation Register Format

Thus after RESET the relocation register will be located at word location 0FFFEH in I/O space.

To relocate the peripheral control block to the memory range 10000-100FFH, for example, the user programs the relocation register with the value 1100H. Since the relocation register is contained within the peripheral control block, it moves to word location 100FEH. Whenever mapping the 80188/80C188 peripheral control block to another location, the programming of the relocation register should be done with a byte write (i.e., OUT DX, AL). Any access to the control block is done 16 bits at a time. Thus, internally, the relocation register will be written with 16 bits of the AX register while externally, the BIU will run only one 8-bit bus cycle. If a word instruction is used (i.e., OUT DX, AX), the relocation register will be written on the first bus cycle. The BIU will then run a second bus cycle which is unnecessary. The address of the second bus cycle will no longer be within the control block (i.e., the control block was moved on the first cycle), and therefore will require the generation of external READY to complete the cycle. For this reason we recommend the use of byte operations for the relocation register. Byte instructions may also be used for the other registers in the control block and will eliminate half of the bus cycles required if a word operation had been specified. Byte operations are only valid on even addresses though, and are undefined on odd addresses.

5.2 PERIPHERAL CONTROL BLOCK REGISTERS

Each of the integrated peripherals' control and status registers are located at a fixed location above the programmed base location of the peripheral control block. There are many locations within the peripheral control block which are not assigned to any peripheral. If a write is made to any of these locations, the bus cycle will be run, but the value will not be stored in any internal location. This means that if a subsequent read is made to the same location, the value written will not be read back.

The processor will run an external bus cycle for any memory or I/O cycle which accesses a location within the integrated control block. This means that the address, data, and control information will be driven on the processor external pins just as if an ordinary bus cycle had been run. Any information returned by an external device will be ignored, however, even if the access was to a location which does not correspond to any of the integrated peripheral control registers. The above is true for the 80188/80C188 except that the word access made to the integrated registers will be performed in a single bus cycle internally. Externally, the BIU runs two bus cycles.

The processor internally generates a READY signal whenever any of the integrated peripherals are accessed; any external READY signal is ignored. This READY will also be returned if an access is made to a location within the 256 byte area of the peripheral control block which does not correspond to any integrated peripheral control register. The processor will insert no wait states for any access within the integrated peripheral control clock except for accesses to the timer registers. Any access to the timer control and counting registers will incur one wait state. This wait state is required to properly multiplex processor and counter element accesses to the timer control registers.

All accesses made to the integrated peripheral control block will be word accesses. Any write to the integrated registers will modify all 16 bits of the register, whether the opcode specified a byte write or a word write. A byte read from an even location causes no problems, but the data returned when a byte read is performed from an odd address within the peripheral control block is undefined. This is true both for the 80186/80C186 and the 80188/80C188. As stated above, even though the 80188/80C188 has an external 8-bit data bus, internally it is still a 16-bit machine. Word accesses by the 80188/80C188 to integrated registers each occur as single bus cycles internally, while externally the BIU runs two bus cycles. The DMA Control Unit cannot be used for either read or write accesses to the peripheral control block.

5.3 PERIPHERAL CONFIGURATION AT RESET

Upon RESET, the chip select/READY logic performs the following actions:

- All chip select outputs are driven HIGH.
- The UMCS register attains the value 0FFFBH. This sets $\overline{UCS}$ chip select line activity for a 1 Kbyte block, three wait states, and external READY consideration.
- No other chip select or READY control registers have any predefined values after RESET. They will not become active until the CPU accesses their control registers.

Upon RESET, the DMA Control Unit performs the following actions:

- The start/stop bit for each channel resets, stopping the channel.
- Any transfer in progress is aborted.

Upon RESET, the Timer Unit performs the following actions:

- All timer enable bits are reset, preventing operation.
- All function select bits are reset to zero. This activity se-

lects max count register A for each timer, which results in the timer output pins going HIGH.

Upon RESET, the Interrupt Control Unit performs the following actions:

- All SFNM bits are reset to zero, disabling Special Fully Nested Mode.
- All priority bits in the various control registers are set to one. This places all sources at lowest priority (level 111).
- All LTM bits are reset to zero, resulting in edge-sense mode.
- All interrupt in-service bits are reset to zero.
- All interrupt mask bits are set to one (masked).
- All Cascade Mode bits are reset to zero (Direct Input Mode).
- All priority mask bits are set to one, implying no levels masked.
- The Interrupt Control Unit is initialized to Master Mode.

Timer Unit 6

CHAPTER 6
TIMER UNIT

The 80186 family includes a Timer Unit which consists of three independent 16-bit timers. These timers operate independently of the CPU. Two have input and output pins allowing counting of external events and generation of arbitrary waveforms. The third can be used as a timer, as a prescaler for the other timers, or as a DMA request source.

The internal Timer Unit on the 80186 family can be modeled by a single counter element, time-multiplexed to three register banks, each of which contains different control and count values. These register banks are, in turn, dual-ported between the counter element and the CPU (see Figure 54). Figure 55 shows the timer element sequencing and the subsequent constraints on input and output signals. There is no connection between the sequencing of the counter element through the timer register banks and the BIU's sequencing through T-states. Timer operation and bus interface operation are completely asynchronous.

6.1 TIMER UNIT PROGRAMMING

Each timer is controlled by a register block (see Figure 56). Each of these registers can be read or written whether or not the timer is operating. All processor accesses to these registers are synchronized to all counter accesses to these registers, meaning that one will never read a count register in which only half of the bits have been modified.

The Bus Interface Unit automatically inserts one wait state for any access to the timer registers to perform this synchronization. Unlike the DMA Unit, LOCKing accesses to timer registers will not prevent the timer's counter elements from accessing the timer registers.

Each timer has a 16-bit count register which is incremented for each timer event. A timer event can be a LOW-to-HIGH transition

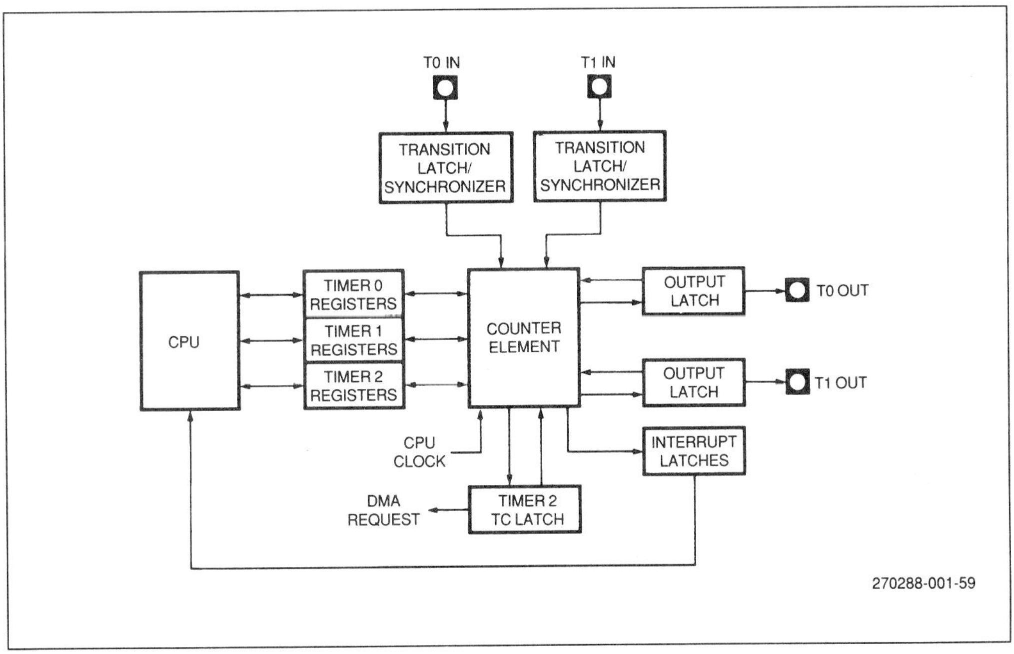

Figure 54. 80186 Family Timer Model

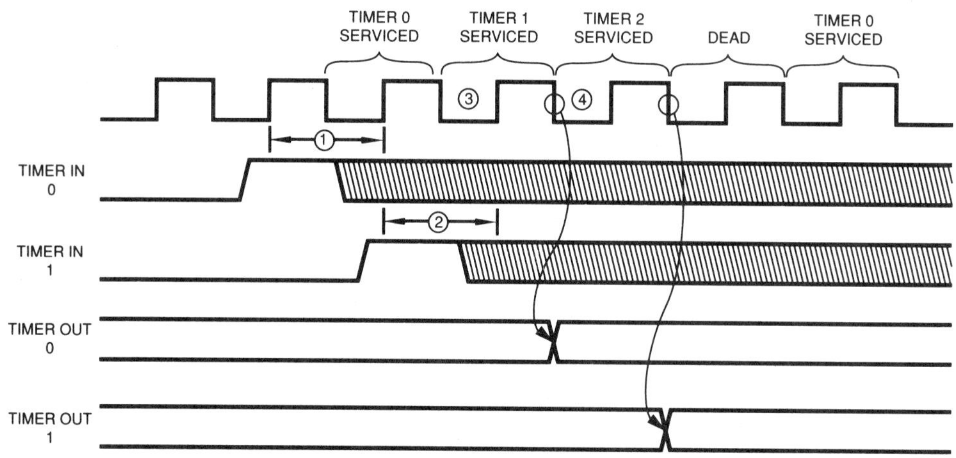

NOTES:
1. Timer In 0 resolution time.
2. Timer In 1 resolution time.
3. Modified count value written into Timer 0 count register.
4. Modified count value written into Timer 1 count register.

Figure 55. Counter Element Multiplexing and Timer Input Synchronization

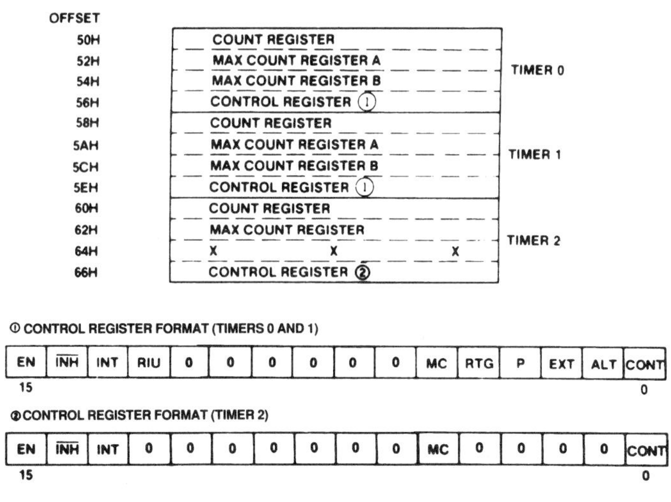

Figure 56. Timer Registers

on a timer input pin (for Timers 0 and 1), a pulse generated every fourth CPU Clock, or a time out of Timer 2 (for Timers 0 and 1). The count register is 16 bits wide, allowing up to 65536 (2^{16}) events to be counted. Upon RESET, the contents of the count registers are indeterminate and they should be initialized to zero before any timer operation.

Each timer includes a maximum count register. Whenever the timer count register is equal to the maximum count register, the count register resets to zero, so the maximum count value is never stored in the count register. This maximum count value may be written while the timer is operating. A maximum count value of 0 implies a maximum count of 65536, a maximum count value of 1 implies a maximum count of 1, etc. Only equivalence between the count value and the maximum count register value is checked. This means that the count value will not be cleared if the value in the count register is greater than the value in the maximum count register. If the timer is programmed in this way, it will count to the maximum count (0FFFFH), increment to 0, then count up to the value in the maximum count register. The TC bit in the timer control register will not be set when the counter overflows to 0, nor will an interrupt be generated from the Timer Unit.

Timers 0 and 1 each contain an additional maximum count register. When both maximum count registers are used, the timer will first count up to the value in maximum count register A, reset to zero, count up to the value in maximum count register B, and reset to zero again. The ALTernate bit in the timer control register determines whether one or both maximum count registers are used. If this bit is LOW, only maximum count register A is used; maximum count register B is ignored. If it is HIGH, both registers are used. The RIU (register in use) bit in the timer control register indicates which maximum count register is presently counting up. This bit is 0 when maximum count register A is being used, 1 when maximum count register B is being used. The RIU bit is read only. It will always be read 0 in single maximum count register mode (since only maximum count register A will be used).

Each timer can generate an interrupt whenever the timer count value reaches a maximum count value. All timers may use maximum count A in single max count mode. Timers 0 and 1 (dual max count mode) may also use maximum count B. In addition, the maximum count (MC) bit in the timer control register is set whenever the timer count reaches a maximum count value. This bit is never automatically cleared, i.e., programmer intervention is required. If a timer generates a second interrupt request before the first interrupt request has been serviced, the first interrupt request to the CPU will be lost.

Each timer has an ENable bit in the timer control register. The timer will count timer events only when this bit is set. Any write to the timer control register will modify the ENable bit only if the INHibit bit is also set. The INHibit bit in the timer control register allows selective updating of the timer ENable bit. The value of the INHibit bit is not stored in a write to the timer control register; it will always be read as logic zero.

Each timer has a CONTinuous bit in the timer control register. If this bit is cleared, the timer ENable bit will be automatically cleared at the end of each timing cycle. If a single maximum count register is used, the end of a timing cycle occurs when the count value resets to zero after reaching the value in maximum count register A. If dual maximum count registers are used, the end of a timing cycle occurs when the count value resets to zero after reaching the value in maximum count register B. If the CONTinuous bit is set, the ENable bit will never be automatically reset. Thus, after each timing cycle, another timing cycle will automatically begin. For example, in single maximum count register mode, the timer will count up to the value in maximum count register A, reset to zero, ad infinitum. In dual maximum count register mode, the timer will count up to the value in maximum count register A, reset to zero, count up to the value in maximum count register B, reset to zero, and repeat.

6.2 TIMER EVENTS

Each timer counts events. All timers can use a transition of the CPU clock as an event. If the internal clock is used, the count increments every fourth CPU clock because of timer element multiplexing. For Timer 2, this is the only timer event which can be used. For Timers 0 and 1, this event is selected by clearing the EXTernal and Prescaler bits in the timer control register.

Timers 0 and 1 can use Timer 2 reaching its maximum count as a timer event. This is selected by clearing the EXTernal bit and setting the Prescaler bit in the timer control register. When this is done, the timer will increment whenever Timer 2 resets to zero having reached its own maximum count. Note that Timer 2 must be initialized and running in order to increment the value in the other timer/counter.

Timers 0 and 1 can also be programmed to count LOW-to-HIGH transitions on the external input pin. Each transition on the external pin is synchronized to the 80186 family processor clock before it is presented to the timer circuitry (see Appendix B for information on synchronizers). The timer counts transitions on the input pin; the input value must go LOW, then HIGH, to cause the timer to increment. Transitions on this line are latched. The maximum count rate for the timer is 1/4 the CPU clock rate measured at CLKOUT.

6.3 TIMER INPUT PIN OPERATION

Timers 0 and 1 each have individual timer input pins. All LOW-to-HIGH transitions on these input pins are synchronized, latched, and presented to the counter element when the particular timer is being serviced by the counter element.

Signals on this input can affect timer operation in three different ways. The manner in which the pin signals are used is determined by the EXTernal and RTG (retrigger) bits in the timer control register. If the EXTernal bit is set, transitions on the input pin will cause the timer count value to increment if the timer is enabled (that is, the ENable bit in the timer control register is set). Thus, the timer counts external events. If the EXTernal bit is cleared, all timer increments are caused by either the CPU clock or by Timer 2 reaching its maximum count. In this mode, the RTG bit determines whether the input pin will enable timer operation, or whether it will retrigger timer operation.

When the EXTernal bit is LOW and RTG bit is also LOW, the timer will count internal timer events only when the timer input pin is HIGH and the ENable bit in the timer control register is set. Note that in this mode, the pin is level sensitive, not edge sensitive. A LOW-to-HIGH transition on the timer input pin is not required to enable timer operation. If the input is tied HIGH, the timer will be continually enabled. The timer enable input signal is completely independent of the ENable bit in the timer control register. **Both** must be HIGH for the timer to count. Examples of uses for the timer in this mode would be a real time clock or a baud rate generator.

When the EXTernal bit is LOW and the RTG bit is HIGH, every LOW-to-HIGH transition on the timer input pin causes the timer count register to reset to zero. This mode of operation can be used to generate a retriggerable digital one-shot. After the timer is enabled (i.e., the ENable bit in the timer control register is set), timer operation (counting) will begin only after the first LOW-to-HIGH transition of the timer input pin has been detected. If another LOW-to-HIGH transition occurs on the input pin before the end of the timer cycle, the timer will reset to zero and begin the timer cycle again. A timer cycle is defined as the time the timer is counting from zero to the maximum count (either max count A or max count B). This means that in the dual max count mode, the RIU bit is not set if the timer is reset by the LOW-to-HIGH transition on the input pin. Should a timer reset occur when RIU is set (indicating max count B), the timer will again begin to count up to max count B before resetting the RIU bit. Thus, when the ALTernate bit is set, a timer reset will retrigger (or extend) the duration of the current max count in use (which means that either the LOW or HIGH level of the timer output will be extended).

If the CONTinuous bit in the timer control register is cleared, the timer ENable bit will automatically be cleared whenever a timer cycle has been completed (max count is reached). If the CONtinuous bit in the timer control register is set, the timer will reset to zero and begin another timer cycle whenever the current cycle has completed.

6.4 TIMER OUTPUT PIN OPERATION

Timers 0 and 1 each have a timer output pin which can perform two functions. The first is a single pulse indicating the end of a timing cycle. The second is a level indication of the maximum count register being used. The timer outputs operate as outlined below whether internal or external clocking of the timer is used. With external clocking, the time between a transition on the timer input pin and a corresponding transition on the timer output pin varies from 2 1/2 to 6 clocks. The exact timing depends on when the input transition occurs relative to timer service by the counter element.

When the timer is in single maximum count register mode, the timer output pin will go LOW for a single CPU clock one clock after the timer is serviced by the counter element when maximum count is reached (see Figure 57).

When the timer is programmed in dual maximum count register mode, the timer output pin indicates which maximum count register is being used. It is LOW if maximum count register B is being used and HIGH if maximum count register A is being used. The timer can generate a repetitive waveform if the CONTinuous bit in the timer control register is set. The frequency and duty cycle of this waveform is easily controlled by the programmer. For example, if maximum count register A contains 10, maximum count register B contains 20, and CLKOUT is 12.5 MHz, the timer generates a 33 per cent duty cycle waveform at 104 kHz. If the timer is programmed to halt upon maximum count, the output pin will go HIGH when the timer halts.

The timer output pins do not float during bus HOLD.

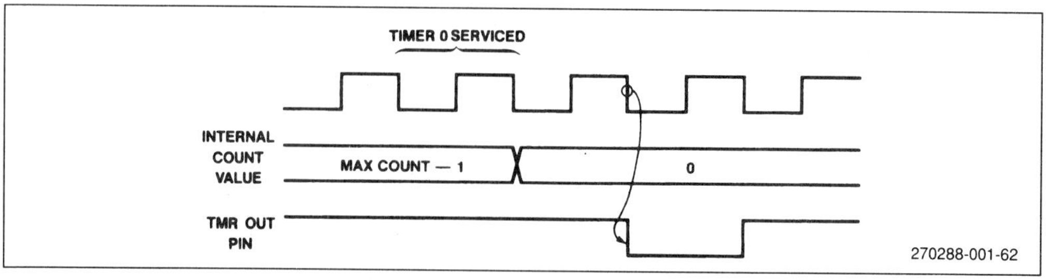

Figure 57. 80186 Timer Out Signal

6.5 EXAMPLE TIMER INITIALIZATION CODE

The 80186 family timers possess great flexibility. It is easy to program them as baud rate generators, digital one-shots, pulse width modulators, event counters, and pulse width measurement applications.

6.5.1 REAL TIME CLOCK

Figure 58 contains sample code to initialize Timer 2 to generate interrupts every millisecond. The CPU then increments memory-based clock variables.

```
$mod186
name                    example_80186_family_timer_code
;
;  This file contains an example 80186 family timer routine to set up the timer
;       and interrupt controller to cause the timer to generate an interrupt
;       every 10 milliseconds, and to service interrupts to implement a real
;       time clock. Timer 2 is used in this example because no input or output
;       signals are required. The code example assumes that the peripheral
;       control block has not been moved from its reset location (FF00-FFFF in
;       I/O space).
;
arg1                equ     word ptr [BP + 4]
arg2                equ     word ptr [BP + 6]
arg3                equ     word ptr [BP + 8]
timer_2int          equ     19                  ; timer 2 has vector type 19
timer_2control      equ     0FF66h
timer_2max_ctl      equ     0FF62h
timer_2count        equ     0FF60h
timer_int_ctl       equ     0FF32h
eoi_register        equ     0FF22h              ; interrupt controller regs
interrupt_stat      equ     0FF30h

data                segment public'data'
                    public  hour_,minute_,second_,msec_
msec_               db      ?
hour_               db      ?
minute_             db      ?
second_             db      ?
data                ends

cgroup              group   code
dgroup              group   data

code                segment public_code_
                    public  set_time
                    assume  cs:code, ds:dgroup

;
;                   set_time(hour,minute,second)
;                   sets the time variables, initializes timer 2 to provide
;                   interrupts every 10 milliseconds, and programs the interrupt
;                   vector for timer 2
;
set_time            proc    near                ; set stack addressability
                    enter   0,0                 ; save registers used
                    push    AX
                    push    DX
                    push    SI
                    push    DS
                    xor     AX,AX               ; set the interrupt vector
                                                ; the timers have unique
                                                ; interrupt vectors even though
                                                ; they share the same control
                                                ; register
                    mov     DS,AX
                    mov     SI,4*timer_2int
                    mov     word ptr DS:[SI], offset timer2_interrupt_routine
                    inc     SI
                    inc     SI
                    mov     DS:[SI],CS
```

Figure 58. Example 80186 Family Real Time Clock Code

```
                  pop     DS

                  mov     AX,arg1                ;set the time values
                  mov     hour_,AL
                  mov     X,arg2
                  mov     minute_,AL
                  mov     AX,arg3
                  mov     second_,AL
                  mov     msec_,0

                  mov     DX,timer_2count        ;clear the
                  xor     AX,AX                  ;count
                  out     DX,AX                  ;register

                  mov     DX,timer_2max_ctl      ; set the max count value
                  mov     AX,2000                ;10 ms / 500 ns(timer 2 counts
                                                 ;at 1/4 the CPU clock rate)
                  out     DX,AX
                  mov     DX,timer_2control      ; set up the control word
                  mov     AX,1110000000000001b   ;enable counting, generate
                                                 ;interrupts on TC, continuous
                                                 ;counting
                  out     DX,AX

                  mov     DX,timer int ctl       ;set up the interrupt
                                                 ;controller
                  mov     AX,0000b               ;unmask interrupts highest
                                                 ;priority interrupt
                  out     DX,AX
                  sti                            ;enable processor interrupts

                  pop     SI
                  pop     DX
                  pop     AX
                  leave
                  ret
set_time          endp

timer_2_interrupt_routine  proc     far
                           push     AX
                           push     DX

                           cmp      msec_,99        ;see if one second has passed
                           jae      bump_second     ;if above or equal...
                           inc      msec_
                           jmp      reset_int_ctl
bump_second:
                           mov      msec_,0         ;reset millisecond
                           cmp      minute_,59      ;see if one minute has passed
                           jae      bump_minute
                           inc      second_
                           jmp      reset_int_ctl
bump_minute:
                           mov      second_,0
                           cmp      minute_,59      ;see if one hour has passed
                           jae      bump_hour
                           inc      minute_
                           jmp      reset_int_ctl
                           pop      DX
                           pop      AX
                           ret
bump_hour:
                           mov      minute_,0
                           cmp      hour_,12        ;see if 12 hours have passed
                           jae      reset_hour
                           inc      hour_
                           jmp      reset_int_ctl
reset_hour:
                           mov      hour_,1
reset_int_ctl:
```

Figure 58. Example 80186 Family Real Time Clock Code (continued)

```
                          mov     DX,eoi_register
                          mov     AX,8000h         ; non-specific end of
                                                   ; interrupt
                          out     DX,AX

                          pop     DX
                          pop     AX
                          iret
timer_2_interrupt_routine endp
code                      ends
                          end
```

270288-001-63

Figure 58. Example 80186 Family Real Time Clock Code (continued)

```
$mod186
name                              example_80186_baud_code
;
;   This file contains an example 80186 family timer routine. This routine sets up
;          the timer as a baud rate generator. In this mode, Timer 1 is used to
;          generate a square wave output with a period of 6.51 usec for use with a
;          serial controller at 9600 baud programmed in divide by 16 mode.This
;          assumes that the procesor is running at 11.0592 MHz.  The code example
;          also assumes that the peripheral control block has not been moved from
;          its reset location (FF00-FFFF in I/O space).
;
timer1_count            equu    0FF58h
timer1_control          equ     0FF5Eh
timer1_max_cnt_a        equ     0FF5Ah
timer1_max_cnt_b        equ     0FF5Ch

code                    segment                         ;public' code'
                        assume  cs:code
;
;  Set_baud() initializes timer 1 as a baud rate generator for a serial port
;          running at 9600 baud
;
set_baud                proc    near
                        push    AX                      ; save registers used
                        push    DX
                        mov     DX,timer1_count         ; clear the
                        xor     AX,AX                   ; count
                        out     DX,AX                   ; register

                        mov     AX,9                    ; set the max count value
                        mov     DX, timer1_max_cnt_a    ; 90.4ns * 18 = 6.5 usec
                        out     DX,AX
                        mov     DX, timer1_max_cnt_b
                        out     DX,AX
                        mov     DX,timer1_control       ; set the control word
                        mov     AX,1100000000000011b    ; enable counting
                                                        ; no interrupt on TC
                                                        ; continuous counting
                                                        ; dual max count registers
                        out     DX,AX

                        pop     DX
                        pop     AX
                                ret
set_baud                        endp
                        code    ends
                                end
```

270288-001-64

Figure 59. Example Baud Rate Initialization Code

6.5.2 BAUD RATE GENERATOR

Figure 59 is an example of code to generate a baud rate clock for serial communications controllers.

6.5.3 EVENT COUNTER

An 80186 family timer can count events using the timer input pins. Sample code for such an application is shown in Figure 60.

```
$mod186
name                        example_80186_family_count_code
;
;  This file contains an example 80186 family timer routine to set up the timer
;        as an external event counter. In this mode, Timer 1 is used to count
;        transitions on its input pin. After the timer has been set up by the
;        routine, the number of events counted can be directly read from the
;        timer count register at location FF58H in I/O space. The timer will
;        count a maximum of 65535 timer events before wrapping around to zero.
;        This code example also assumes that the peripheral control block has not
;        been moved from its reset location (FF00-FFFF in I/O space).
;
timer1_control          equu    0FF5Eh
timer1_max_cnt          equ     0FF5Ah
timer1_cnt_reg          equ     0FF58H

code                    segment public'code'
                        assume  cs:code
;
;                       set_count()initializes the 80186 timer1 as an event counter
;
set_count               proc    near                    ;save registers used
                        push    AX
                        push    DX

                        mov     DX,timer1_max_cnt       ;set the max count value
                        mov     AX,0                    ;allows the timer to count
                                                        ;all the way to FFFFH
                        out     DX,AX
                        mov     DX,timer1_control       ;set the control word
                        mov     AX,1100000000000101b    ;enable counting
                                                        ;no interrupt on TC
                                                        ;continuous counting
                                                        ;single max count register
                                                        ;external clocking
                        out     DX,AX

                        xor     DX,timer1_cnt_reg       ;zero AX
                        mov     DX,timer1_cnt_reg       ;and zero the count in the
                                                        ;timer
                        out     DX, AX
                        pop     DX
                        pop     AX
                        ret

set_count               endp
code                    ends
                        end
```

270288-001-65

Figure 60. Example 80186 Family Event Counter Code

Chip Select/Ready Logic 7

CHAPTER 7
CHIP SELECT/READY LOGIC

The 80186 family includes a Chip Select Unit which provides 13 hardware chip select signals for memory and I/O accesses generated by the CPU and DMA Unit. This unit is programmable such that it can fulfill the chip select requirements (in terms of memory device or bank size and speed) of many small and medium sized 80186 family processor systems. Using integrated chip selects has the advantage over externally generated chip selects because the chip select signals appear earlier in the bus cycle.

The chip selects are driven **only** for internally generated bus cycles. Any cycles generated by an external device (that is, an external bus master) will not cause the chip selects to go active. Thus, any external bus masters must be responsible for their own chip select generation. Also, during a bus HOLD, the processor does not float the chip select lines. Therefore, logic must be included to enable the devices which the external bus master wishes to access (see Figure 61).

the block size was 128K (four 32 Kbyte areas) the base address could be 0 or 20000H, but not 10000H. With MCS3-0 programmed for a 512K block and either UCS or LCS programmed for a 256K block, the maximum memory area under control of the memory chip selects is 768K.

The memory chip selects are controlled by 4 registers in the peripheral control block (see Figure 63). These include one each for UCS and LCS, the values of which determine the size of the memory blocks addressed by these lines. The other registers are used to control the size and base address of the mid-range memory block.

On RESET, only UCS is active. It is programmed to be active for a block at the top 1 Kbyte of memory, to insert three wait states to all memory fetches, and to factor external READY for every memory fetch (see Section 7.3 for more information

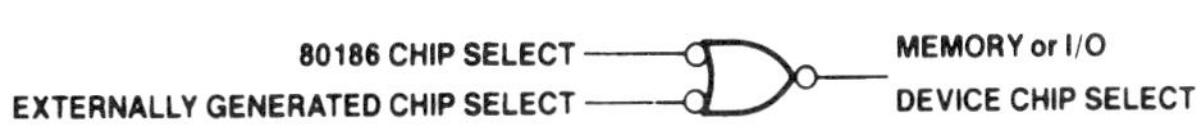

270288-001-66

Figure 61. 80186 External Chip Select/Device Chip Select Generation

7.1 MEMORY CHIP SELECTS

The 80186 family provides six discrete memory chip select lines. These signals are the Upper Memory Chip Select (UCS), Lower Memory Chip Select (LCS), and the Mid-Range Chip Selects 0-3 (MCS0-3). They are meant to be connected to the three major areas of the system memory (see Figure 62) but are not limited to this application.

The upper limit of UCS and the lower limit of LCS are fixed at 0FFFFFH and 00000H in memory space, respectively. The other limit is set by the memory size programmed into the control register for the chip select line. UCS and LCS are active for block sizes up to 256 Kbytes.

Mid-range memory chip selects are active when a memory reference is made within a programmed 8 to 512 Kbyte block. The user programs both the base address and the block size of the memory area. Each of the four chip select lines is active for one of the four equal contiguous divisions of the mid-range block. Therefore, if the total block size is 32 Kbytes, each chip select is active for 8K of memory with MCS0 being active for the first range and MCS3 being active for the last range. The only limitation is that the base address must be programmed to be an integer multiple of the total block size. For example, if

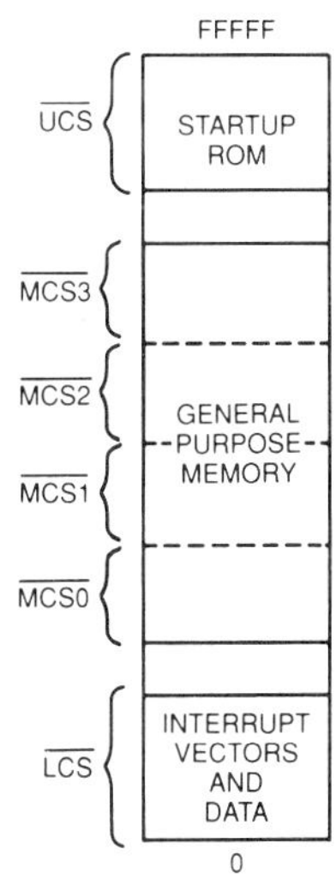

270288-001-67

Figure 62. 80186 Family Memory Areas and Chip Selects

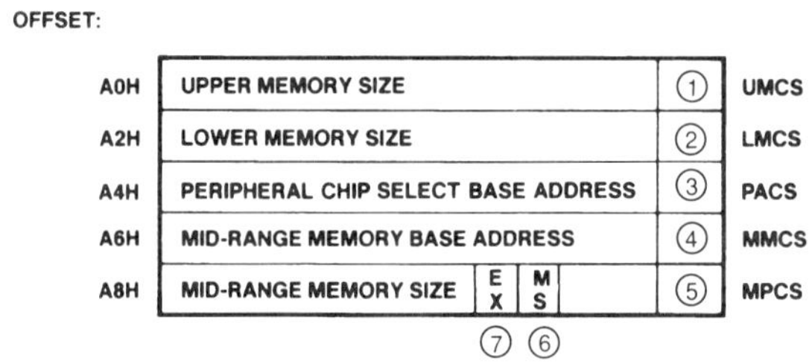

270288-001-68

NOTES:
1. Upper memory READY bits.
2. Lower memory READY bits.
3. PCS0-PCS3 READY bits.
4. Mid-range memory READY bits.
5. PCS4-PCS6 READY bits.
6. MS: 1 = Peripherals active in memory space.
   0 = Peripherals active in I/O space.
7. EX: 1 = 7PCS lines.
   0 = PCS5 = A1, PCS6 = A2.

Not all bits of every field are used.

Figure 63. Chip Select Control Registers

on internal READY generation). None of the other chip select lines will be active until all necessary registers have been accessed. A read to an uninitialized chip select register will enable the chip select function controlled by that register. Three of the mid-range chip select pins are unavailable on the 80C186 when it is in Enhanced Mode (see Section 7.5).

7.2 PERIPHERAL CHIP SELECTS

The 80186 family provides seven discrete chip select lines which are meant to be connected to peripheral components in a system based on an 80186 family processor. Each of these lines is active for one of seven continuous 128 byte areas in memory or I/O space above a programmed base address.

The peripheral chip selects are controlled by two registers in the internal peripheral control block (see Figure 63). These registers set the base address of the peripherals and map the peripherals into memory or I/O space. Both of these registers must be accessed before any of the peripheral chip selects will become active.

A bit in the MPCS register allows PCS5 and PCS6 to become latched A1 and A2 outputs. When this option is selected, PCS5 and PCS6 reflect the state of A1 and A2 throughout a bus cycle. This allows external peripheral register selection in a system in which the addresses are not latched. Upon RESET, PCS5 and PCS6 are driven HIGH.

7.3 READY GENERATION

The 80186 family includes a READY Generation Unit. This unit generates an internal READY signal for all accesses to memory or I/O areas to which the chip select circuitry responds.

For each READY generation area, the internal unit may insert up to three wait states. In addition, the READY generation circuit may be programmed to ignore or include the state of the external READY pins. When using both internal and external READY generation, both elements must be fulfilled before a bus cycle will end. Follow Table 16 to program the READY control bits. The external READY condition is always required upon RESET for accesses involving the top 1K of memory. Therefore, at least one of the READY pins must be connected to functional READY circuitry or be tied HIGH until UCS is reprogrammed during the initialization sequence.

Table 16. 80186 Family Wait State Programming

R2	R1	R0	Number of Wait States
0	0	0	0 + external READY
0	0	1	1 + external READY
0	1	0	2 + external READY
0	1	1	3 + external READY
1	0	0	0 (no external READY required)
1	0	1	1 (no external READY required)
1	1	0	2 (no external READY required)
1	1	1	3 (no external READY required)

7.4 OVERLAPPING CHIP SELECT AREAS

It is customary that chip select areas do not overlap each other. It is imperative that chip selects do not overlap any locations of the integrated 256-byte peripheral control block.

Whenever two chip select areas do overlap, the processor activates both lines during accesses in the overlapped region. The user must program the READY bits for both areas to the same value; otherwise, the processor response to an access in the overlapped region is indeterminate.

If any of the chip select areas overlap the integrated 256-byte control block, the timing on the chip select lines is altered. An access to the control block will temporarily activate the corresponding chip select pin, but it will go inactive prematurely.

7.5 CHIP SELECTS AND THE 80C186 IN ENHANCED MODE

The 80C186 MCS0, MCS1 and MCS3 pins change function when the device is configured for Enhanced Mode (see Appendix C.2 for more about Enhanced Mode). The 80C188 MCS pins function the same in both modes. These pins are configured to support an asynchronous numerics floating point processor extension (see Table 17). Thus, the 80C186 does not provide the complete range of middle chip selects normally available. However, the functionality of the MCS2 pin and the programming features of the MPCS and MMCS registers are still available.

Table 17. MCS Pin Definitions

Pin #	Compatible Mode	Enhanced Mode
35	MCS3	NPS, Numerics Processor Select
36	MCS2	MCS2
37	MCS1	ERROR, Numerics Processor Error
38	MCS0	PEREQ Processor Extension Request

In Enhanced Mode, it is still possible to program the starting address, block size and READY requirements of the middle chip selects. This allows the user to take advantage of the wait state generation logic on the 80C186 even though most of the MCS pins are not available. It is also possible to use MCS2 which is active for one fourth the block size (see Figure 62).

If the chip select circuitry is programmed so the reserved numerics processor port addresses 00F8H-00FFH fall within the PCS address range, a PCS pin will go active during I/O operations to the 80C187. However, the 80C186 NPS line does not go active for non-numerics accesses. It is the responsibility of the system designer to ensure that no bus contention occurs during numerics processor operations.

7.6 EXAMPLE SYSTEM INITIALIZATION CODE

Figure 64 contains code which initializes 80186 family chip select circuitry. Since only the upper memory chip select is active at RESET, it is customary to program memory chip selects first, followed by peripheral chip selects and the DRAM Refresh Control Unit (80C186/80C188). Then, depending on which units are used, the Interrupt Controller, timers, and DMA Control Unit may be programmed as required.

```
$mod186
name                     example_80186_family_system_init
;
; This file contains a system initialization routine for the 80186. It
;       initializes the integrated chip select registers.
;
restart                  segment at OFFFFh               ;This is the processor reset
                                                         ;address at OFFFF0H
;
                         org      0
                         jmp      far ptr initialize
restart                  ends
;
                         extrn    monitor:far
init_hw                  segment at OFF0h
                         assume   CS:init_hw
;
; This segment initializes the chip selects. It must be located in the top 1K
;       to ensure that the ROM remains selected in the 80186 family processor
;       system until the proper size of the select area can be programmed.
;
UMCS_reg                 equ      OFFA0H                 ;chip select register locations
LMCS_reg                 equ      OFFA2H
PACS_reg                 equ      OFFA4H
MPCS_reg                 equ      OFFA8H
UMCS_value               equ      OF038H                 ;64K, no wait states
LMCS_value               equ      07F8H                  ;32K, no wait state
PACS_value               equ      007EH                  ;peripheral base at 400H, 2 ws
MPCS_value               equ      81B8H                  ;PCS5 and 6 supplied.
                                                         ;peripherals in I/O space
initialize               proc     far
                         mov      DX,UMCS_reg            ;program the UMCS register
                         mov      AX,UMCS_value
                         out      DX,AX

                         mov      DX,LMCS_reg            ;program the LMCS register
                         mov      AX,LMCS_value
                         out      DX,AX

                         mov      DX,PACS_reg            ;set up the peripheral chip
                                                         ;selects (note the mid-range
                                                         ;memory chip selects are not
                                                         ;needed in this system, and
                                                         ;are thus not initialized)
                         mov      AX,PACS_value
                         out      DX,AX
                         mov      DX,MPCS_reg
                         mov      AX,MPCS_value
                         out      DX,AX
;
; Now that the chip selects are all set up, the main program of the computer may
;       be executed.
;
initialize               endp
init_hw                  ends
                         end
```

270288-001-69

Figure 64. 80186 System Initialization Code

DMA Control Unit 8

CHAPTER 8
DMA CONTROL UNIT

An 80186 family processor includes a DMA Unit consisting of two independent DMA channels. These channels operate independently of the CPU and drive all integrated bus interface components (Bus Interface Unit, chip selects, etc.) exactly as the CPU does (see Figure 65). This means that bus cycles initiated by the DMA Unit are the same as bus cycles initiated by the CPU (except that S6 = 1 during all DMA-initiated cycles). Interfacing to the DMA Unit itself is very simple, since except for the addition of the DMA request connection, it is exactly the same as interfacing to the CPU.

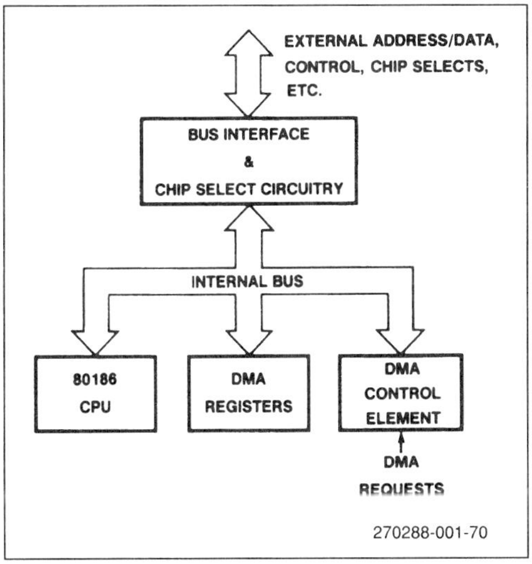

Figure 65. CPU/DMA Channel Internal Model

8.1 DMA FEATURES

Each of the two DMA channels provides the following features:

- Independent 20-bit source and destination pointers which access the I/O or memory location from which data will be fetched or to which data will be deposited.
- Programmable auto-increment, auto-decrement or neither, relative to the source and destination pointers after each DMA transfer.
- Programmable termination of DMA activity after a certain number of DMA transfers.
- Programmable CPU interruption at DMA termination.
- Byte or word DMA transfers to or from even or odd memory or I/O addresses.
- Programmable generation of DMA requests by the source of the data, the destination of the data, Timer 2 (see Chapter 6), or by the DMA Unit itself.

8.2 DMA UNIT PROGRAMMING

Each of the DMA channels contains several registers to control channel operation. These registers are included in the 80186 family integrated peripheral control block (see Section 5.2). These registers include the source and destination pointer registers, the transfer count register, and the control register. The layout of the bits in these registers is given in Figures 66 and 67.

The 20-bit source and destination pointers access the complete one Mbyte address space of the 80186 processor family and all 20 bits are affected by the auto-increment or auto-decrement unit of the DMA. The address space is seen as a flat, linear array without segments. Even though the usual I/O addressability is 64 Kbytes, it is possible to perform I/O addresses over a one Mbyte address range. Therefore, one must program the upper four bits of the pointer registers to 0 if routine I/O addresses are desired.

After every DMA transfer the 16-bit DMA transfer count register is decremented by 1, whether a byte transfer or a word transfer has occurred. If the TC bit in the DMA control register is set, the DMA ST/$\overline{STOP}$ bit (see below) will be cleared when this register goes to 0, causing all DMA activity to cease. A transfer count of zero allows 65536 (216) transfers. If the TC bit is cleared, the transfer count register will decrement to zero, then roll over to 0FFFFH; transfers will continue indefinitely.

Upon RESET, the contents of the DMA pointer registers and transfer count registers are indeterminate; initialization of all the bits should be practiced.

The DMA control register (see Figure 67) contains bits which control various channel characteristics. Each data source and destination pointer can point to memory or I/O space, and be incremented, decremented, or left alone after each DMA transfer. The register also contains a bit which selects byte or word transfers. Two synchronization bits determine the source of the DMA requests (see Section 8.7). The terminal count (TC) bit determines whether DMA activity will cease after a pro-

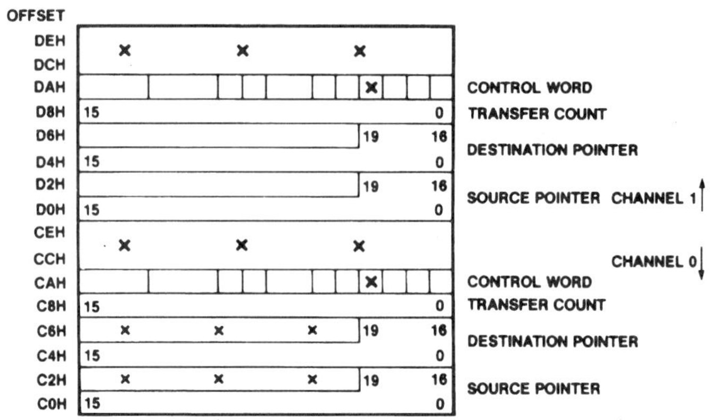

270288-001-71

Figure 66. 80186 Family DMA Registers

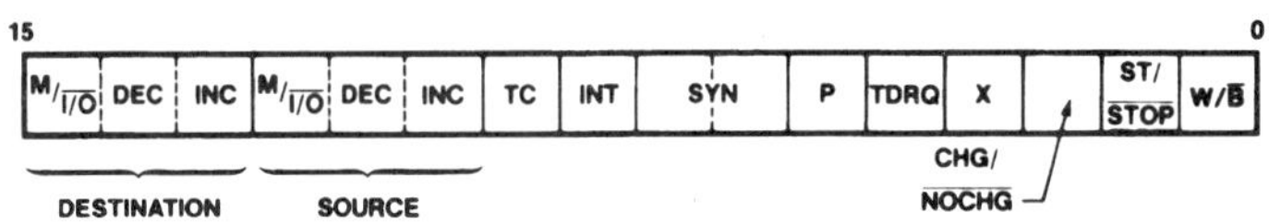

270288-001-72

Figure 67. DMA Control Register Format

grammed number of DMA transfers, and the INT bit enables interrupts to the processor upon terminal count. An interrupt will not be generated to the CPU unless **both** the INT bit and TC bit are set.

The control register also contains a start/stop (ST/$\overline{STOP}$) bit which enables DMA transfers. Whenever this bit is set, the channel is armed, that is, a DMA transfer will occur whenever a DMA request is made to the channel. A companion bit, the CHG/$\overline{NOCHG}$ bit, allows the DMA control register to be changed without modifying the state of the ST/$\overline{STOP}$ bit. The ST/STOP bit will only be modified if the CHG/$\overline{NOCHG}$ bit is also set during the write to the DMA control register. The CHG/$\overline{NOCHG}$ bit is write only. It will always be read back as a 0. Set the ST/$\overline{STOP}$ bit only after programming all other DMA Control Unit registers because DMA transfers may start immediately. This bit is automatically cleared when the transfer count register reaches zero and the TC bit in the DMA control register is set, or when the transfer count register reaches zero and unsynchronized DMA transfers are programmed.

All DMA Unit programming registers are directly accessible by the CPU. This means the CPU can, for example, modify the DMA source pointer register after 137 DMA transfers have occurred, and have the new pointer value used for the 138th DMA transfer. If more than one register for a DMA channel is being modified while DMA activity is possible, the register values should be placed in memory locations and moved into the DMA registers using a LOCKed string move instruction. This prevents a DMA transfer from occurring after only some of the register values have changed. A read/modify/write operation (AND, for example) to a memory-mapped pointer register should also be LOCKed.

8.3 DMA CHANNEL PRIORITY

The P bit in the DMA control register determines the channel priority if DMA requests are received on both channels simultaneously. A one in this position sets higher priority relative to the other channel while a zero specifies lower priority relative to the other channel. If both channels are programmed at the same priority, they will alternate cycles. This alternation starts with Channel 1 unless Channel 1 is already running a transfer. In source or destination synchronized operation, the alternation scheme only applies when DRQ0 and DRQ1 are sampled active simultaneously.

8.4 DMA TRANSFERS

Every DMA transfer consists of two independent bus cycles, a fetch cycle and a deposit cycle (see Figure 68). During the fetch cycle, the byte or word data is accessed according to the source pointer register. The data is read into an internal temporary register which is not accessible by the CPU. During the deposit cycle, the data is written to memory or I/O space at the address in the destination pointer register. These two bus cycles cannot be separated by a bus HOLD, a refresh cycle, or any other condition except RESET. DMA bus cycles are identical to bus cycles initiated by the CPU except that the S6 status line is driven to a logic 1 state.

DMA transfer rates depend on processor bus width and the DMA Control Unit operating mode. Maximum DMA rates (expressed as Mbytes/sec) can be calculated by multiplying the processor clock rate (in MHz at CLKOUT) by the appropriate factor in Table 18.

8.5 DMA REQUESTS

DMA transfers may be initiated in three ways: by direct register programming, by external requests on a DMA request (DRQ) pin, or by timeouts of Timer 2. Continuous transfer operation is referred to as unsynchronized mode and is selected by

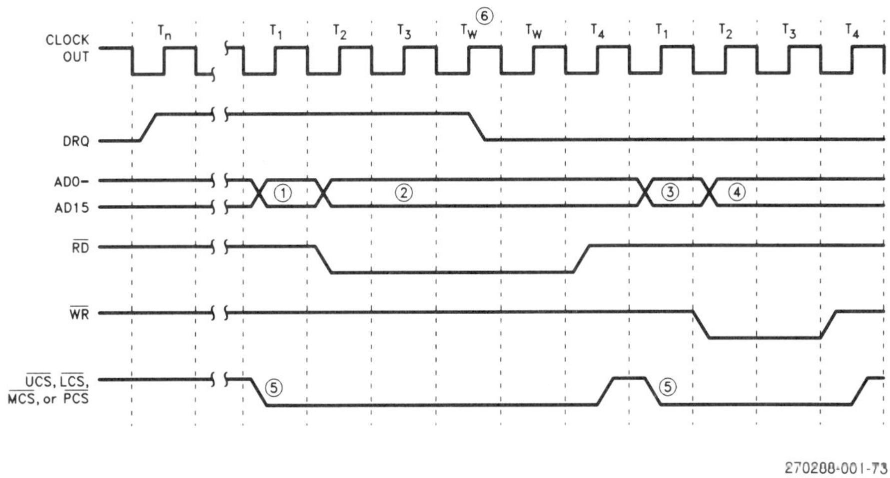

NOTES:
1. Source address.
2. Source data.
3. Destination address.
4. Destination data.
5. If a source or destination address overlaps and active chip select region, the chip select will go active.
6. Wait states are inserted by programming the chip select/READY logic for an active address region, or by the external READY pins.

Figure 68. Example DMA Transfer Cycle on the 80186/80C186

Table 18. Maximum DMA Transfer Rate Factor

Type of Synchronization	80188/80C188	80186/80C186
Unsynchronized	1/8	1/4
Source Synchronized	1/8	1/4
Destination Synchronized, CPU Does Not Need Bus	1/10	1/5
Destination Synchronized, CPU Needs Bus	1/12	1/6

synchronization bits in DMA control register. These bits can also select source or destination synchronized requests on the DRQ pin. The processor synchronizes external requests to the CPU clock before presenting them to the DMA logic.

8.5.1 DMA REQUEST TIMING AND LATENCY

Before any DMA request can be generated, the internal bus must be granted to the DMA Unit. A certain amount of time is required for the processor to grant this internal bus to the DMA Unit. The time between a DMA request being issued and the DMA transfer being run is known as DMA latency. Many of the issues concerning DMA latency are the same as those concerning bus latency (see Section 3.8.2). External HOLD and refresh always have bus priority over DMA transfers. Thus, the latency time of an internal DMA cycle will suffer during an external bus HOLD.

Each DMA channel has a programmed priority relative to the other DMA channel. Both channels may be programmed to be the same priority, or one may be programmed to be of higher priority than the other channel. If both channels are active, DMA latency will suffer on the lower priority channel. If both channels are simultaneously active and both channels are of the same programmed priority, DMA transfer cycles will alternate between the two channels (i.e., the first channel will perform a fetch and deposit, followed by a fetch and deposit by the second channel, etc.).

The following sections describe DMA synchronization in detail.

The minimum DMA latency is four clocks as shown in Figure 69. The DRQ signal is sampled on every falling clock edge and it takes this amount of time for it to propagate through the bus control logic, independent of any wait states associated with current bus activity. In other words, a DMA cycle will start at the next available T_I state as long as a higher priority activity is not pending and the DRQ signal was sampled active four clocks previously.

If DRQ is sampled active at point 1 in Figure 69, the DMA cycle can be executed four clocks later even if the DMA request goes inactive before then. If the DMA cycle does not start when shown (if, for instance, an 80C186/80C188 DRAM refresh cycle starts instead), DRQ is not latched and must remain active until four clocks before the **next** DMA bus cycle T1 opportunity.

8.5.2 DMA ACKNOWLEDGE

80186 family processors generate no explicit DMA acknowledge (DACK) signal. Instead, the processor performs a read or write directly to the DMA requesting device. A DMA acknowledge signal can be generated by decoding an address or by using a $\overline{PCS}$ line (see Figure 70). Note that ALE must be used to factor DACK in some cases because addresses are not guaranteed stable when chip selects go active.

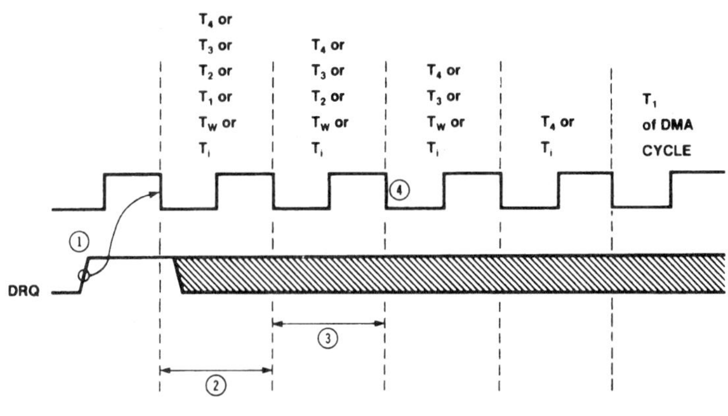

270288-001-74

NOTES:
1. T_{INVCL} = DMA request to clock low.
2. Synchronizer resolution time.
3. DMA unit priority arbitration and overhead.
4. Bus interface Unit latches DMA request and decides to run DMA cycle.

Figure 69. DMA Request Timing (Showing Minimum Response Time)

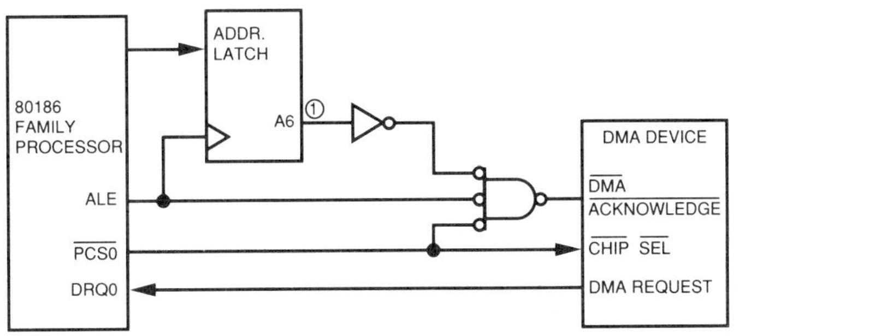

NOTE:
1. A6 is arbitrary and is only used to differentiate DMA and non-DMA bus cycles.

Figure 70. DMA Acknowledge Synthesis

8.6 INTERNALLY GENERATED DMA REQUESTS

DMA transfer requests may originate from two of the integrated peripherals in the 80186 family. The source may be either the DMA Control Unit or Timer 2.

The DMA channel can be programmed so that whenever Timer 2 reaches its maximum count, a DMA request will be generated. This feature is selected by setting the TDRQ bit in the DMA channel control register. A DMA request generated in this manner will be latched in the DMA Control Unit, so that once the timer request has been generated, it cannot be cleared except by running the DMA cycle or by clearing the TDRQ bit. Before any DMA requests are generated in this mode, Timer 2 must be initialized and enabled.

A timer-requested DMA cycle run from either DMA channel will reset the timer request. Thus, if both channels are using Timer 2 to request a DMA cycle, only one DMA channel will execute a transfer for every timeout. Another implication is that if a second Timer 2 timeout occurs before a DMA channel has a chance to run a DMA transfer, the first request will be lost.

The DMA channel can also be programmed to provide its own DMA requests. In this mode, DMA transfer cycles will run continuously at the maximum bus bandwidth until the preprogrammed number of DMA transfers have occurred. This mode is selected by programming the synchronization bits in the DMA control register for unsynchronized transfers. Note that in this mode, the DMA Control Unit will monopolize the CPU bus, i.e., the CPU will not be able to perform opcode fetching, memory operations, etc., while the DMA transfers are occurring. Also notice that the DMA Control Unit will only perform the number of transfers indicated in the maximum count register regardless of the state of the TC bit in the DMA control register.

8.7 EXTERNALLY SYNCHRONIZED DMA TRANSFERS

There are two types of externally synchronized DMA transfers, source synchronized and destination synchronized. These modes are selected by programming the synchronization (SYN) bits in the DMA channel control register. The only difference between the two is the time at which the DMA request pin is sampled to determine if another DMA transfer is immediately required after the present DMA transfer. On source synchronized transfers, this is done such that two transfers may occur immediately after each other. On destination synchronized transfers, a certain amount of idle time is automatically inserted between two DMA transfers to allow time for the DMA requesting device to drive its DMA request inactive.

8.7.1 SOURCE SYNCHRONIZED DMA TRANSFERS

In a source synchronized DMA transfer, the data source requests the DMA cycle. In this type of transfer, the processor reads the device requesting the DMA transfer during the fetch cycle of the transfer. It takes four CPU clock cycles from the time the processor samples the DMA request pin until the time the DMA transfer begins and a bus cycle takes a minimum of four clock cycles. Therefore, the earliest time the DMA request pin will be sampled for another DMA transfer will be at T_1 of the deposit cycle of the DMA transfer (assuming no wait states). This allows three CPU clock cycles (assuming no wait states) between the time the DMA requesting device receives acknowledgement of its request (at the beginning of T_2 of the

DMA fetch cycle), and the time it must drive the request line inactive if no more DMA transfers are desired (see Figure 71.)

8.7.2 DESTINATION SYNCHRONIZED DMA TRANSFERS

In destination synchronized DMA transfers, the data destination requests the DMA transfer. An example of this would be a floppy disk write from main memory to the disk. In this type of transfer, the device requesting the transfer is written during the deposit cycle of the DMA transfer. This causes a problem, since the DMA requesting device will not receive notification of the DMA cycle being run until three clock cycles before the end of the DMA transfer (if no wait states are being inserted into the deposit cycle of the DMA transfer) and it takes four clock cycles to determine if another DMA cycle should run immediately following the current transfer. To get around this problem, the DMA Unit relinquishes the bus after each destination synchronized DMA transfer for at least two CPU clock cycles. This allows the requesting device time to drop its DMA request if it does not immediately desire another DMA transfer.

When the bus is relinquished by the DMA Unit, the CPU may resume bus operation. Typically, a CPU-initiated bus cycle is inserted between each destination synchronized DMA transfer. If no CPU bus activity is required, however, the DMA Unit inserts two CPU clock cycles between the deposit of one DMA transfer and the fetch cycle of the next DMA transfer. The critical time at which DRQ is sampled to decide whether to run the next DMA cycle is two clocks before the end of the deposit cycle, regardless of wait states. Figure 71 shows the DMA request going away too late to prevent the immediate generation of another DMA transfer. Wait states lengthen the amount of time from the beginning of the deposit cycle to the time the DRQ pin is sampled for a decision on the next transfer. Thus, wait states can be inserted into the DMA cycle to increase the amount of time the requesting device has to drop the DRQ line after receiving DMA acknowledge.

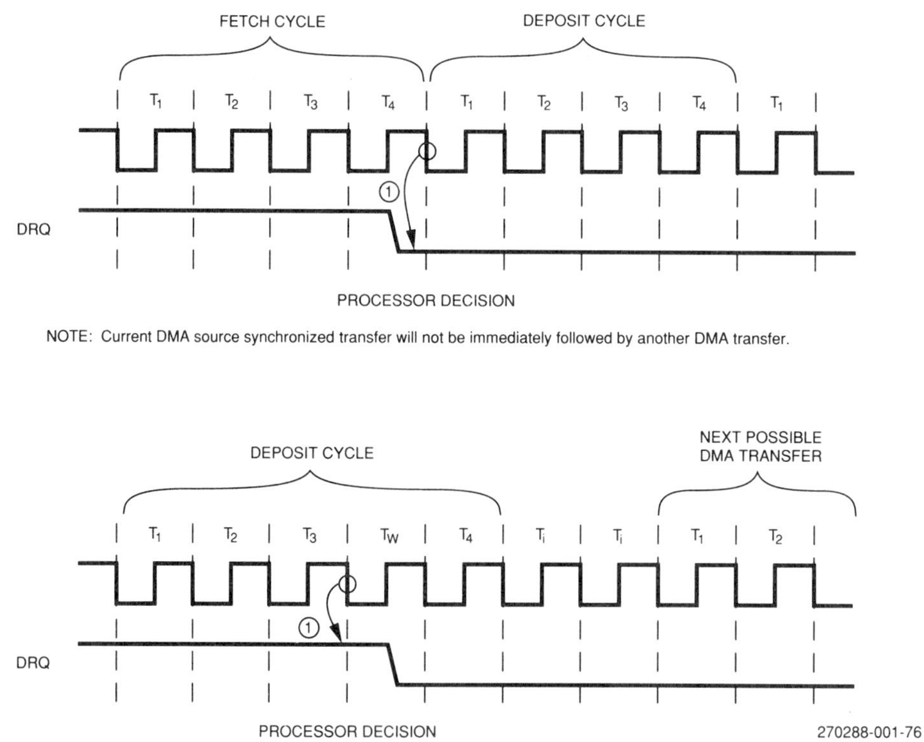

NOTE: Current DMA source synchronized transfer will not be immediately followed by another DMA transfer.

NOTE: Current DMA destination synchronized transfer will be followed immediately by another DMA transfer.

Figure 71. Source and Destination Synchronized DMA Request Timing

8.8 DMA HALT AND NMI

Whenever a Non-Maskable Interrupt is received on an 80186 family microprocessor, all DMA activity will be suspended at the end of the current DMA transfer. This is performed by the NMI automatically setting the DMA Halt (DHLT) bit in the Interrupt Controller status register (see Section 9.5.2.10). The timing of NMI required to prevent a DMA cycle from occurring is shown in Figure 72. After the NMI has been serviced, the DHLT bit can be cleared by the programmer to resume DMA activity (i.e., it is not automatically cleared when entering the NMI service routine). The DHLT bit is automatically cleared when the IRET instruction is executed. In either case, DMA activity resumes exactly as it left off, i.e., none of the DMA control registers are modified. This DHLT bit may also be set by the programmer to prevent DMA activity during critical sections of code. Do not write to the DHLT bit in the controller status register while timer interrupts are enabled; a conflict with the internal use of the register may lead to incorrect timer interrupt processing. The DHLT bit does not function when the integrated Interrupt Control Unit is configured for Slave Mode.

8.9 EXAMPLE DMA INTERFACE CODE

Figure 73 contains sample code to initialize the DMA Control Unit to perform transfers between the system and a floppy disk controller.

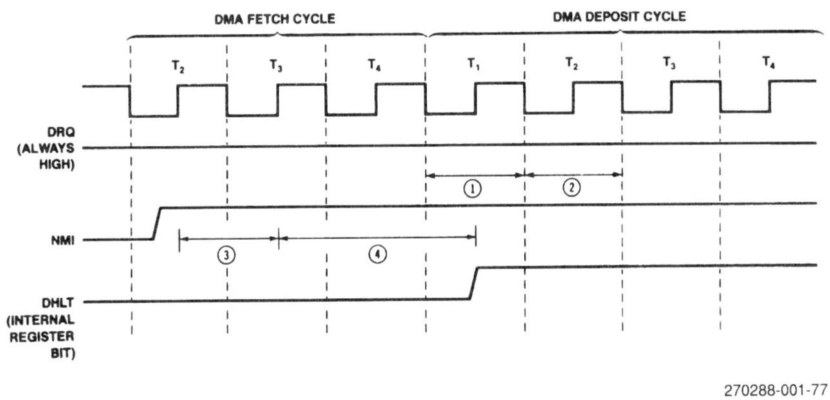

NOTES:
1. DMA request synchronization.
2. Decision: Will DMA cycle be run?
   Answer: No DMA request is active but DHLT is set (from NMI request).
3. NMI synchronization time.
4. Logic delay time from synchronized NMI unit DHLT set (note: DHLT is in the interrupt control status register).

Figure 72. NMI and DMA Interaction

```
$mod186
name                    assembly_example_80186_family_DMA_support
;
;  This file contains an example procedure which initializes the DMA controller
;       to perform the DMA transfers between an 80186 family system and the 8272
;       Floppy Disk Controller (FDC). It assumes that the peripheral control
;       block has not been moved from its reset location.
;
arg1                    equu    word ptr[BP + 4]
arg2                    equ     word ptr[BP + 6]
arg3                    equ     word ptr[BP + 8]
DMA_FROM_LOWER          equ     0FFC0h                  ; DMA register locations
DMA_FROM_UPPER          equ     0FFC2h
DMA_TO_LOWER            equ     0FFC4h
DMA_TO_UPPER            equ     0FFC6h
DMA_COUNT               equ     0FFC8h
DMA_CONTROL             equ     0FFCAh
DMA_TO_DISK_CONTROL     equ     01486h                  ; destination synchronization
                                                        ; source to memory, incremented
                                                        ; destination to I/O
                                                        ; no terminal count
                                                        ; byte transfers
DMA_FROM_DISK_CONTROL equ       0A046h                  ; source synchronization
                                                        ; source to  I/O
                                                        ; destination to memory,
                                                        ; incremented, no terminal count
                                                        ; byte transfers
FDC_DMA                 equ     6B8h                    ; FDC DMA address
FDC_DATA                equ     688h                    ; FDC data register
FDC_STATUE              equ     680h                    ; FDC status register

cgroup                  group   code
code                    segment public'code'
                        public  set_dma_
                        assume  cs:cgroup
;
;                       set_dma (offset,to) programs the DMA channel to point one
;                       side to the disk DMA address, and the other to memory
;                       pointed to by ds:offset. If "to"= 0 then will be a transfer
;                       from disk to memory; if "to"= 1 then will be a transfer from
;                       memory to disk. The parameters to the routine are passed on
;                       the stack.
;
set_dma_                proc    near
                        enter   0,0                     ; set stack addressability
                        push    AX                      ; save registers used
                        push    BX
                        push    DX
                        test    arg2,1                  ; check to see direction of
                                                        ; transfer
;                       jz      from_disk
;                       performing a transfer from memory to the disk controller
;
                        mov     AX,DS                   ; get the segment value
                        rol     AX,4                    ; generate the upper 4 bits of
                                                        ; the physical address in the
                                                        ; lower 4 bits of the register
                        mov     BX,AX                   ; save the result...
                        mov     DX,DMA_FROM_UPPER       ; prgm the upper 4 bits of the
                        out     DX,AX                   ; DMA source register
                        and     AX,0FFF0h               ; form the lower 16 bits of the
                                                        ; physical address
                        add     AX,arg1                 ; add the offset
                        mov     DX,DMA_FROM_LOWER       ; prgm the lower 16 bits of the
                        out     DX,AX                   ; DMA source register
                        jnc     no_carry_from           ; check for carry out of
                                                        ; addition
                        inc     BX                      ; if carry out, then need to adj
                        mov     AX,BX                   ; the upper 4 bits of the
                                                        ; pointer
```

Figure 73. Example DMA Interface Code

```
                mov     DX,DMA_FROM_UPPER
                out     DX,AX
no_carry_from:
                mov     AX,FDC_DMA              ; prgm the low 16 bits of DMA
                mov     DX,DMA_TO_LOWER         ; destination register
                out     DX,AX
                xor     AX,AX                   ; zero the uppper 4 bits of
the
                mov     DX,DMA_TO_UPPER         ; DMA destination register
                out     DX,AX
                mov     AX,DMA_TO_DISK_CONTROL; prgm the DMA ctl reg
                mov     DX,DMA_CONTROL          ; note:DMA may begin directly
                out     DX,AX                   ; after this word is output
                pop     DX
                pop     BX
                pop     AX
                leave
                ret
from_disk:
;
;               performing a transfer from the disk to memory
;
                mov     AX,DS
                rol     AX,4
                mov     DX,DMA_TO_UPPER
                out     DX,AX
                mov     BX,AX
                and     AX,0FFF0h
                add     AX,arg1
                mov     DX,DMA_TO_LOWER
                out     DX,AX
                jnc     no_carry_to
                inc     BX
                mov     AX,BX
                mov     DX,DMA_TO_UPPER
                out     DX,AX
no_carry_to:
                mov     AX,FDC_DMA

                mov     DX,DMA_FROM_LOWER
                out     DX,AX
                xor     AX,AX
                mov     DX,DMA_FROM_UPPER
                out     DX,AX
                mov     AX,DMA_FROM_DISK_CONTROL
                mov     DX,DMA_CONTROL
                out     DX,AX
                pop     DX
                pop     BX
                pop     AX
                leave
                ret
set_dma_        endp

code            ends
                end
```

270288-001-78

Figure 73. Example DMA Interface Code (continued)

Interrupts 9

CHAPTER 9
INTERRUPTS

80186 family interrupts can be software- or hardware-initiated. Software interrupts originate from three sources:

- Execution of INT instructions.
- A direct result of program execution, that is, execution of a breakpointed instruction.
- An indirect result of program logic, for example, attempted division by zero.

Hardware interrupts originate from either the integrated peripherals or external logic. In the 80186 family, an integrated Interrupt Control Unit performs the tasks which would otherwise be left to an external 8259 Interrupt Controller. Hardware interrupts are classified as either non-maskable or maskable.

All interrupts, whether software- or hardware-initiated, result in the transfer of control to a new program location. A 256-entry vector table (see Figure 74), which contains address pointers to the interrupt routines, resides in memory locations 0 through 3FFH. Each entry in this table consists of two 16-bit address values (four bytes) that are loaded into the code segment (CS) and the instruction pointer (IP) registers when an interrupt is accepted.

All interrupts save the machine status by pushing the current contents of the flags onto the stack. The 80186 family CPU then clears the interrupt enable and trap bits in the flags register to prevent subsequent maskable and single step interrupts. Next, the CPU establishes the routine return linkage by pushing the current CS and IP register contents onto the stack before loading the new CS and IP register values from the vector table.

9.1 INTERRUPT CONTROL MODEL

80186 family software interrupts are presented directly to the CPU, while hardware interrupts are managed through the integrated Interrupt Controller.

The tasks performed by the integrated Interrupt Controller include synchronization of interrupt requests, prioritization of interrupt requests, and management of interrupt acknowledge sequences. Nesting is provided so interrupt service routines for lower priority interrupts may themselves be interrupted by higher priority interrupts. The integrated Interrupt Controller can be a master to two external 8259A or 82C59A Interrupt Controllers or can be a slave to an external master controller.

The integrated Interrupt Controller block diagram is shown in Figure 75. It contains registers and a control element. Four inputs are provided for external interfacing to the interrupt controller. Their functions change according to the mode of the Interrupt Controller. Like the other 80186 family integrated peripheral registers, the Interrupt Controller registers are available for CPU reading or writing at any time.

9.2 INTERRUPT CHARACTERISTICS RELATED TO INTERRUPT TYPE

The interrupts handled directly by the CPU are varied and specific, while the interrupts handled by the integrated Interrupt Controller are processed like each other.

9.2.1 INTERRUPTS HANDLED DIRECTLY BY THE CPU

The integrated Interrupt Controller does not intervene in interrupt processing related to INT instructions, instruction traps and exceptions, and the Non-Maskable Interrupt.

9.2.1.1 INSTRUCTION-GENERATED TRAPS AND EXCEPTIONS

Software interrupts have higher priority than hardware interrupts, with the exception of NMI. There are eight dedicated software interrupts associated with instruction execution or attempted instruction execution, leaving room in the vector table from Type numbers 32 through 255 for user-defined interrupts.

The predefined software interrupts in the 80186 family are listed below with brief descriptions. When an interrupt is invoked, the CPU will transfer control to the memory location specified by the vector associated with the specific type. The user must provide the interrupt service routine and initialize the interrupt vector table with the appropriate service routine address. The user may additionally invoke these interrupts through hardware or software. If the preassigned function is not used in the system, the user may assign some other function to the associated type. However, for compatibility with future Intel products, interrupt Types 0-31 should not be reassigned as user defined interrupts.

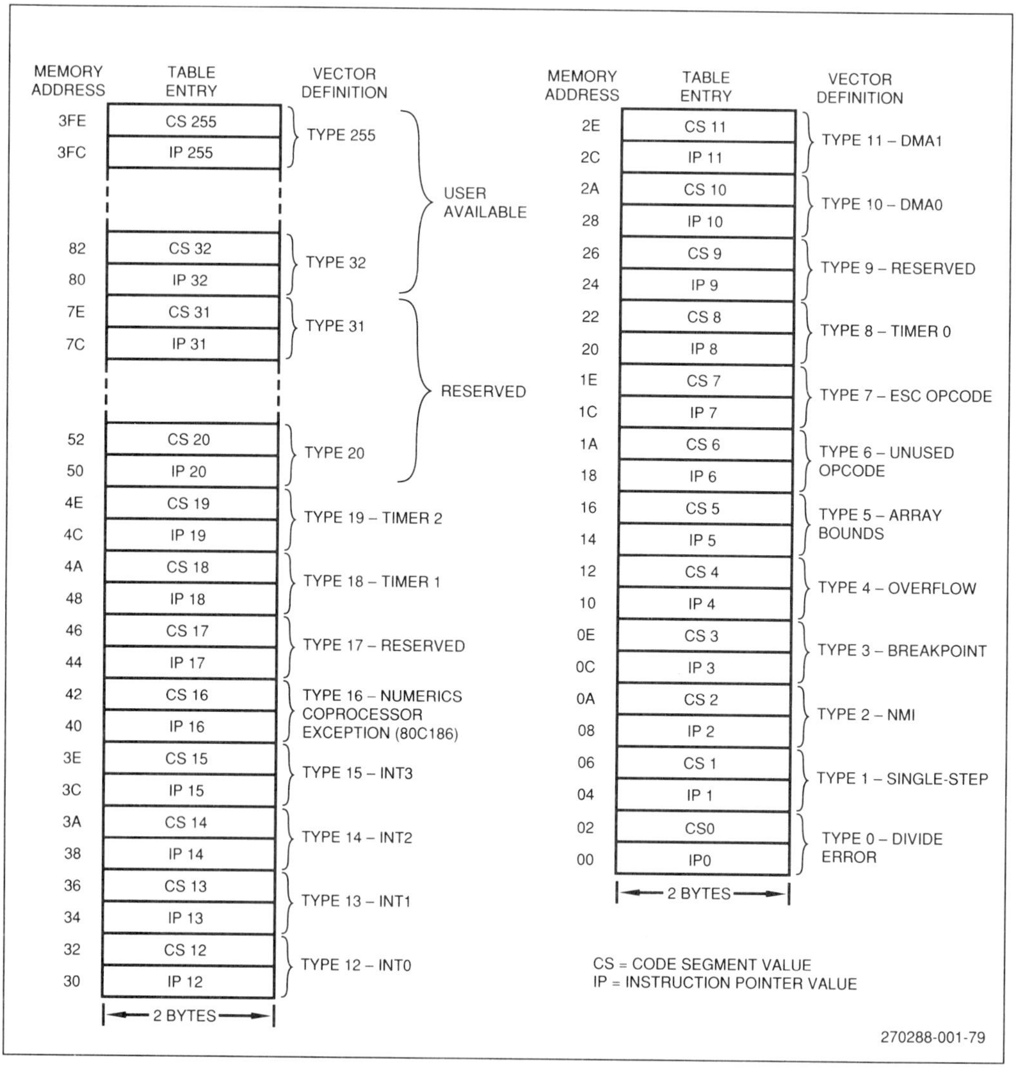

Figure 74. Interrupt Vector Table

DIVIDE ERROR - TYPE 0:

Type 0 interrupts are invoked by an attempted division in which the quotient exceeds the maximum value (e.g., division by zero). The interrupt is non-maskable and is entered as part of the execution of the divide instruction. If divide errors are common in an application and interrupts are not re-enabled by the interrupt service routine, add the interrupt routine execution time to the worst case divide instruction execution time to calculate interrupt latency for hardware interrupts.

SINGLE STEP - TYPE 1:

This interrupt occurs one instruction after the trap flag (TF) is set in the flag register. It is used to allow software single stepping through a sequence of code. Single stepping is initiated by copying the flags onto the stack, setting the TF bit on the stack and popping the flags. The interrupt routine should be the single step routine. The interrupt sequence saves the flags and program counter, then resets TF to allow the single step routine to execute normally. To return to the routine under test, an interrupt return restores the IP register, CS register,

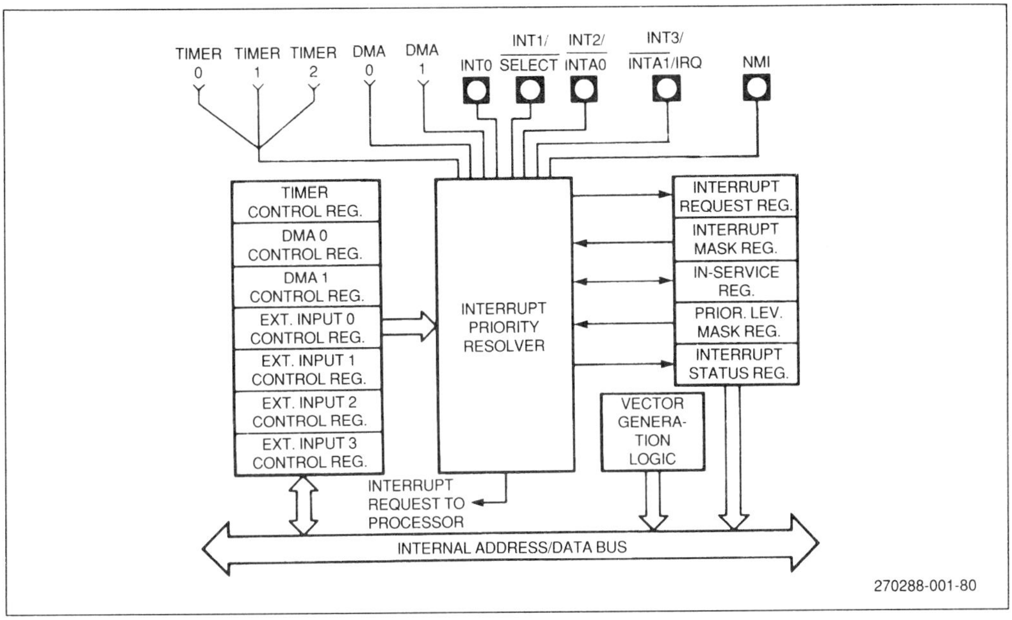

Figure 75. 80186 Processor Family Interrupt Controller Block Diagram

and flags (with TF set). This allows the execution of the next instruction in the program under test before trapping back to the single step routine.

BREAKPOINT INTERRUPT - TYPE 3:

This is a special version of the INT instruction. Since it requires only a single byte of code space, the breakpoint interrupt can map into the smallest instruction for absolute breakpoint resolution. This interrupt is not maskable.

INTERRUPT ON OVERFLOW - TYPE 4:

This non-maskable interrupt occurs if the overflow flag (OF) is set in the flag register and the INTO instruction is executed. This instruction allows trapping to an overflow error service routine.

ARRAY BOUNDS EXCEPTION - TYPE 5:

If an array index is outside the array bounds during the BOUND instruction, a Type 5 interrupt results. The array bounds are located in memory at a location indicated by one of the instruction operands. The other operand indicates the value of the index to be checked.

UNUSED OPCODE EXCEPTION - TYPE 6:

Attempted execution of undefined opcodes generates this interrupt.

ESCAPE OPCODE EXCEPTION - TYPE 7:

This exception is the result of attempted ESCape opcode (D8H-DFH) execution. On the 80186/80188 and the 80C186 in Enhanced Mode, the ESC trap is enabled by setting a bit in the relocation register. On the 80C186 in Compatible Mode and the 80C188 in any mode, ESC instructions always generate this trap. (See Appendix C.2 for more on Enhanced and Compatible Modes.) The return address of this exception will point to the ESC instruction causing the exception. If a segment override prefix preceded the ESC instruction, the return address will point to the segment override prefix.

NUMERICS COPROCESSOR EXCEPTION (80C186 ONLY) - TYPE 16:

When the execution of numerics (ESCape) instruction causes an unmasked exception in the 80C187 Numerics Processor Extension, the result is an interrupt Type 16. Although this is classified as a software interrupt, signaling is performed in hardware from the 80C187 to the 80C186 on the $\overline{\text{ERROR}}$ pin.

In general, this exception is detected by the 80C186 upon execution of the instruction subsequent to the one causing the error condition.

9.2.1.2 NON-MASKABLE INTERRUPT (NMI)

The Non-Maskable Interrupt (NMI), a hardware interrupt, is interrupt Type 2. It has the highest priority among hardware interrupts and is typically reserved for catastrophic events such as impending power failure or timeout of a system watch-dog timer. NMI cannot be prevented by programming and multiple NMI inputs will lead to nesting of NMI interrupt service routines. Noise on the NMI pin can cause unnecessary system upsets.

NMI must be asserted for one CLKOUT period in order to be internally synchronized. The signal is edge-triggered and level-latched. The vectoring sequence for NMI starts at the next available instruction edge after NMI is latched. The interrupt response time for NMI is 42 processor clocks.

The processor will start recognizing the NMI input pin at the same clock edge on which the RES input goes inactive. If NMI is asserted within 10 clocks after RESET goes inactive, the processor will vector to the NMI service routine before it executes the first instruction. This procedure is useful when it is desired to begin execution somewhere other than the default starting address of 0FFFF0H.

9.2.1.3 USER-DEFINED SOFTWARE INTERRUPTS

The user can generate an interrupt through the software with a two byte interrupt instruction INT nn. The first byte is the INT opcode while the second byte (nn) contains the type number of the interrupt to be performed. The INT instruction is not maskable by the interrupt-enable flag. This instruction can be used to transfer control to routines that are dynamically relocatable and whose location in memory is not known by the calling program. This technique also saves the flags of the calling program on the stack prior to transferring control. The called procedure must return control with an interrupt return (IRET) instruction to remove the flags from the stack and fully restore the state of the calling program.

All interrupts invoked through software (all interrupts discussed thus far with the exception of NMI) are not maskable with IF and initiate the transfer of control at the end of the instruction in which they occur. They do not initiate interrupt acknowledge bus cycles and will disable subsequent maskable interrupts by resetting the flags IF and TF. The vectors for these interrupts are implied in the instruction.

9.2.2 INTERRUPTS HANDLED BY THE INTEGRATED INTERRUPT CONTROLLER

The 80186 family integrated Interrupt Controller receives and prioritizes hardware interrupts from four external pins and five integrated peripheral sources. The Interrupt Controller was designed to allow these interrupts to be flexibly managed. For example, it is possible to mask one or more interrupt sources and handle them by polling while allowing vectored interrupts for all the other sources to proceed.

Requests on interrupt pins INT0-3 **are not latched**. If a normally LOW INT input is pulsed HIGH briefly while that interrupt is disabled or another interrupt is in service, that request will not be saved, even if the corresponding bit gets temporarily set in the interrupt request register. It is necessary to hold the INT input active until the processor starts the vectoring sequence, either by running interrupt acknowledge cycles or reading the new CS and IP values from the interrupt vector table. The 80186 processor family does not employ a default vector as does the 8259A or 82C59A.

All interrupt requests from the integrated peripherals **are latched** in the integrated Interrupt Controller for presentation to the CPU.

9.3 OTHER INTERRUPT CHARACTERISTICS

To understand how interrupts participate in the overall microprocessor system, it is necessary to understand latency, masking and priority.

9.3.1 INTERRUPT LATENCY

Interrupt latency time it takes the 80186 family processor to begin its response after it receives an interrupt. This is different from interrupt response time, the time from reception of the interrupt until it actually executes the first instruction of the interrupt service routine.

Two factors affecting interrupt latency are the instruction being executed and the state of the interrupt-enable flip-flop. The interrupt-enable flip-flop must be explicitly set by issuing the STI instruction. Since interrupt vectoring automatically clears the flip-flop, it is necessary to set the flip-flop within the interrupt service routine if nested interrupts are desired.

In general, an interrupt can be acknowledged only when the CPU finishes executing an instruction, i.e., interrupts are acknowledged at the first available instruction boundary. For the purpose of determining instruction boundaries, prefixes

(LOCK, REP, and segment override) are considered to be part of the following instruction. Thus, interrupt latency time can be as long as 69 CPU clocks, the amount of time it takes the processor to execute an integer divide instruction with a segment override prefix. There are a number of exceptions to these rules.

MOVs and POPs to a segment register cause interrupt processing to be delayed until after the next instruction. This delay allows a 32-bit pointer to be loaded to the SS and SP stack registers without the danger of an interrupt occurring between the two loads.

The WAIT instruction causes the CPU to suspend processing while checking the $\overline{\text{TEST}}$ pin for a logic LOW condition. If an interrupt is detected, the processor will vector to the interrupt service routine with the return pointer aimed back to the WAIT instruction. The 80C186/80C188, does not check the $\overline{\text{ERROR}}$ pin for 80C187 exceptions during the WAIT instruction.

When the repeat prefix (REP) is used in front of a string operation, the processor does allow interrupt vectoring between repetitions, including those which are LOCKed. If multiple prefixes precede a repeated string operation and the instruction is interrupted, only the prefix immediately preceding the string primitive is restored.

With the 80C186/80C187 processor combination, interrupts on the external interrupt pins INT0-3 can be serviced after the 80C186 starts a numerics instruction. However, once communication is completely established with the 80C187 (i.e., the 80C187 is not busy), interrupts are blocked until the end of the instruction.

Interrupt latency is also affected by activity of the integrated peripheral set. Interrupt latency is increased if the processor does not have control of the bus due to the HOLD/HLDA protocol. Bus cycles associated with the interrupt vectoring sequence cannot break in between the fetch and deposit cycles of a DMA transfer. Finally, the 80C186/80C188 will not accept interrupts during DRAM refresh bus cycles.

9.3.2 INTERRUPT MASKS AND NESTING

To provide a high degree of flexibility in designing complex interrupt structures, the 80186 family has an elaborate mechanism to control the enabling and disenabling of individual interrupts. The programmer must understand this structure to utilize the processor most efficiently in a heavily interrupt-driven system. The rules of masking are as follows:

- The non-maskable interrupt (NMI), cannot be prevented by programming, as its name implies.
- Software interrupts, both user-defined and execution exception, cannot be masked.
- All other hardware interrupts are subject to the condition of the interrupt-enable flag which is set by the STI instruction and cleared by the CLI instruction. Since every interrupt vectoring sequence clears the flag, programmer intervention is required to enable interrupt nesting. The flag is automatically restored upon execution of the IRET instruction.
- The integrated Interrupt Controller has a priority mask register which disables interrupts below a programmable priority.
- The integrated Interrupt Controller has a mask register with programmable bits for each possible interrupt source, including the DMA Control Unit, timers, and the external interrupt pins. (Timers share a mask bit in Master Mode.)
- The integrated Interrupt Controller has a control register for each interrupt source. (Timers share a control register in Master Mode.) Each control register addresses the same mask bit as does the mask register.

Interrupts under control of the integrated Interrupt Controller are nestable subject to the states of their in-service bits. Additionally, INT0 and INT1 have a provision called Special Fully Nested Mode (SFNM), which allows successive interrupts on those pins to ignore the state of their in-service bits.

9.3.3 INTERRUPT PRIORITY

When considering the precedence of interrupts for multiple simultaneous interrupts, apply the following guidelines:

1. Of the non-maskable interrupts (NMI, instruction trap, and user-defined software), single step has the highest priority (will be serviced first), followed by NMI, followed by all other software interrupts.
2. The interrupts controlled by the 80186 family integrated Interrupt Controller are all maskable hardware interrupts. Their priorities levels are lower than the non-maskable interrupts.

A simultaneous NMI and single step trap will cause the NMI service routine to follow single step. A simultaneous software trap and single step trap will cause the software interrupt service routine to follow single step. Finally, simultaneous NMI and software trap will cause the NMI service routine to be executed followed by the software interrupt service routine. An exception to this priority structure occurs if all three interrupts are pending. For this case, transfer of control to the software interrupt service routine followed by the NMI trap will cause both the NMI and software interrupt service routines to be executed without single stepping. Single stepping resumes upon execution of the instruction following the instruction causing the software interrupt (the next instruction in the routine being single stepped).

If the user does not wish to single step before hardware interrupt service routines, the single step routine need only disable interrupts during execution of the program being single stepped and re-enable interrupts on entry to the single step routine. Disabling the interrupts within the program under test prevents entry into the interrupt service routine while single step (TF = 1) is active. To prevent single stepping before NMI service routines, the single step routine must check the return address and return control to that routine without single step enabled. As examples, consider Figures 76 and 77. In Figure 76 single step and NMI occur simultaneously. In Figure 77, NMI, a timer interrupt and a divide error all occur while single stepping a divide instruction.

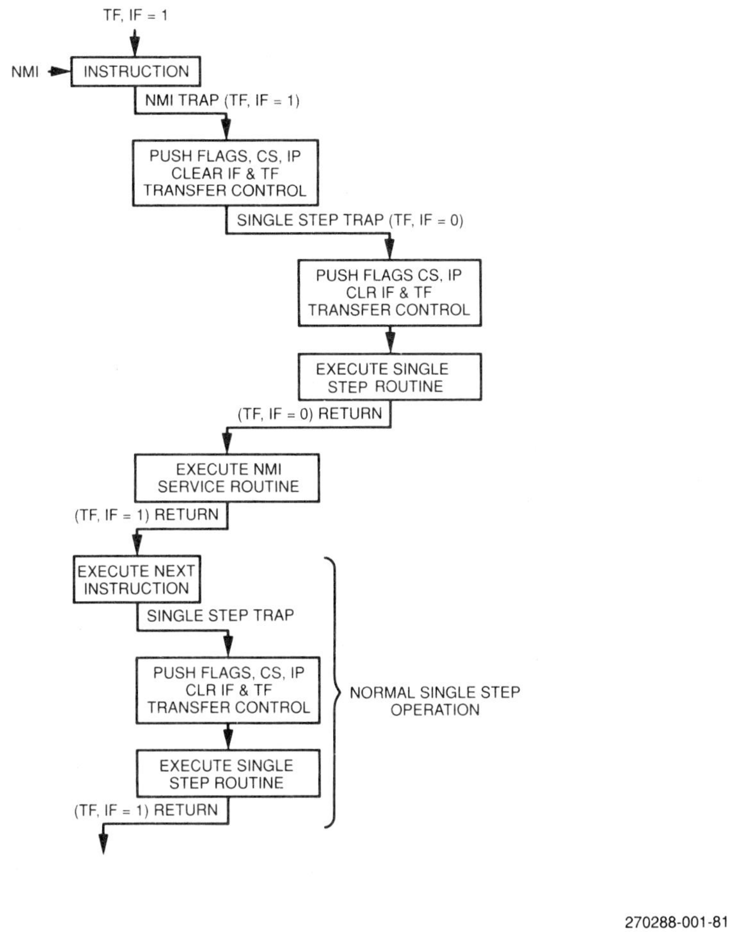

Figure 76. NMI During Single Stepping and Normal Single Step Operation

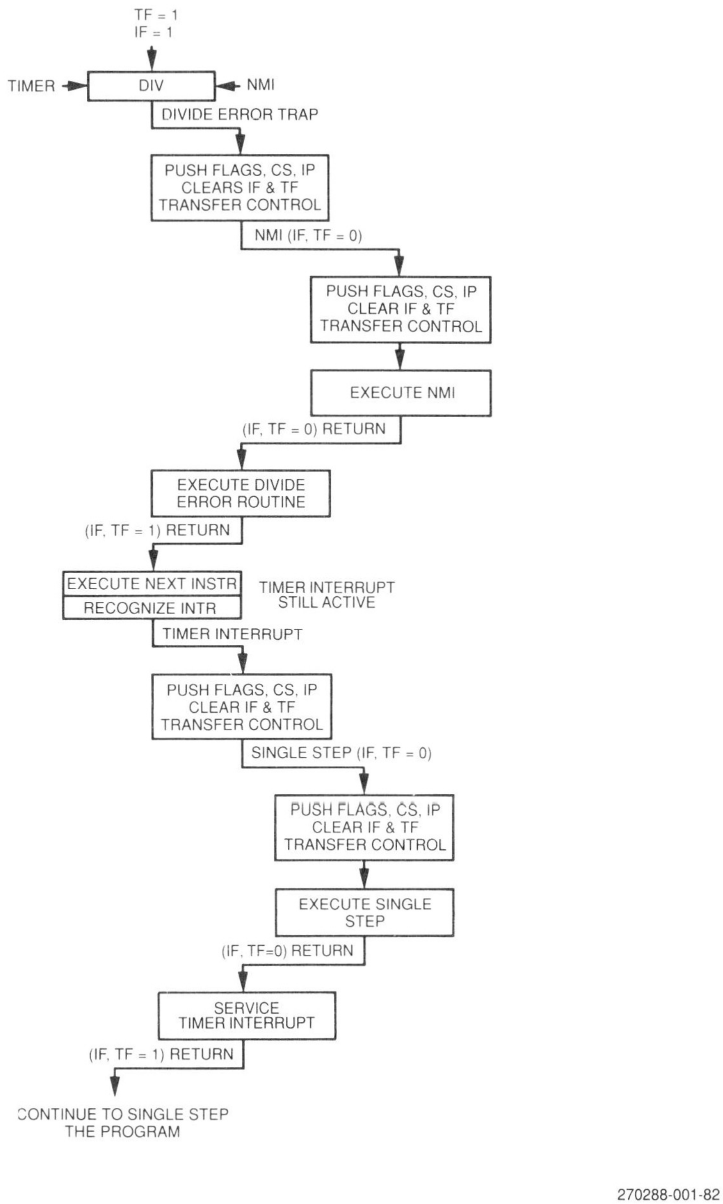

Figure 77. NMI, Timer, Single Step and Divide Error Simultaneous Interrupts

9.4 INTERRUPT CONTROL UNIT OPERATION MODES

The Interrupt Control Unit operates in either of two major modes, Master Mode and Slave Mode. The system designer must choose the operation mode early on since the two modes differ greatly with respect to overall function, pin definition, and programming registers.

In Master Mode, the Interrupt Control Unit acts as the master interrupt controller for the system, receiving and arbitrating hardware interrupts generated both internally and externally. The Interrupt Controller presents interrupts directly to the CPU of the 80186 family processor. As many as two 8259A (or 82C59A) Interrupt Controllers may act as slaves to the master processor. Master Mode is the default configuration.

In Slave Mode, the integrated 80186 family Interrupt Control Unit operates as a slave to an external master 8259A Interrupt Controller, receiving hardware interrupts only from the integrated peripherals. The CPU presents interrupt requests to the 8259A, which may receive interrupts from other sources as well. The 8259A arbitrates all the interrupt sources and requests interrupt service from the CPU. Setting the SLAVE/MASTER bit in the relocation register (see Section 5.1) selects Slave Mode.

9.5 MASTER MODE

Master Mode is the simplest and most popular configuration of the Interrupt Control Unit.

9.5.1 MASTER MODE EXTERNAL CONNECTIONS

In Master Mode the four external interrupt pins are configurable according to two options, direct and cascade. With the pins configured in Direct Input Mode the integrated Interrupt Controller provides interrupt vectors. With the pins configured in Cascade Mode, interrupt types are furnished by an external Interrupt Controller. Mixed mode operation (two pins as direct inputs and two pins as an INT/INTA pair) is also possible.

9.5.1.1 DIRECT INPUT MODE

When the Cascade Mode bits are cleared, the interrupt input pins are configured as direct interrupt pins (see Figure 78). Whenever an interrupt is received on the input line, the integrated controller will do nothing unless the interrupt is enabled, and it is the highest priority pending interrupt. At this time, the Interrupt Controller will present the interrupt to the CPU and wait for an interrupt acknowledge. When the acknowledge occurs, it will present the interrupt vector address to the CPU. In Direct Input Mode, the CPU will not run any external interrupt acknowledge (INTA) cycles.

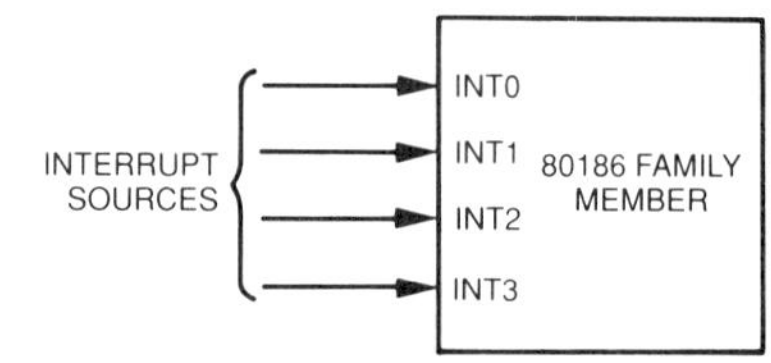

Figure 78. Direct Input Mode Interrupt Connections

9.5.1.2 CASCADE MODE

The INT2/$\overline{\text{INTA0}}$ and INT3/$\overline{\text{INTA1}}$ lines are dual purpose; they can function as direct input lines, or they can function as interrupt acknowledge outputs. When the Cascade Mode bit is set, the interrupt input lines are configured in Cascade Mode. In this mode, the interrupt input line is paired with an interrupt acknowledge line. $\overline{\text{INTA0}}$ provides the interrupt acknowledge for an INT0 input, and $\overline{\text{INTA1}}$ provides the interrupt acknowledge for an INT1 input. Figure 79 shows this connection.

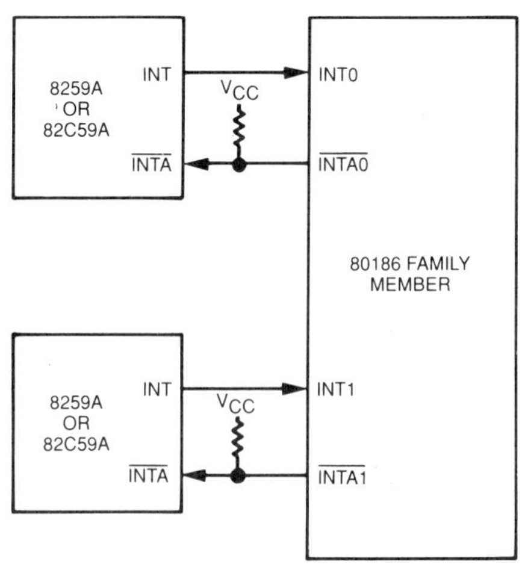

Figure 79. 80186 Family Cascade Mode Interface

The 8259A or 82C59A Interrupt Controllers may each be further cascaded to eight more Interrupt Controllers. Cascading Interrupt Controllers in this way allows up to 64 interrupt levels.

INT0 with INT2/$\overline{\text{INTA0}}$ and INT1 with INT3/$\overline{\text{INTA1}}$ may be individually programmed into interrupt request/acknowledge pairs, or programmed as direct inputs. For example, INT0 and INT2/$\overline{\text{INTA0}}$ may be programmed as an interrupt and interrupt acknowledge pair, while INT1 and INT3/$\overline{\text{INTA1}}$ each provide separate internally vectored interrupt inputs.

9.5.2 MASTER MODE PROGRAMMING

The Interrupt Controller registers for Master Mode are defined according to Figure 80.

9.5.2.1 CONTROL REGISTERS IN MASTER MODE

Each interrupt source to an 80186 family processor has a control register in the internal controller. These registers contain three bits which select one of eight interrupt priority levels for the device (0 is highest priority, 7 is lowest priority), and a mask bit to enable the interrupt (see Figure 81). When the mask bit is zero, the interrupt is enabled; when it is one, the interrupt is masked. All interrupt sources have default priority levels.

There are seven control registers in the integrated Interrupt Controller. In Master Mode, four of these serve the external interrupt inputs, one each for the two DMA channels, and one for the collective timer interrupts.

MASTER MODE	OFFSET ADDRESS
INT3 CONTROL REGISTER	3EH
INT2 CONTROL REGISTER	3CH
INT1 CONTROL REGISTER	3AH
INT0 CONTROL REGISTER	38H
DMA1 CONTROL REGISTER	36H
DMA0 CONTROL REGISTER	34H
TIMER CONTROL REGISTER	32H
INTERRUPT CONTROLLER STATUS REGISTER	30H
INTERRUPT REQUEST REGISTER	2EH
IN-SERVICE REGISTER	2CH
PRIORITY MASK REGISTER	2AH
MASK REGISTER	28H
POLL STATUS REGISTER	26H
POLL REGISTER	24H
EOI REGISTER	22H
(1)	20H

NOTE:
1. Unsupported in this mode; values written may or may not be stored.

270288-001-85

Figure 80. Interrupt Controller Registers for Master Mode

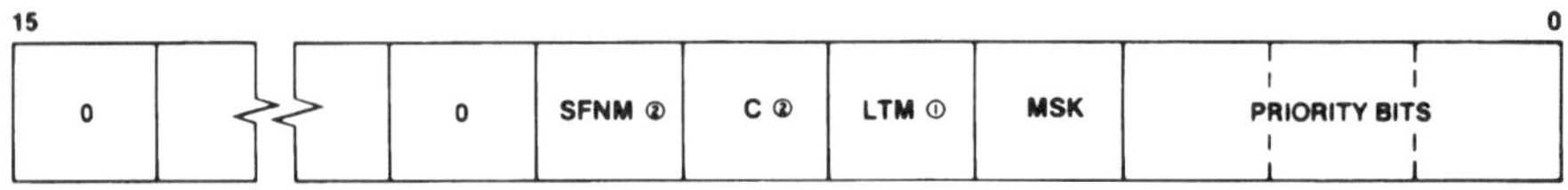

270288-001-86

NOTE:
1. This bit present only in INT0-INT3 control registers.
2. These bits present only in INT0-INT1 control register.

Figure 81. Interrupt Controller Control Register Format

The control registers for the external interrupt pins contain special bits not present for other interrupt sources. Setting the LTM bit in these registers selects level-triggered operation as opposed to edge-triggered operation. The INT0 and INT1 control registers contain C and SFNM bits to select Cascade and Special Fully Nested Modes, respectively.

Setting the LTM bit in these registers selects level-triggered operation over edge-triggered operation. With edge-triggered operation, a LOW-to-HIGH transition must occur before the interrupt will be recognized. The interrupt input must also be LOW for one clock before the active-going edge. With level-triggered operation, only a HIGH level is required to generate an interrupt. In both types of operation, the interrupt input must remain active until acknowledged.

With level-triggered operation only, an interrupt request input left active until after the end-of-interrupt causes another interrupt request.

9.5.2.2 CASCADE MODE

When programmed in this mode, the 80186 family processor will provide two interrupt acknowledge pulses in response to external interrupts. These pulses will be provided on the INT2/INTA0 line, and will also be reflected by interrupt acknowledge status being generated on the S0-S2 status lines. The interrupt type will be read on the second pulse. Similarly, the processor will provide two interrupt acknowledge pulses on INT3/INTA1 in response to an interrupt request on the INT1 line.

When an interrupt is received on a cascaded interrupt pin, the priority mask bits and the in-service bits in the particular interrupt control register will be set. This prevents the controller from generating a CPU interrupt request from a lower priority interrupt. Also, any subsequent interrupt requests on the same interrupt input line will not cause the integrated Interrupt Controller to generate an interrupt request to the 80186 family CPU. This means that if the external Interrupt Controller receives a higher priority interrupt request on one of its interrupt request lines and presents it to the 80186, the Interrupt Controller will not present it to the CPU until the in-service bit for the interrupt line has been cleared.

9.5.2.3 SPECIAL FULLY NESTED MODE

When both the Cascade Mode bit and the SFNM bit are set, the interrupt input lines are configured in Special Fully Nested Mode. The external interface in this mode is exactly as in Cascade Mode. The only difference is in the conditions which allow an external interrupt to interrupt the CPU.

When an interrupt is received from a Special Fully Nested Mode interrupt line, it will interrupt the CPU if it is the highest priority pending interrupt regardless of the state of the in-service bit for the source in the Interrupt Controller. When the processor acknowledges an interrupt from a Special Fully Nested Mode interrupt line, it sets corresponding bits in the priority mask and in-service registers. This prevents the Interrupt Controller from accepting a lower priority interrupt. However the Interrupt Controller will allow additional requests generated by the same external source to interrupt the CPU. This means that if the external (cascaded) Interrupt Controller receives higher priority interrupts on its interrupt request lines and presents them to the integrated controller's request line, these interrupts will be nested.

If the SFNM bit is set and the Cascade Mode bit is not set, the controller will provide internal interrupt vectoring. It will also ignore the state of the in-service bit in determining whether to present an interrupt request to the CPU. In other words, it will use the SFNM conditions of interrupt generation with an internally vectored interrupt response, i.e., if the interrupt pending is the highest priority type pending, it will cause a CPU interrupt regardless of the state of the in-service bit for the interrupt. This operation is only applicable to INT0 and INT1, which have SFNM bits in their control registers.

9.5.2.4 REQUEST REGISTER IN MASTER MODE

The Interrupt Controller includes an interrupt request register (see Figure 82). This register contains seven active bits, one for every interrupt source with an interrupt control register. Whenever an interrupt request is made, the bit in the interrupt request register is set regardless of whether the interrupt is enabled. Interrupt request bits are automatically cleared when the interrupt is acknowledged by starting the interrupt vectoring sequence. The programmer can set or clear the D1 and D0 bits of the request register to request or cancel DMA interrupt requests.

9.5.2.5 MASK REGISTER IN MASTER MODE

The Interrupt Controller mask register (see Figure 83) contains a mask bit for each interrupt source associated with an interrupt control register. The bit for an interrupt source in the mask register is the same bit as provided in the interrupt control register; modifying a mask bit in the control register will also modify it in the mask register, and vice versa.

9.5.2.6 PRIORITY MASK REGISTER IN MASTER MODE

The interrupt priority mask register (see Figure 84) contains three bits which indicate the lowest priority an interrupt must have to cause an interrupt request to be serviced. Interrupts which have a lower priority will be masked. Upon RESET, the register is set to the lowest priority of 7 to enable interrupts of any priority. This register may be read or written.

9.5.2.7 IN-SERVICE REGISTER IN MASTER MODE

The Interrupt Controller contains an in-service register (see Figure 85). A bit in the in-service register is associated with each interrupt control register so that when an interrupt request by the device associated with the control register is acknowledged by the processor (either by interrupt acknowledge cycles or by reading the poll register) the bit is set. The bit is reset when the CPU issues an End Of Interrupt to the Interrupt Controller. This register may be both read and written, i.e., the CPU may set in-service bits without an interrupt ever occurring, or may reset them without using the EOI function of the Interrupt Controller.

9.5.2.8 POLL AND POLL STATUS REGISTERS

The Interrupt Controller contains both a poll register and a poll status register (see Figure 86). These registers contain the same information. They have a single bit to indicate an interrupt is pending and five bits to indicate the type of the pending interrupt. The request bit is set if an interrupt of sufficient priority has been received. It is automatically cleared when the interrupt is acknowledged. If an interrupt is pending, the

OFFSET: 2EH

15										0
X	X	X	I3	I2	I1	I0	D1	D0	X	TMR

270288-001-87

Figure 82. Interrupt Request Register Format

OFFSET: 28H

15										0
X	X	X	I3	I2	I1	I0	D1	D0	X	TMR

270288-001-88

Figure 83. Interrupt Mask Register Format

OFFSET: 2AH

15							0
X	X	X	X	X	PRM2	PRM1	PRM0

270288-001-89

Figure 84. Interrupt Controller Priority Mask Register Format

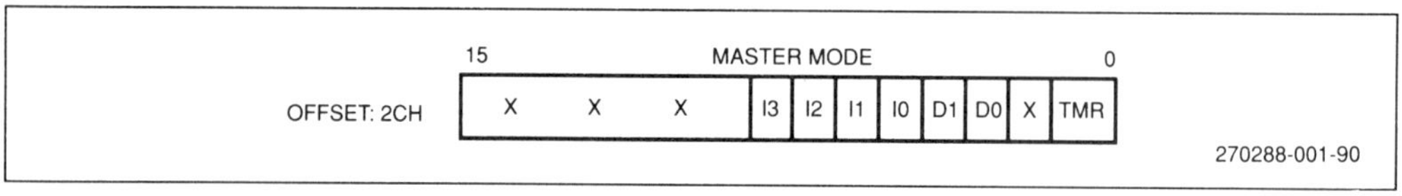

Figure 85. Interrupt Controller In-Service Register Format

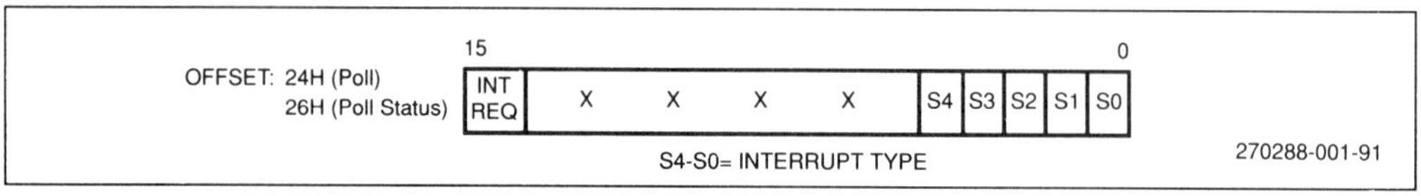

Figure 86. Poll and Poll Status Register Format

remaining bits contain information about the highest priority pending interrupt. These registers are read-only.

Reading the poll register will acknowledge the pending interrupt to the Interrupt Controller just as if the processor had started the interrupt vectoring sequence. The processor will not actually run any interrupt acknowledge cycles, and will not vector through a location in the interrupt vector table. The contents of the interrupt request, in-service, poll, and poll status registers will change appropriately.

Reading the poll status register will merely transmit the status of the polling bits without modifying any of the other Interrupt Controller registers.

9.5.2.9 END OF INTERRUPT REGISTER IN MASTER MODE

The Interrupt Controller contains an End Of Interrupt register (see Figure 87). The programmer issues an End Of Interrupt (EOI) to the controller by writing to this register. After receiving the EOI, the Interrupt Controller automatically resets the in-service bit for the interrupt. The value of the word written to this register determines whether the EOI is specific or non-specific. A non-specific EOI is requested by setting the non-specific bit in the word written to the EOI register. In a non-specific EOI, the in-service bit of the highest priority interrupt set is automatically cleared, while a specific EOI allows the in-service bit cleared to be explicitly specified. If the highest priority interrupt is reset, the poll and poll status registers change to reflect the next lowest priority interrupt to be serviced. If a less than highest priority interrupt in-service bit is reset, the poll and poll status registers will not be modified (because the highest priority interrupt to be serviced has not changed). This register is write-only.

9.5.2.10 INTERRUPT STATUS REGISTER IN MASTER MODE

The Interrupt Controller also contains an interrupt status register (see Figure 88). This register contains four programmable bits. Three bits show which timer is causing an interrupt. This is required because in Master Mode, the timers share a single interrupt control register. A bit in this register is set to indicate which timer generated an interrupt. The bit associated with a timer is automatically cleared after the interrupt request for the timer is acknowledged. More than one of these bits may be set at a time. The fourth bit is the DMA halt bit. When set, this bit prevents any DMA activity. It is automatically set whenever a NMI is received by the Interrupt Controller. It can also be set by the programmer. This bit is automatically cleared whenever the IRET instruction is executed. All implemented bits in the interrupt status register are read/write. Do not perform the write operation when interrupts from the timer/counters are possible; a conflict with internal use of the register may lead to incorrect timer interrupt processing.

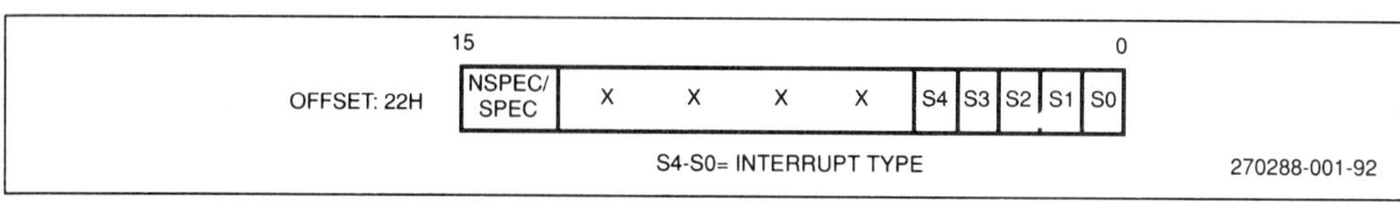

Figure 87. End of Interrupt Register Format

OFFSET: 30H	15 DHLT	X	X	X	X	X	X	T2	T1	0 T0

270288-001-93

Figure 88. Interrupt Status Register Format

9.5.3 MASTER MODE INTERRUPT SOURCES

The 80186 family Interrupt Controller receives requests and arbitrates among many different interrupt request sources, both internal and external. External interrupts are processed by the integrated Interrupt Controller only in Master Mode. Each interrupt source may be programmed to be a different priority level.

9.5.3.1 INTERNAL SOURCES

The internal interrupt sources are the three timers and the two DMA channels. An interrupt from any of these interrupt sources is latched in the Interrupt Controller. The state of the pending interrupt can be obtained by reading the interrupt request register. Also, latched DMA interrupts can be reset by the processor by writing to the interrupt request register. Note that all timers share a common bit in the interrupt request register in Master Mode. The Interrupt Controller status register may be read to determine which timer is actually causing the interrupt request. Each timer has a unique interrupt vector (see Section 9.0). Thus, polling is not required to determine which timer has caused the interrupt in the interrupt service routine. Also, because the timers share a common interrupt control register, they are placed at a common priority level relative to other interrupt sources. Among themselves they have a fixed priority, with Timer 0 as the highest priority timer and Timer 2 as the lowest priority timer.

9.5.3.2 EXTERNAL SOURCES

The Interrupt Controller will accept external interrupt requests only when it is programmed in Master Mode. In this mode, the external pins associated with the Interrupt Controller may serve either as direct interrupt inputs, or as cascaded interrupt inputs from other Interrupt Controllers. These options are selected by programming the C and SFNM bits in the INT0 and INT1 control registers (see Figure 81).

When programmed as direct interrupt inputs, the four interrupt inputs are each controlled by an individual interrupt control register. As stated earlier, each of these registers contain bits which select the priority level for the interrupt and a mask bit. In addition, each of these control registers contains a bit which selects edge- or level-triggered mode for the interrupt input.

When edge-triggered operation is selected, a LOW-to-HIGH transition must occur on the interrupt input before an interrupt is generated, while in level-triggered mode, only a HIGH level needs to be maintained to generate an interrupt. In edge-triggered mode, the input must remain LOW at least one clock cycle before the input is rearmed. In both modes, the interrupt level must remain HIGH until the interrupt is acknowledged, i.e., the interrupt request **is not latched** in the Interrupt Controller. The status of the interrupt input can be shown by reading the interrupt request register. Since interrupt requests on these inputs **are not latched** by the Interrupt Controller, if an input goes inactive, the interrupt request (and its request bit) will also go inactive.

If the C (Cascade) bit of either the INT0 or INT1 control register is set, the interrupt input is cascaded to an external Interrupt Controller. In this mode, whenever the interrupt presented on the INT0 or INT1 line is acknowledged, the integrated Interrupt Controller will not provide the interrupt type for the interrupt. Instead, two INTA bus cycles will be run, with $\overline{INTA0}$ or $\overline{INTA1}$ lines providing the interrupt acknowledge pulses for the INT0 and INT1 interrupt requests, respectively. This allows up to 128 individually vectored interrupt sources if two banks of 8 external Interrupt Controllers each are used.

9.5.4 MASTER MODE INTERRUPT RESPONSE

The 80186 family processor can respond to an interrupt in two different ways. The first response will occur if the internal controller is providing the interrupt vector information with the controller in Master Mode. The second response will occur if the CPU reads interrupt type information from an external Interrupt Controller. In both instances the interrupt vector information driven by the integrated Interrupt Controller is not available outside the microprocessor.

When the integrated Interrupt Controller receives an interrupt, it will automatically set the in-service bit and reset the interrupt request bit. In addition, unless the interrupt control register for the interrupt is set in Special Fully Nested Mode, the Interrupt Controller will prevent any interrupts from occurring from the same interrupt line until the in-service bit for that line has been cleared.

9.5.4.1 INTERNAL VECTORING IN MASTER MODE

In Master Mode, the interrupt types associated with all the interrupt sources are fixed and unalterable. These types are given in Table 19. In response to an internal CPU interrupt acknowledge the Interrupt Controller will generate the vector address rather than the interrupt type. On 80186 family microprocessors the interrupt vector address is the interrupt type multiplied by four.

Table 19. 80186 Family Interrupt Vector Types

Interrupt Name	Vector Type	Relative Priority
Timer 0	8	0(a)
Timer 1	18	0(b)
Timer 2	19	0(c)
DMA 0	10	1
DMA 1	11	2
INT 0	12	3
INT 1	13	4
INT 2	14	5
INT 3	15	6

In Master Mode, no external Interrupt Controller need know when the integrated controller is providing an interrupt vector, nor when the interrupt acknowledge is taking place. As a result, no interrupt acknowledge bus cycles will be generated. The first external indication that an interrupt has been acknowledged will be the processor reading the interrupt vector from the interrupt vector table in memory.

Interrupt response to an internally vectored interrupt is 42 clock cycles because the processor does not run interrupt acknowledge cycles. This is faster than the interrupt response when external vectoring is required, or if the Interrupt Controller is run in Slave Mode.

If two interrupts of the same programmed priority occur, the default priority scheme (shown in Table 19) is used.

9.5.4.2 EXTERNAL VECTORING IN MASTER MODE

External interrupt vectoring occurs whenever the Interrupt Controller is placed in Cascade Mode. With external vectoring, the 80186 family processor generates two interrupt acknowledge cycles, reading the interrupt type off the lower 8 bits of the address/data bus on the second interrupt acknowledge cycle (see Figure 89). In the 8259A or 82C59A, the upper five bits are user-programmable and the lower three bits are determined by a defined interrupt request level. Interrupt acknowledge bus cycles have the following characteristics:

- The two interrupt acknowledge cycles are LOCKed.
- Two idle T-states are always inserted between the two interrupt acknowledge cycles.
- Wait states will be inserted in an interrupt acknowledge cycle if READY is not returned to the processor.

Also notice that the processor provides two interrupt acknowledge signals, one for interrupts signaled by the INT0 line, and one for interrupts signaled by the INT1 line (on the INT2/$\overline{\text{INTA0}}$ and INT3/$\overline{\text{INTA1}}$ lines, respectively). These two interrupt acknowledge signals are mutually exclusive. Interrupt acknowledge status will be driven on the status lines ($\overline{\text{S0}}$-$\overline{\text{S2}}$) when either INT2/$\overline{\text{INTA0}}$ or INT3/$\overline{\text{INTA1}}$ signal an interrupt acknowledge. The interrupt type generated on the second INTA cycle is read by the CPU and then multiplied by four. The resultant value is used as a pointer into the interrupt vector table.

When the Interrupt Controller is operating in Cascade Mode and an interrupt occurs during an instruction that has been LOCKed by software, the $\overline{\text{LOCK}}$ signal timing shown in Figure 89 may be altered. Some peripheral devices used with 80186 family members require contiguous INTA cycles to allow correct Interrupt Controller response. In such cases, the external circuitry in Figure 90 should be used to ensure that DMA or HOLD requests are blocked from stealing the bus during INTA cycles.

9.5.4.3 MASTER MODE INTERRUPT RESPONSE TIME

The interrupt response time for the 80186 family is 42-55 CPU clocks when the Interrupt Controller is in Master Mode. Figure 91 shows how the total is obtained. The clock count changes when the processor replaces the indicated idle states with bus cycles for other tasks such as DMA. The processor does not necessarily flush the queue until the very last moment, so prefetching may continue for a while during the vectoring sequence. Also, the clock count must be adjusted for wait states or for the 80188/80C188. For the 80188/80C188, double the number of clocks given for each bus cycle accessing the stack or memory.

These clock counts are also applicable to software interrupts and NMI (notice there are no INTA cycles).

9.5.5 EXAMPLE MASTER MODE INITIALIZATION

The code to initialize the Interrupt Control Unit for a combination of direct inputs and Cascade Mode inputs is given in Figure 92. Refer to Figures 78 and 79 for the corresponding

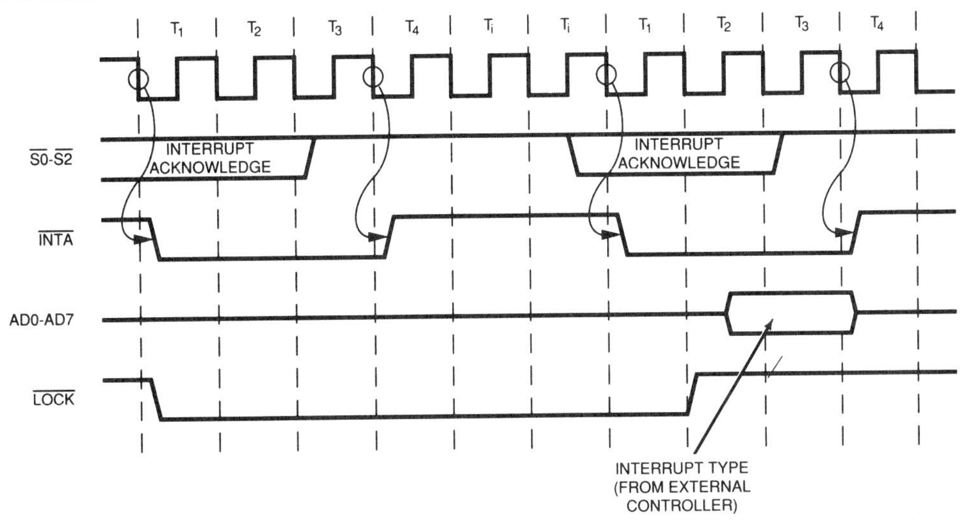

Figure 89. Cascaded Interrupt Acknowledge Timing

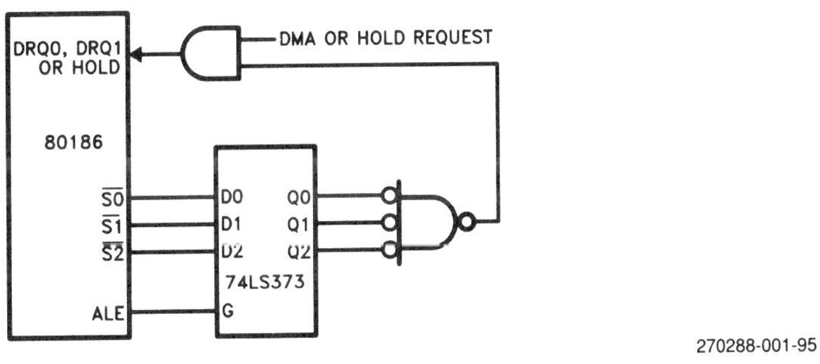

Figure 90. Circuit Blocking DMA or HOLD Request Between INTA Cycles

hardware configurations. Notice that a READY signal must be returned to the processor to prevent the generation of wait states in response to the interrupt acknowledge cycles. This configuration provides 10 external input lines: two provided by the Interrupt Controller itself (pins INT1 and INT3), and eight from the external 8259A (cascaded at pins INT0 and INTA0). The 80186 integrated Interrupt Control Unit is the master system Interrupt Controller. The 8259A will only receive interrupt acknowledge pulses in response to interrupts it has generated. The 8259A may be cascaded again as a master to as many as eight additional 8259A Interrupt Controllers (configured as slaves).

9.6 SLAVE MODE

Although Master Mode is more commonly used in 80186 family applications, Slave Mode has a number of unique functions that make it attractive in some larger system designs.

```
                                                                            CLOCKS
Interrupt presented to the interrupt controller --------------------------------->
                                                                               5
Interrupt presented to CPU ------------------------------------------------------>
                                          INTA                                 4  ⎫ CASCADE
                                          IDLE                                 2  ⎬ MODE
                                          INTA                                 4  ⎪ ONLY
                                          IDLE                                 5  ⎭
                                          READ IP                              4
                                          IDLE                                 3  (5 IF NOT CASCADE MODE)
                                          READ CS                              4
                                          IDLE                                 4
                                          PUSH FLAGS                           4
IF←0, TF←0                                IDLE                                 3
                                          PUSH CS                              4
                                          PUSH IP                              4
First instruction fetch                   IDLE                                 5
from interrupt routine ---------------------------------------------------------->
                                                                        ---------
                                                                        Total 42-55
                                                                  270288-001-96
```

Figure 91. 80186 Family Master Mode Interrupt Response Time

```
$mod186
name                    example_80186_family_interrupt_code
;
; This routine configures the interrupt controller to provide two cascaded
;       interrupt inputs (through an external 8259A internal controller on
;       pins INT0 and INT2/INTA0) and two direct interrupt inputs (on pins INT1
and
;       INT3). The default priority levels are used. Because of this, the
;       priority level programmed into the control register is set to 111, the
;       level all interrupts assume at reset.
;
int0_control            equ     0FF38H
int_mask                equ     0FF28H
;
code                    segment                 ;public'code'
                        assume  CS:code
set_int_                proc    near
                        push    DX
                        push    AX

                        mov     AX,0100111B     ;Cascade Mode
                                                ;interrupt unmasked
                        mov     DX,int0_control
                        out     DX,AX

                        mov     AX,01001101B    ;now unmask the other external
                                                ;interrupts
                        mov     DX,int_mask
                        out     DX,AX
                        pop     AX
                        pop     DX
                        ret
set_int_                endp
code                    ends
                        end
                                                                  270288-001-97
```

Figure 92. Example 80186 Family Interrupt Initialization for Master Mode

9.6.1 SLAVE MODE EXTERNAL CONNECTIONS

When the SLAVE/$\overline{\text{MASTER}}$ bit in the peripheral relocating register is set, the Interrupt Control Unit is in Slave Mode. In this mode, all four Interrupt Controller input lines are used to perform the necessary handshaking with the external master Interrupt Controller. Figure 93 shows the hardware configuration of the interrupt lines with an external controller in Slave Mode. This discussion uses only the Slave Mode functional pin names.

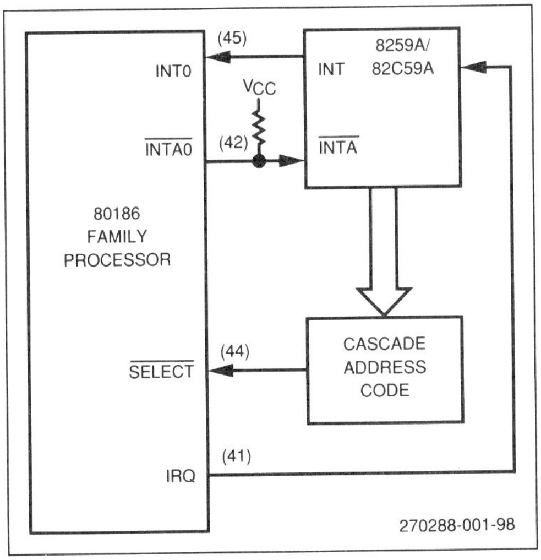

Figure 93. Slave Mode Interface

Because the integrated Interrupt Control Unit is a slave controller, it must be able to generate an interrupt input for an external Interrupt Controller. It also must be signaled when it has the highest priority pending interrupt to know when to place its interrupt vector on the bus. These two signals are provided by the IRQ and $\overline{\text{SELECT}}$ lines, respectively. The external master Interrupt Controller must be able to interrupt the CPU, and needs to know when the interrupt request is acknowledged. The INT0 and $\overline{\text{INTA0}}$ lines provide these two functions.

9.6.2 SLAVE MODE PROGRAMMING

The Interrupt Controller registers for Slave Mode are defined according to Figure 94. In many cases, the names and functions of registers at specific addresses is different from those in Master Mode.

9.6.2.1 CONTROL REGISTERS IN SLAVE MODE

In Slave Mode, the integrated Interrupt Controller uses five control registers. Unlike in Master Mode, each timer has its own individual control register. These registers contain three bits which select one of eight interrupt priority levels for the device (0 is highest priority, 7 is lowest priority), and a mask bit to enable the interrupt (see Figure 95). When the mask bit is zero, the interrupt is enabled; when it is one, the interrupt is masked.

9.6.2.2 REQUEST REGISTER IN SLAVE MODE

The Interrupt Controller includes an interrupt request register (see Figure 96). This register contains seven active bits, one for every interrupt source with an interrupt control register. Whenever an interrupt request is made, the bit in the interrupt request register is set regardless of whether the interrupt is enabled. These interrupt request bits are automatically cleared when the interrupt is acknowledged. The D1 and D0 bits for the request register can also be set (requesting a DMA interrupt), or cleared (removing a DMA interrupt request) by programming.

9.6.2.3 MASK REGISTER IN SLAVE MODE

The Interrupt Controller mask register (see Figure 97) contains a mask bit for each interrupt source associated with an interrupt control register. The bit for an interrupt source in the mask register is the same bit as provided in the interrupt control register; modifying a mask bit in the control register will also modify it in the mask register, and vice versa.

9.6.2.4 PRIORITY MASK REGISTER IN SLAVE MODE

The interrupt priority mask register (see Figure 98) contains three bits which indicate the lowest priority an interrupt may have that will cause an interrupt request to actually be serviced. Interrupts received which have a lower priority will be masked. Upon RESET, this register is set to the lowest priority of 7 to enable interrupts of any priority. This register may be read or written.

9.6.2.5 IN-SERVICE REGISTER IN SLAVE MODE

The Interrupt Controller contains an in-service register (see Figure 99). There is an in-service bit for every interrupt control register. An interrupt acknowledge (either by INTA cycles or

SLAVE MODE	OFFSET ADDRESS
①	3EH
①	3CH
TIMER 2 CONTROL REGISTER	3AH
TIMER 1 CONTROL REGISTER	38H
DMA1 CONTROL REGISTER	36H
DMA0 CONTROL REGISTER	34H
TIMER 0 CONTROL REGISTER	32H
INTERRUPT CONTROLLER STATUS REGISTER	30H
INTERRUPT REQUEST REGISTER	2EH
IN-SERVICE REGISTER	2CH
PRIORITY MASK REGISTER	2AH
MASK REGISTER	28H
①	26H
①	24H
SPECIFIC EOI REGISTER	22H
INTERRUPT VECTOR REGISTER	20H

NOTE:
1. Unsupported in this mode; values written may or may not be stored.

270288-001-99

Figure 94. Interrupt Controller Registers for Slave Mode

15	14	13		8	7	6	5	4	3	2	1	0
0	0	0	• • • •	0	0	0	0	0	MSK	PR2	PR1	PR0

270288-001-100

Figure 95. Control Word Format (Slave Mode)

OFFSET: 2EH

15								0
X	X	X	TMR 2	TMR 1	D0	D1	X	TMR 0

270288-001-101

Figure 96. Interrupt Controller Request Register Format (Slave Mode)

OFFSET: 28H

15								0
X	X	X	TMR 2	TMR 1	D0	D1	X	TMR 0

270288-001-102

Figure 97. Interrupt Controller Mask Register Format (Slave Mode)

OFFSET: 2AH	15							0
	X	X	X	X	X	M2	M1	M0

270288-001-103

Figure 98. Interrupt Controller Priority Mask Register Format (Slave Mode)

a read of the interrupt poll register) sets an in-service bit. The bit is reset when the CPU issues an End Of Interrupt to the Interrupt Controller. This register may be both read and written, i.e., the CPU may set in-service bits without an interrupt ever occurring, or may reset them without using the EOI function of the Interrupt Controller.

9.6.2.6 END OF INTERRUPT REGISTER IN SLAVE MODE

The programmer issues an End of Interrupt (EOI) by writing to the End of Interrupt register (see Figure 100). After receiving the EOI, the Interrupt Controller automatically resets the in-service bit for the interrupt. In Slave Mode, the in-service bit for a particular interrupt is specified by explicitly writing the interrupt type bits (see Table 20) of the interrupt to this register. The EOI register is write-only.

9.6.2.7 INTERRUPT STATUS REGISTER IN SLAVE MODE

The Interrupt Controller also contains an interrupt status register (see Figure 101). This register contains three programmable bits that indicate which timer is causing an interrupt. The bit associated with a timer is automatically cleared after the interrupt request for the timer is acknowledged. More than one of these bits may be set a time. All implemented bits in the interrupt status register are read/write. Do not perform the write operation when interrupts from the timer/counters are possible; a conflict with internal use of the register may lead to incorrect timer interrupt processing.

Table 20. Slave Mode Interrupt Type Bits 2-0

Interrupt Source	Type Bits 2-0
Timer 0	000
(reserved)	001
DMA 0	010
DMA 1	011
Timer 1	100
Timer 2	101

9.6.2.8 INTERRUPT VECTOR REGISTER

In Slave Mode only, the Interrupt Controller contains an interrupt vector register (see Figure 102). This register specifies the 5 most significant bits of the interrupt vector type number to be placed on the CPU bus in response to an interrupt acknowledge. The three least significant bits are fixed according to Table 20.

OFFSET: 2CH	15								0
	X	X	X	TMR 2	TMR 1	D0	D1	X	TMR 0

270288-001-104

Figure 99. In-Service and Mask Register Format

OFFSET: 22H	15								0
	X	X	X	X	X	X	VT2	VT1	VT0

270288-001-105

Figure 100. End of Interrupt Register Format (Slave Mode)

OFFSET: 30H

15															0
X		X		X		X		X		X			T2	T1	T0

270288-001-106

Figure 101. Interrupt Status Register Format (Slave Mode)

OFFSET: 20H

15															0
X		X		X		X		T4	T3	T2	T1	T0	0	0	0

270288-001-107

Figure 102. Interrupt Vector Register Format (Slave Mode)

9.6.3 SLAVE MODE INTERRUPT SOURCES

When the Interrupt Controller is configured in Slave Mode, it accepts interrupt requests only from the integrated peripherals. Any external requests go through an external Interrupt Controller. This external Interrupt Controller requests interrupt service directly from the 80186 family CPU through the INT0 line. Once in Slave Mode, the integrated Interrupt Control Unit cannot affect the function of this line. The integrated Interrupt Control Unit must request interrupt service from the external Interrupt Controller just like any other external interrupt sources in the system. This interrupt request is made on the IRQ line (see Figure 93).

The internal interrupt sources are the three timers and the two DMA channels. An interrupt from any of these interrupt sources is latched in the Interrupt Controller. The state of the pending interrupt can be obtained by reading the interrupt request register. Also, writing to the interrupt request register can reset latched interrupts.

9.6.4 SLAVE MODE INTERRUPT RESPONSE

When the integrated Interrupt Controller receives an interrupt, the in-service bit is automatically set and the interrupt request bit is reset. The Interrupt Controller will prevent any interrupts from occurring from the same source until the in-service bit for that line has been cleared. Vector information driven by an 80186 family device is not available outside the microprocessor.

9.6.4.1 INTERNAL VECTORING IN SLAVE MODE

In Slave Mode, the interrupt types associated with the various interrupt sources are alterable. The five most significant bits are taken from the interrupt vector register, and the three least significant bits are defined according to Table 20. The CPU calculates the vector address before servicing the interrupt because the Interrupt Controller gives only the interrupt type in this mode.

In Slave Mode, the integrated Interrupt Controller will present the interrupt type to the CPU in response to the two interrupt acknowledge bus cycles run by the processor. During the first interrupt acknowledge cycle, the external master Interrupt Controller determines which slave Interrupt Controller will place its vector type number on the microprocessor bus. During the second acknowledge cycle, the processor reads the vector type from its bus. Thus, these two interrupt acknowledge cycles must be run, since the integrated controller will present the interrupt type information only when the external Interrupt Controller signals the integrated controller that it has the highest pending interrupt request (see Figure 103). Correct master-slave interface requires decoding of the slave addresses (CAS0-2). External circuitry must decode the slave address because of microprocessor pin limitations. $\overline{\text{SELECT}}$ is used as a slave-select input. In this configuration the slave vector address is transferred internally, but the READY input must be supplied externally. $\overline{\text{INTA0}}$ is used as an acknowledge output, suitable to drive the $\overline{\text{INTA}}$ input of the 8259A or 82C59A. The processor samples the $\overline{\text{SELECT}}$ line during the falling edge of the clock at the beginning of T3 of the second interrupt acknowledge cycle. $\overline{\text{SELECT}}$ must be stable before and after this edge.

These two interrupt acknowledge cycles run back-to-back, and will be LOCKed with the $\overline{\text{LOCK}}$ output active. The two interrupt acknowledge cycles will always be separated by two idle T-states, and wait states will be inserted into the interrupt acknowledge cycle if a READY is not returned by the processor bus interface. The two idle T-states are inserted to allow compatibility with an external 8259 or 82C59A Interrupt Controller.

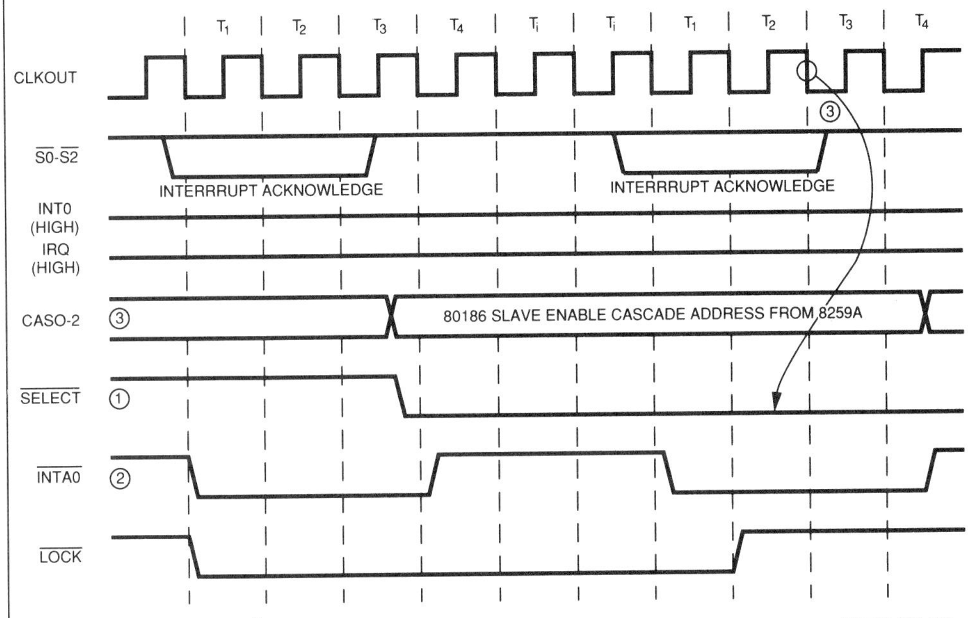

NOTES: 1. Pin 44 (INT1/SELECT) assumes the SELECT function in Slave Mode.
2. Pin 42 (INT2/INTA0) functions as interrupt acknowledge INTA0 in Slave Mode.
3. Cascade address is driven by the external interrupt controller.
4. SELECT must be driven before phase 2 of T_2 of the second INTA cycle.
5. SELECT read by processor.
6. ALE is generated for each INTA cycle.
7. RD is inactive.

Figuro 103. Slave Mode Interrupt Acknowledge Timing

9.6.4.2 EXTERNAL VECTORING IN SLAVE MODE

External interrupt vectoring occurs whenever the 80186 family Interrupt Control Unit is placed in Slave Mode and the integrated controller is not selected by the external master Interrupt Controller. In this mode, the processor generates two interrupt acknowledge cycles, reading the type number off the lower 8 bits of the address/data bus on the second interrupt acknowledge cycle (see Figure 103). Notice that the two interrupt acknowledge cycles are LOCKed, and that two idle T-states are always inserted between the two interrupt acknowledge bus cycles. Notice, too, that wait states will be inserted in the interrupt acknowledge cycle if a READY is not returned to the processor. Interrupt acknowledge status will be driven on the status lines (S0-S2) when INTA0 signals an interrupt acknowledge.

When the Interrupt Control Unit is operating in Slave Mode and an interrupt occurs during an instruction that has been LOCKed by software, the LOCK signal timing shown in Figure 103 may be altered. Some peripheral devices used with the 80186 family require contiguous INTA cycles to allow correct Interrupt Controller response. In such cases, the external circuitry in Figure 90 should be used to ensure that DMA or HOLD requests are blocked from stealing the bus during INTA cycles.

9.6.4.3 SLAVE MODE INTERRUPT RESPONSE TIME

Because interrupt acknowledge cycles must be run for Slave Mode and the integrated controller presents an interrupt type rather than a vector address, the interrupt response time is 55 CPU clocks. Figure 104 shows how the total is obtained. The clock count changes when the processor replaces the indicated idle states with bus cycles for other tasks such as DMA. The processor does not necessarily flush the queue until the very last moment, so prefetching may continue for a while during the vectoring sequence. Also, the clock count must be adjusted for wait states or for the 80188/80C188. For the 80188/80C188, double the number of clocks given for each bus cycle accessing the stack or memory.

9.6.5 EXAMPLE SLAVE MODE INITIALIZATION

As shown in Figure 105, the initialization of Slave Mode requires setting only one bit in the relocation register.

Event	Bus Cycle	CLOCKS
Interrupt presented to the interrupt controller --->		
		5
Interrupt presented to CPU --->		
	INTA	4
	IDLE	2
	INTA	4
	IDLE	5
	READ IP	4
	IDLE	3
	READ CS	4
	IDLE	4
	PUSH FLAGS	4
IF←0, TF←0	IDLE	3
	PUSH CS	4
	PUSH IP	4
First instruction fetch	IDLE	5
from interrupt routine --->		
		Total 55

270288-001-109

Figure 104. Interrupt Response Time For Slave Mode

```
$mod186
name                    example_80186_family_interrupt_code
;
; This routine configures the interrupt controller into Slave Mode. This code
;       does not initialize any of the integrated peripheral control registers,
;       nor does it initialize the external 8259A interrupt controller
;
relocation_reg          equ     0FFFEH
;
                        code    segment                 ;public'code'
                        assume  CS:code
set_slave               proc    near
                        push    DX
                        push    AX

                        mov     DX,relocation_reg
                        in      AX,DX                   ;read old contents of register
                        or      AX,0100000000000000B    ;set the Slave/Master mode bit
                        out     DX,AX

                        pop     AX
                        pop     DX
                        ret
set_slave               endp
code                    ends
                        end
```

270288-001-110

Figure 105. Example 80186 Family Interrupt Initialization for Slave Mode

9.7 INTERRUPT CONTROLLER FLOW CHARTS

Figure 106 shows an interrupt request generation flow chart and Figure 107 shows an interrupt acknowledge sequence flow chart. Each interrupt source processed by an 80186 family integrated Interrupt Controller follows each flow chart independently.

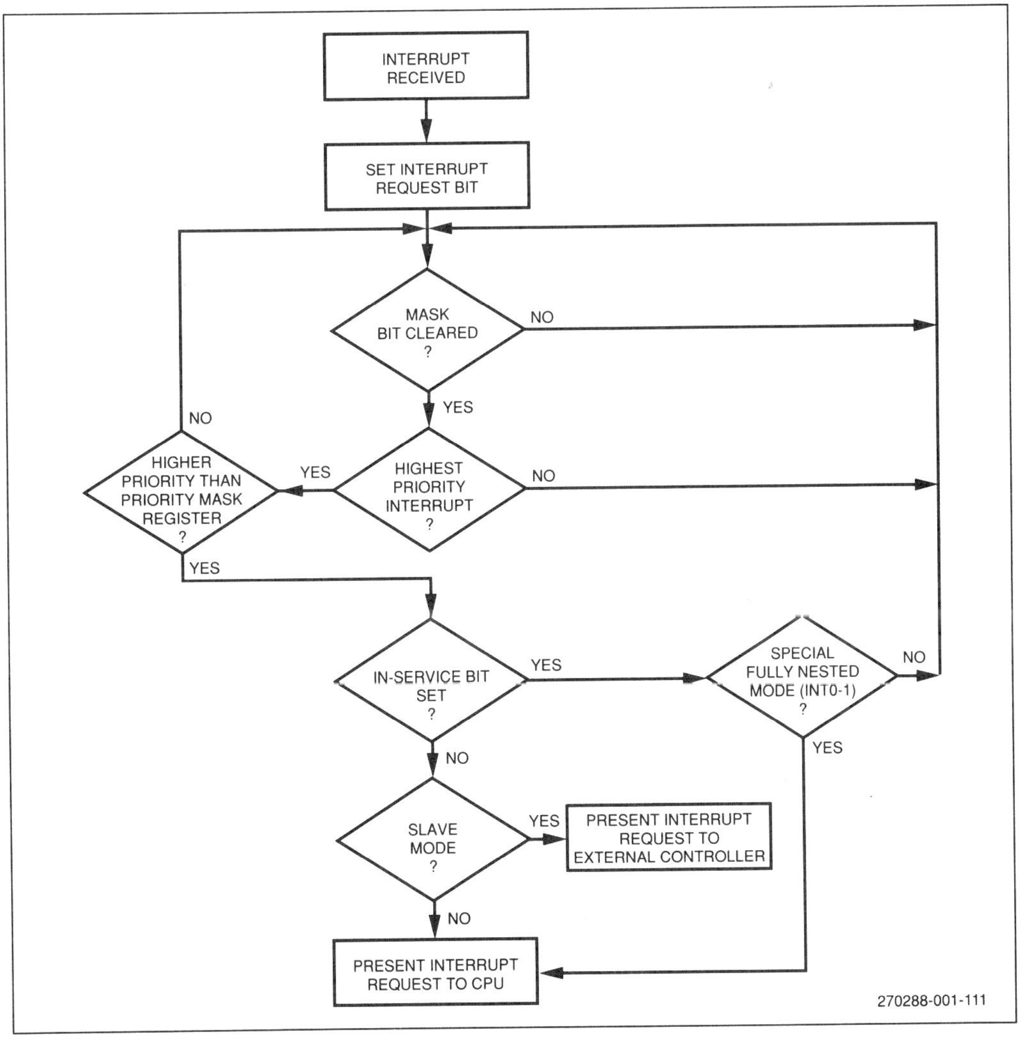

Figure 106. Interrupt Request Sequencing

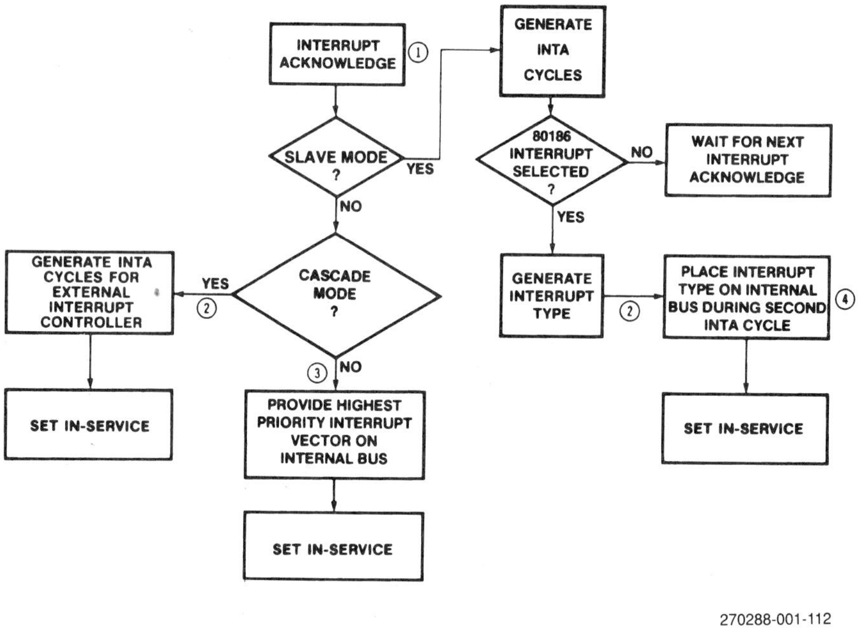

NOTES:
1. Before actual interrupt acknowledge is run by CPU.
2. Two interrupt acknowledge cycles will be run; the interrupt type is read by the CPU on the second cycle.
3. Interrupt acknowledge cycles will not be run; the interrupt vector address is placed on an internal bus and is not available outside the processor.
4. Interrupt type is not driven on external bus in Slave Mode.

Figure 107. Interrupt Acknowledge Sequencing

Refresh Control Unit (80C186/80C188 Only) 10

CHAPTER 10
REFRESH CONTROL UNIT (80C186/80C188 ONLY)

To simplify the design of a dynamic memory controller, the 80C186 incorporates integrated address and clock counters into a Refresh Control Unit (RCU). Its relationship to the BIU is shown in Figure 108. To the memory interface a refresh request looks exactly like a memory read bus cycle. Integration of the RCU into the 80C186 means that chip selects, wait state logic, and status lines may be used by an external DRAM controller. The external DRAM controller generates the $\overline{RAS}$, CAS, and enable signals actually needed by the DRAMs.

The three control registers are MDRAM, CDRAM, and EDRAM (see Figure 109). These registers define the operating characteristics of the RCU. The EDRAM register programs the base address (upper 7 bits) of the refresh address (see Figure 109). This allows the refresh address to be mapped to any 4 kilobyte boundary within the one megabyte 80C186/80C188 address space. The MDRAM register is not altered whenever the refresh address bits (A1 through A9 in Figure 110) roll over. In other words, the refresh address does not act like a linear counter found in a typical DMA controller.

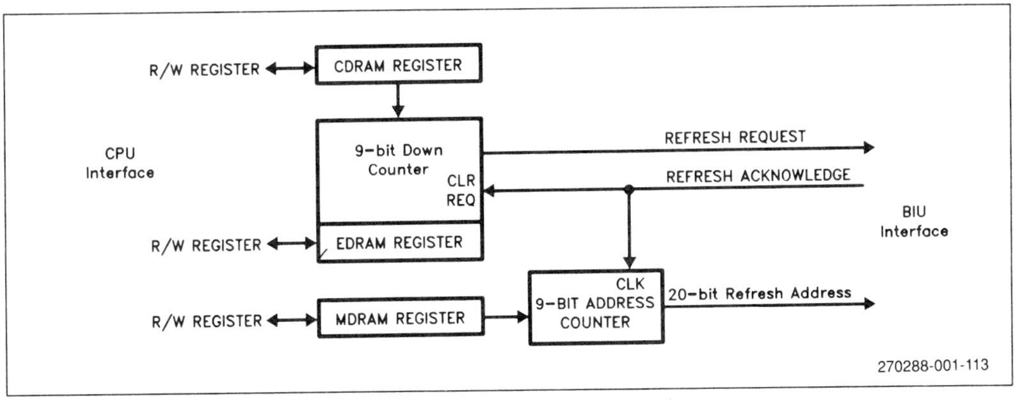

Figure 108. Refresh Control Unit Block Diagram

The 9-bit address counter is used in the formation of refresh addresses. Thus, any dynamic memory whose refresh address requirements (rows of memory cells)do not exceed nine bits can be directly supported by the 80C186. The 9-bit address counter, a 6-bit base register, and six fixed bits define a full 20-bit refresh address. The 9-bit counter decrements every clock cycle and generates a refresh request to the BIU whenever it reaches 1. When the bus is free, the BIU will run the refresh (dummy read) bus cycle. Refresh requests have a higher priority than any other bus request (i.e., CPU, DMA, HOLD).

10.1 REFRESH CONTROL UNIT PROGRAMMING

There are three registers in the Peripheral Control Block that control the RCU. These registers are only accessible when the 80C186 or 80C188 are operating in Enhanced Mode (see Appendix C.2 for more on Enhanced Mode). Otherwise, a read or write to these registers is ignored.

The CDRAM register defines the interval between refresh requests by initializing the value loaded into the 9-bit down counter. Thus, the higher the value, the longer the amount of time between requests. The down counter is decremented every falling edge of CLKOUT, regardless of the activity of the CPU or BIU. When the counter decrements to 1, a request is generated and the counter is again loaded with the value in the CDRAM register. The amount of time between refresh requests can be calculated using the equation shown in Figure 111. The minimum value that can be programmed into the CDRAM register is 18 (12H) regardless of the operating frequency. This minimum count ensures that the BIU has enough time to execute the refresh bus cycle. The BIU cannot queue DRAM refresh requests. If another request is generated before the current request is executed, the current request is lost. However, the address associated with the request is not lost; the refresh address changes only after the BIU runs a refresh bus cycle. Thus it is possible to miss refresh requests, but not refresh addresses.

OFFSET:

	15															0	
E4H	E	0	0	0	0	0	0	T8	T7	T6	T5	T4	T3	T2	T1	T0	EDRAM Register (1)
E2H	0	0	0	0	0	0	0	C8	C7	C6	C5	C4	C3	C2	C1	C0	CDRAM Register (2)
E0H	M6	M5	M4	M3	M2	M1	M0	0	0	0	0	0	0	0	0	0	MDRAM Register (3)

Notes:

1. Bits 0-8: T0-T8, Refresh request count. These bits are read-only and represent the current value of the down counter. Any write to these bits is ignored.
   Bit 15 : E, enables the operation of the refresh control unit.
2. Bits 0-8: C0-C8, define the number of CLKOUT cycles between each refresh request.
3. Bits 9-15: M0-M6, are used to define address bits A13-A19 (respectively) of the 20-bit memory address. These bits clear to zero on RESET.

270288-001-114

Figure 109. Refresh Control Unit Registers

Address Bit	19	18	17	16	15	14	13	12	11	10	9	8	7	6	5	4	3	2	1	0
Physical Refresh Address	M6	M5	M4	M3	M2	M1	M0	0	0	0	CA8	CA7	CA6	CA5	CA4	CA3	CA2	CA1	CA0	1

Bit 0: Always driven to 1 (HIGH). This is true for both the 80C186 and the 80C188.
Bits 1-9: CA0-CA8, generated by the 9-bit linear-feedback shift counter.
Bits 10-12: Always driven to 0 (LOW).
Bits 13-19: M0-M6, defined by the MDRAM register.

270288-001-115

Figure 110. Physical Address Generation

$$\frac{R_{PERIOD}(\mu s) \times f(MHz)}{\#\ \text{Refresh Rows} + \#\ (\text{Refresh Rows} \times \%\ \text{Overhead})} = \text{CDRAM Register Value}$$

R_{PERIOD} = Maximum refresh period specified by DRAM manufacturer (microseconds).
f = Operating frequency of 80C186 in MHz.
# Refresh Rows = Total number of rows to be refreshed.
% Overhead = Derating factor to compensate for missed refresh requests (typically 1-5%).

270288-001-116

Figure 111. Equation to Calculate Refresh Interval

The EDRAM register has two functions, depending on whether it is being written or read. During writes to the EDRAM register, only the Enable bit is active. Setting the Enable bit turns on the RCU while clearing the Enable bit deactivates the RCU. When the RCU is enabled, the contents of the EDRAM register are loaded into the 9-bit down counter and refresh requests are generated when the counter reaches 1. Disabling the RCU stops and clears the counter. A read of the EDRAM register will return the current value of the Enable bit as well as the current value of the 9-bit down counter (zero if the RCU is not enabled). Writing to EDRAM register when RCU is running does not modify the count value in the 9-bit counter.

10.2 REFRESH CONTROL UNIT OPERATION

Figure 112 illustrates the two major functions of the Refresh Control Unit that are responsible for initiating and controlling the refresh bus cycles.

The down counter is loaded on the falling edge of CLKOUT, when either the Enable bit is set or the counter decrements to 1. Once loaded, the down counter will decrement every falling edge of CLKOUT (as long as the Enable bit remains set).

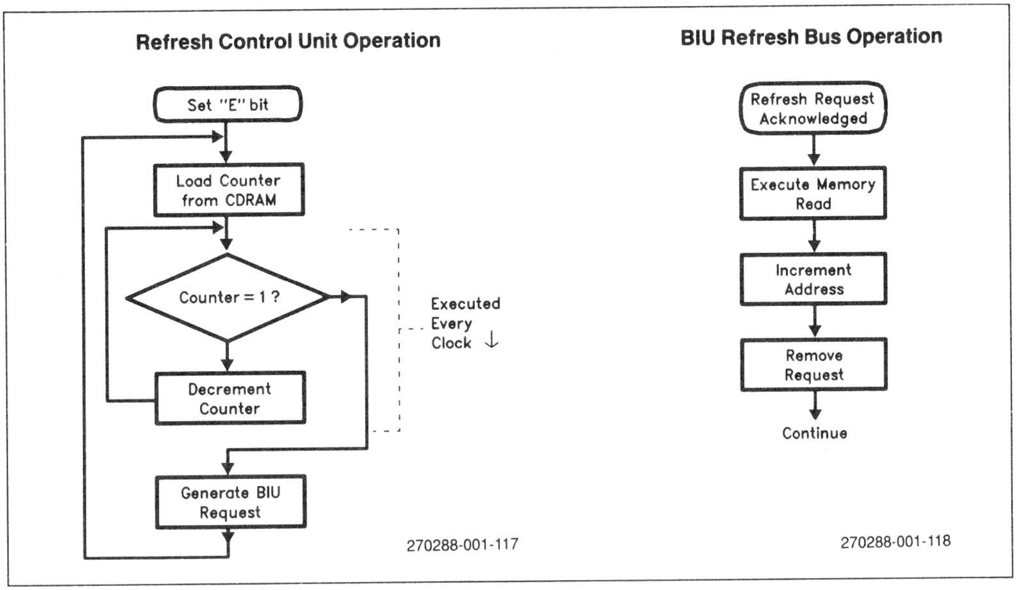

Figure 112. Flowchart of RCU Operation

When the counter decrements to 1, two things happen. First, a request is generated to the BIU to run a refresh bus cycle. The request remains active until the bus cycle is run. Second, the downcounter is reloaded with the value contained in the CDRAM register. At this time, the down counter will again begin counting down every clock cycle. It does not wait until the request has been serviced. This is done to ensure that each refresh request occurs at the correct interval. Otherwise, the time between refresh requests would also be a function of varying bus activities. When the BIU services the refresh request, it will clear the request and increment the refresh address.

Refresh bus cycles are specially encoded to distinguish them from ordinary read cycles according to Table 21.

Table 21. Identification of 80C186/80C188 DRAM Refresh Cycles

	$\overline{BHE}$/$\overline{RFSH}$	A0
80C186	1	1
80C188	0	1

NOTE:
$\overline{BHE}$ applies to the 80C186 and $\overline{RFSH}$ applies to the 80C188.

10.3 REFRESH ADDRESSES

The physical address that is generated during a refresh bus cycle is shown in Figure 110, and applies to both the 80C186 and 80C188. The refresh address bits CA0 through CA8 are generated using a linear-feedback shift counter which does not increment the addresses linearly from 0 through 1FFH (although they do follow a predicable algorithm). Further, note that for the 80C188, address bit A0 does not toggle during refresh operation, which means that it cannot be used as part of the refresh (row) address applied to the dynamic memory device. Typically, A0 is used as part of memory decoding in 80C188 applications, unlike 80C186 applications which use A0 along with $\overline{BHE}$ to select an upper or lower bank.

10.4 REFRESH OPERATION AND BUS HOLD

When another bus master has control of the bus, the HLDA signal is kept active as long as the HOLD input remains active. If a refresh request is generated while HOLD is active, the 80C186 will drive the HLDA signal inactive to indicate to the current bus master that the 80C186 wishes to regain control of the bus (see Figure 113). Only when the HOLD input is removed will the BIU begin the refresh bus cycle.

Therefore, it is the responsibility of the system designer to ensure that the 80C186 can regain the bus if a refresh request is signalled. The sequence of HLDA going inactive while

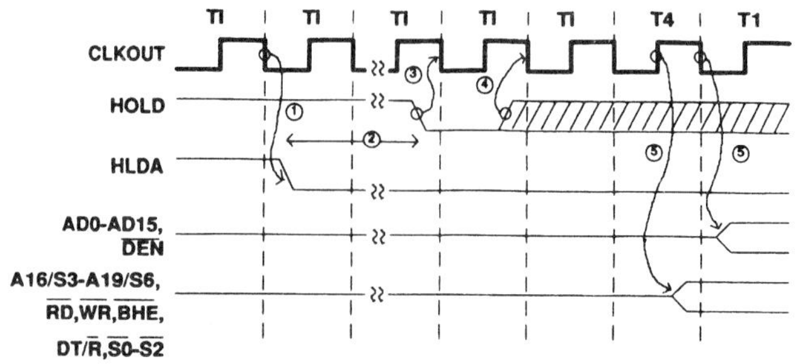

270288-001-119

NOTES:
1. HLDA deasserted, signaling need to run DRAM refresh cycles; less than T_{CLHAV}.
2. External bus master terminates use of the bus.
3. HOLD deasserted; greater than T_{HVCL}.
4. HOLD may be reasserted after one clock.
5. Lines come out of float in order to run DRAM refresh cycle.

Figure 113. Release of 80C186/80C188 HOLD to Run Refresh Cycle

HOLD is active can be used to signal a pending refresh. If HOLD is again asserted, the 80C186 will give up the bus after the refresh bus cycle has been run (provided another refresh request is not generated during that time).

10.5 EXAMPLE RCU INITIALIZATION CODE

Sample code to initialize the 80C186/80C188 DRAM Refresh Control Unit is included in Figure 114.

```
$mod186
name                          example_80C186_dru_code
;
;  This file contains example code to initialize the 80C186 DRAM refresh control
;        unit. For the purposes of our example, we will assume that the
;        specifications for our system call for 512 kbytes of DRAM to be located
;        at a base address of 256k.  We choose 256k X 4 DRAMs so that two devices
;        are low-byte addressed and two devices are high-byte addressed.  Reading
;        the fine print on the DRAM data sheet we see that 256 refresh cycles are
;        required every 4 ms.  This information also tells us the memory cells in
;        the DRAMs are physically arranged as 256 (2**8) rows by 1024 (2**10)
;        columns. To calculate the maximum number of clocks between refresh
;        cycles, we multiply the total refresh period by the 80C186 CLKOUT
;        frequency and divide by the number of rows.  For an 80C186 running at
;        12.5 MHz, the minimum refresh rate is 4E-03 * 12.5E+06 / 256 = 195
;        clocks.
;
mdram               equu    0FFE0h
cdram               equ     0FFE2h
edram               equ     0FFE4h

code                segment public'code'
                    assume  cs:code

init_rcu            proc    near
                    push    AX
                    push    CX                          ;save registers used
                    push    DX
                    push    DI
;
;  Notice that we don't initialize the middle chip select.  On the 80186 family,
;        the MCS block can be initialized to a size of 512 kbytes, but the block
;        cannot be located at a starting address of 256k. Since the programmable
;        ready logic is unavailable, the system must provide READY to either the
;        SRDY or ARDY pins in hardware.
;
                    mov     DX,mdram                    ;set upper 7 address bits
                    mov     AX,4000h                    ;for a starting address of
                    out     DX, AX                      ;of 256k

                    mov     DX,cdram                    ;set the clock pre-scaler
                    mov     AX,185                      ;to refresh at 185 clock
                    out     DX,AX                       ;intervals, just to be sure

                    mov     DX,edram                    ;write a one to enable the
                    mov     AX,8000h                    ;RCU
                    out     DX, AX

                    mov     CX, 8                       ;8 dummy cycles are
                    xor     DI,DI                       ;required by the DRAMs
exercise_ram:       mov     word ptr [DI], 0            ;before actual use
                    loop    exercise_ram

                    pop     DI
                    pop     DX
                    pop     CX
                    pop     AX
                    ret
init_rcu            endp
code                ends
                    end
```

270288-001-120

Figure 114. Example DRAM Refresh Initialization Code

Power-Save Unit (80C186/80C188 Only) 11

CHAPTER 11
POWER-SAVE UNIT (80C186/80C188 ONLY)

The Power-Save Unit is intended to benefit applications by lowering power consumption while maintaining regular operation of the CPU. The 80C186 power-save mechanism lowers current needs by reducing the operating frequency.

The Power-Save Unit is an internal clock divider as shown in Figure 115. power-save operation changes the internal operating frequency of the processor, so it affects integrated peripherals as well as the CPU. Affected units include the timers, DRAM refresh control, DMA, and BIU. Thus by using the power-save feature, the net effect is similar to changing the input clock frequency.

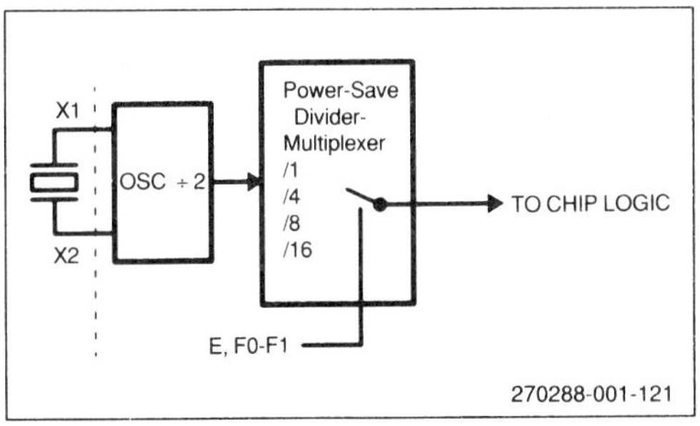

Figure 115. Simplified Power-Save Internal Operation

11.1 POWER-SAVE UNIT PROGRAMMING

The PDCON register (see Figure 116) controls the operation of the Power-Save Unit. This register is available for programming when the 80C186 or 80C188 is in Enhanced Mode (see Appendix C.2 for more on Enhanced Mode). Reads or write to the PDCON register in Compatible Mode result in no operation, and the value returned will be all ones.

When the Enable bit in the PDCON register is set, the Power-Save Unit is active and, depending on the condition of the F0 and F1 bits, the operating clock of the 80C186 changes from normal operation. When the Enable bit is cleared, the 80C186 will operate at the standard divide-by-two clock rate. The Enable bit is automatically cleared whenever a non-masked interrupt occurs. Thus, if the power-save feature is enabled and an unmasked interrupt of sufficient priority is received, the Enable bit clears and the processor executes at full speed. This allows interrupts to be processed at maximum speed. A return from the interrupt does not automatically set the Enable bit. This must be done as part of the interrupt routine. Software interrupts do not clear the Enable bit.

The F0 and F1 bits determine the divisor of the Power-Save Unit. Figure 117 provides a list of the various combinations of the bits and their division factors. Note that the divisor relates to CLKOUT, not the input clock at pin X1. Selecting a divisor of 1 does not reduce the power consumption. The operating clock of the 80C186 must not be divided below the minimum operating frequency specified in the data sheet (500 kHz). Figure 116 also indicates the minimum crystal frequency which will allow the use of a specific divisor.

11.2 POWER-SAVE OPERATION

When the Enable bit in the PDCON register is set, the clock divider circuitry will turn on during the write to the PDCON register (refer to Figure 116). At the falling edge of T_3 of the register write, CLKOUT will change to reflect the new divisor. If any values of F0-F1 other than zero have been programmed,

OFFSET: F0H

15															0
E	0	0	0	0	0	0	0	0	0	0	0	0	0	F1	F0

Bits 0-1: Clock Division Select

F1	F0	Divsion Factor	Minimum X1 Frequency
0	0	divide by 1	1 MHz
0	1	divide by 4	4 MHz
1	0	divide by 8	8 MHz
1	1	divide by 16	16 MHz

Bits 2-14: Reserved, read bask as zero.
Bit 15: Enable (set) power-save mode. Cleared (disabled) on reset.

270288-001-122

Figure 116. Power-Save Register Format

the CLKOUT period will increase, starting with the LOW phase. CLKOUT is glitch-free.

The Power-Save Unit remains active until one of three events happens: the Enable bit in the PDCON register is cleared, new values for F0 and F1 are programmed, or an unmasked interrupt is received. In the first two cases, the changes directly follow Figure 117. When an unmasked interrupt is received, the operating frequency is changed as shown in Figure 116, but may occur at T_3 of **any** bus cycle in progress just after the interrupt. Thus, it is not possible to determine exactly when, in the event of an interrupt, the Power-Save Unit will be disabled.

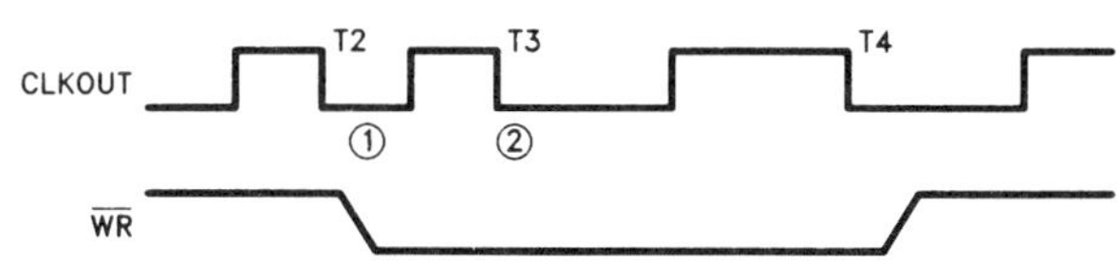

NOTES:
1. Write to PDCON register (as viewed on the bus).
2. Low going edge of T_3 starts new clock divider.

270288-001-123

Fgure 117. Power-Save Clock Transition

11.3 EXAMPLE POWER-SAVE INITIALIZATION CODE

Figure 118 illustrates the programming of the Power-Save Unit for a typical 80C186 system.

```
$mod186
name                    example_80C186_power_save_code
;
;  This file contains example code to initialize the 80C186 power-save unit. We
;       will initially assume that our system is operating at a clock frequency
;       of 8 MHz (16 MHz at X1) and that we wish to change the processor to a
;       background mode, with reduced power consumption.
;
pdcon                   equ      0FFF0h

code                    segment public'code'
                        assume   cs:code

init_ps                 proc     near
                        push     AX                     ;save registers used
                        push     DX
;
;  At the beginning of the procedure the user should reprogram those peripherals
;       which will be affected by the slower clock, including timers and the
;       DRAM refresh unit.  Of particular concern is any external logic clocked
;       by both CLKIN and CLKOUT.
;
                        mov      DX,pdcon               ;set bits 0 and 1 for a
                        mov      AX,8003h               ;divisor of 16, which
                        out      DX,AX                  ;yields a processor clock
                                                        ;of 500 kHz, the minimum
                                                        ;specification for the
                                                        ;80C186.
;
;  As soon as the out DX, AX operation takes place, the clock frequency is
;       reduced.  The original clock frequency will be restored upon an unmasked
;       interrupt or reprogramming the pdcon register.
;
                        pop      DX
                        pop      AX
                        ret

init_ps                 endp
code                    ends
        end
```

270288-001-124

Figure 118. Example 80C186 Power-Save Initialization Code

12 Hardware Provisions for Floating Point Math

CHAPTER 12
HARDWARE PROVISIONS FOR FLOATING POINT MATH

The 80186 microprocessor family was designed for general-purpose microprocessing. In most data controller applications, the actual arithmetic performed on data values is fairly simple, while fast, efficient data movement and control instructions are very important. However, some applications require more powerful arithmetic instructions and more complex data types than provided by a general purpose data processor. Characteristics of such applications include the following:

- Numeric data vary over a wide range of values or include non-integral values.
- Algorithms produce very large or very small intermediate results.
- Computations must be very precise, i.e., a large number of significant digits must be retained.
- Computations must be extremely reliable without undue dependence on programmed algorithms.
- Overall math performance exceeds the power provided by a general-purpose processor and software alone.

The 80186 family supports these needs by providing the necessary hardware interfaces to either a numerics coprocessor (the 8087) or a numerics coprocessor extension (the 80C187).

12.1 USING THE 80186/80188 WITH THE 8087 NUMERICS COPROCESSOR

Use of the 8087 numerics coprocessor with an 80186 or 80188 adds 68 floating-point instructions and eight 80-bit floating-point registers to the basic architecture. An 8087 can increase the math performance of an 80186/80188 system by 50 to 100 times. The detailed operation of 80186(80188)/8087 hardware and software is transparent to the system user.

12.1.1 OVERVIEW OF NUMERICS COPROCESSING

The 80186 or 80188 interfaces to the 8087 through an 82188 Integrated Bus Controller (See Figure 119). Due to the 33 percent duty cycle restriction of the 8087 (specifically the 8087-1 speed selection) and clock input restrictions of the 82188, this combination is limited in speed to 8 MHz.

12.1.2 8087 INSTRUCTION SET

8087 instructions are divided into six functional groups: data transfer, arithmetic, comparison, transcendental, constant, and processor control. Typical 8087 instructions accept one or two operands and produce a single result. Operands are most often located in memory or the 8087 stack. The operands of some instructions are predefined; for example, FSQRT always takes the square root of the number in the top stack element. Others allow, or require, the programmer to explicitly code the operand(s) along with the instruction mnemonic. Still others accept one explicit operand and one implicit operand, usually the top stack element.

As with the basic 80186 family instruction set, there are two types of operands, source and destination. Source operands are not altered by the instruction. Even when an instruction converts the source operand from one format to another (e.g., real to integer), the conversion is actually performed in an internal work area to avoid altering the source operand. A destination operand is distinguished from a source operand because its contents may be altered when it receives the result of the operation; that is, the destination is replaced by the result.

12.1.2.1 DATA TRANSFER INSTRUCTIONS

These instructions move operands among elements of the 8087 register stack, and between stack top and memory. Any of the seven data types can be converted to temporary real (see Section 12.1.3) and loaded onto the stack in a single operation; they can be stored to memory in the same manner. Data transfer instruction are summarized in Table 22.

12.1.2.2 ARITHMETIC INSTRUCTIONS

The 8087's arithmetic instruction set (Table 23) provides a wealth of variations on the basic add, subtract, multiply, and divide operations, and a number of other useful functions. These range from a simple absolute value to a square root instruction that executes faster than ordinary division. Other arithmetic instructions perform exact modulo division, round real numbers to integers, and scale values by powers of two.

Table 23 summarizes the available operation and operand forms provided for basic arithmetic. In addition to the four normal operations, two "reversed" instructions make subtraction and division "symmetrical" like addition and multiplication.

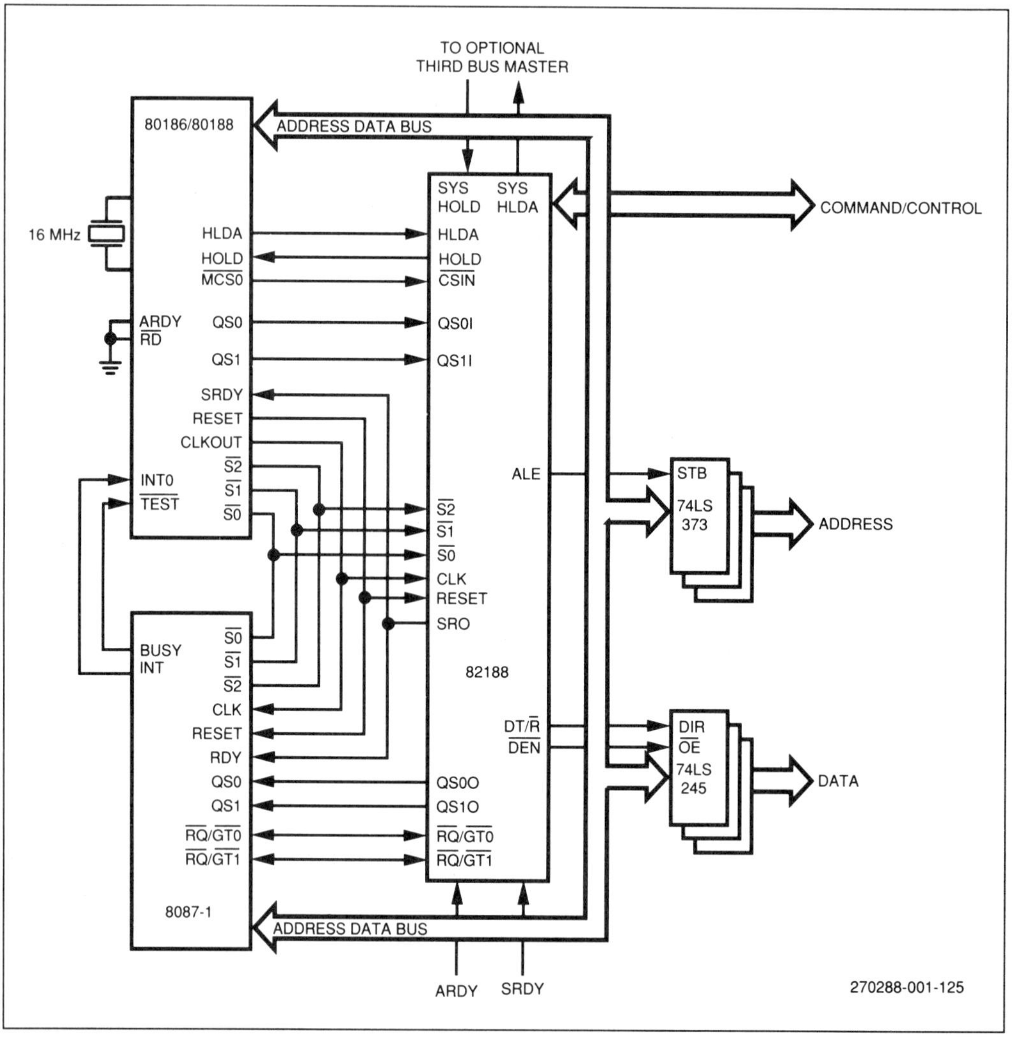

Figure 119. 80186 (80188) – 82188–8087 Circuit Diagram

The variety of instruction and operand forms give the programmer unusual flexibility:

- Operands may be located in registers or memory.
- Results may be deposited in a choice of registers.
- Operands may be a variety of data types, including temporary real, long real, short real, short integer, or word integer, with automatic type conversion to temporary real performed by the 8087.

12.1.2.3 COMPARISON INSTRUCTIONS

Each of these instructions (Table 24) analyzes the stack top element, often in relationship to another operand, and reports the result in the status word condition code. The basic operations are compare, test (compare with zero), and examine (report tag, sign, and normalization).

Table 22. Data Transfer Instructions

REAL TRANSFERS	
FLD	Load real
FST	Store real
FSTP	Store real and pop
FXCH	Exchange registers
INTEGER TRANSFERS	
FILD	Integer load
FIST	Integer store
FISTP	Integer store and pop
PACKED DECIMAL TRANSFERS	
FBLD	Packed decimal (BCD) load
FBSTP	Packed decimal (BCD) store and pop

Table 24. Comparison Instructions

Instruction	Description
FCOM	Compare real
FCOMP	Compare real and pop
FCOMPP	Compare real and pop twice
FICOM	Integer compare
FICOMP	Integer compare and pop
FTST	Test
FXAM	Examine

12.1.2.4 TRANSCENDENTAL INSTRUCTIONS

The instructions in this category perform the time-consuming core calculations for common trigonometric, hyperbolic, inverse hyperbolic, logarithmic, and exponential functions. Prologue and epilogue software may be used to reduce arguments to the range accepted by the instructions and to adjust the result to correspond to the original arguments if necessary. The transcendentals operate on the top one or two stack elements and they return their results to the stack. Table 25 lists the transcendental instructions.

Table 25. Transcendental Instructions

Instruction	Description
FPTAN	Partial tangent
FPATAN	Partial arctangent
F2XM1	2^X-1
FYL2X	$Y \cdot \log_2 X$
FYL2XP1	$Y \cdot \log_2(X+1)$

Table 23. Arithmetic Instructions

ADDITION	
FADD	Add real
FADDP	Add real and pop
FIADD	Integer add
SUBTRACTION	
FSUB	Subtract real
FSUBP	Subtract real and pop
FISUB	Integer subtract
FSUBR	Subtract real reversed
FSUBRP	Subtract real reversed and pop
FISUBR	Integer subtract reversed
MULTIPLICATION	
FMUL	Multiply real
FMULP	Multiply real and pop
FIMUL	Integer multiply
DIVISION	
FDIV	Divide real
FDIVP	Divide real and pop
FIDIV	Integer divide
FDIVR	Divide real reversed
FDIVRP	Divide real reversed and pop
FIDIVR	Integer divide reversed
OTHER OPERATIONS	
FSQRT	Square root
FSCALE	Scale
FPREM	Partial remainder
FRNDINT	Round to integer
FXTRACT	Extract exponent and significand
FABS	Absolute value
FCHS	Change sign

12.1.2.5 CONSTANT INSTRUCTIONS

Each of these instructions (Table 26) loads a commonly used constant onto the stack. The values have full temporary real precision (80 bits) and are accurate to approximately 19 decimal digits. Since a temporary real constant occupies 10 memory bytes, the constant instructions, only two bytes long, save memory space. These instructions simplify programming as well.

Table 26. Constant Instructions

FLDZ	Load +0.1
FLD1	Load +1.0
FLDPI	Load π
FLDL2T	Load $\log_2 10$
FLDL2E	Load $\log_2 e$
FLDLG2	Load $\log_{10} 2$
FLDLN2	Load $\log_e 2$

12.1.2.6 PROCESSOR CONTROL INSTRUCTIONS

Most of these instructions (Table 27) are not used in computations; they are provided principally for system-level activities. These include initialization, exception handling and task switching.

Table 27. Processor Control Instructions

FINIT/FNINIT	Initialize processor
FDISI/FNDISI	Disable interrupts
FENI/FNENI	Enable interrupts
FLDCW	Load control word
FSTCW/FNSTCW	Store control word
FSTSW/FNSTCW	Store status word
FCLEX/FNCLEX	Clear exceptions
FSTENV/FNSTENV	Store environment
FLDENV	Load environment
FSAVE/FNSAVE	Save state
FRSTOR	Restore state
FINCSTP	Increment stack pointer
FDECSTP	Decrement stack pointer
FFREE	Free register
FNOP	No operation
FWAIT	CPU wait

12.1.3 8087 DATA TYPES

An 80186(80188)/8087 or 80C186/80C187 system supports the following seven data types:

- Word Integer - A signed binary numeric value contained in a 16-bit word. All operations assume a 2's complement representation.
- Short Integer - A signed binary numeric value contained in a 32-bit double word. All operations assume a 2's complement representation.
- Long Integer - A signed binary numeric value contained in a 64-bit quad word. All operations assume a 2's complement representation.
- Packed Decimal - A signed numeric value contained in an 80-bit BCD format.
- Short Real - A signed, floating point numeric value contained in a 32-bit format.
- Long Real - A signed, floating point numeric value contained in a 64-bit format.
- Temporary Real - A signed, floating point numeric value contained in an 80-bit format. Temporary real is the native 8087/80C187 format.

Figure 120 graphically represents these data types.

12.1.4 80186(80188)/8087 INTERFACE

The 8087 is comprised of two elements, a Control Unit and a Numeric Execution Unit. The Numeric Execution Unit executes all numeric instructions, while the Control Unit receives and decodes instructions, reads and writes memory operands, and executes coprocessor control instructions. These two elements operate independently of one another. This allows the Control Unit to maintain synchronization with the 80186 or 80188 CPU while the Numeric Execution Unit is busy processing instructions.

The 8087 is referred to as a numerics coprocessor because it operates synchronously with the host processor. The CPU's status lines (S0-S2) and queue status lines (QS0-QS1) allow the 8087 to monitor and decode instructions in synchronization and without any CPU overhead. The 8087 maintains its own prefetch queue identical to the one in the 80186 or 80188. When a numerics instruction is encountered, the 8087 processes them independently of the CPU (Figure 121).

No special configuration is necessary for the 8087 to determine whether the data bus is eight or sixteen bits; the 8087 examines the 80186/80188 $\overline{BHE}$/S7 line at RESET to adjust its queue length and external data path accordingly.

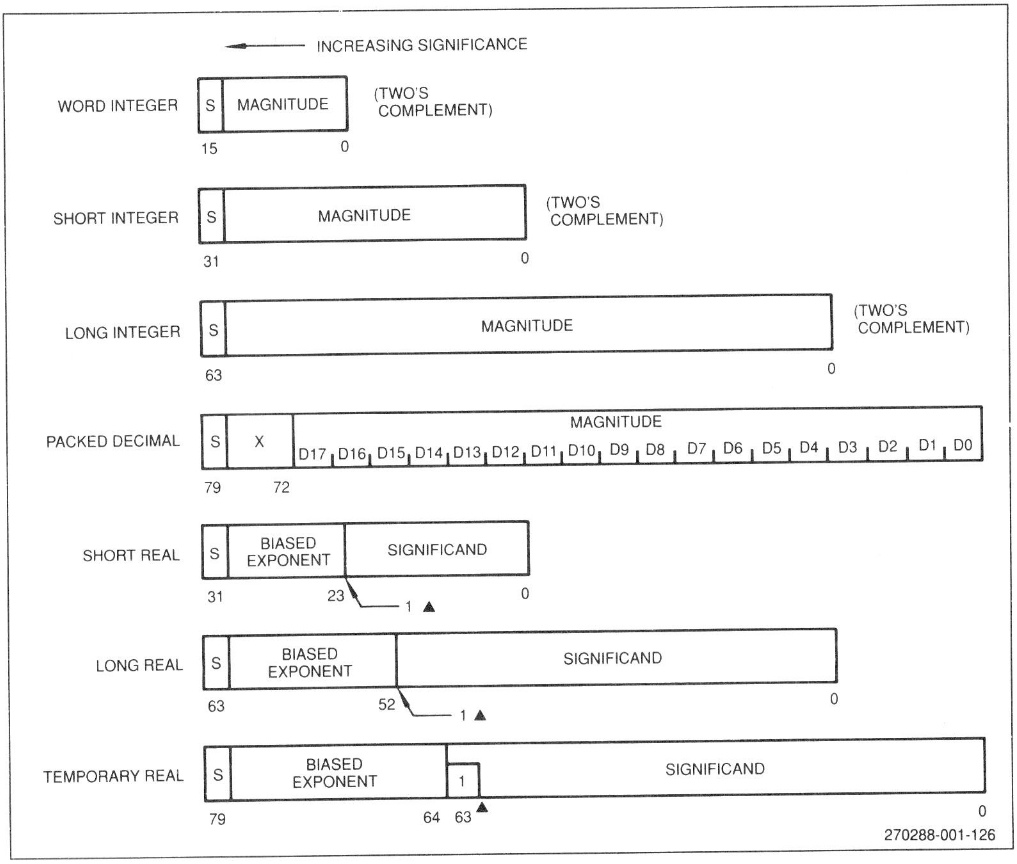

Figure 120. 8087/80C187 Supported Data Types

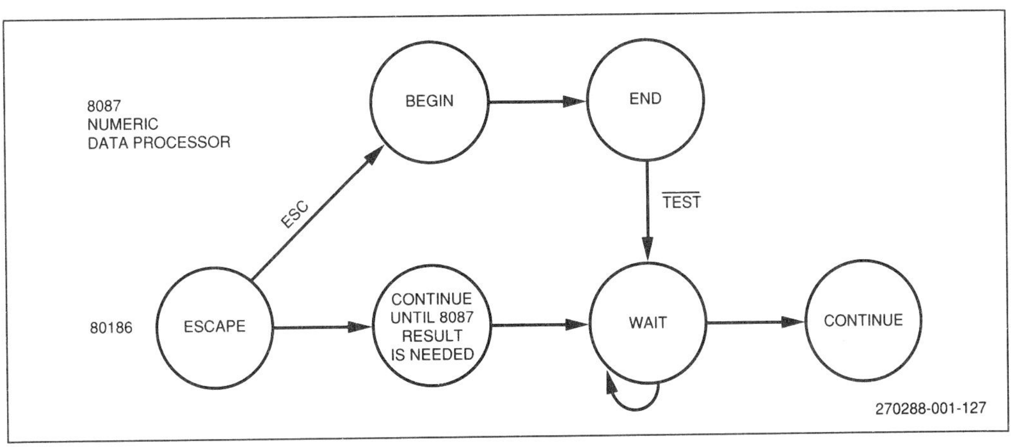

Figure 121. 8087 Coprocessor Operation

12.1.5 80186(80188) BUS CYCLES DURING NUMERICS COPROCESSING

The 8087 is an alternate bus master which directly performs all coprocessor reads and writes to memory. When the Numeric Execution Unit begins executing an instruction, it activates the 8087 BUSY signal. This signal is used in conjunction with the WAIT or FWAIT instruction to resynchronize both processors when the Numeric Execution Unit has completed its current instruction.

The 82188 performs several functions necessary to integrate the 8087 into an 80186 system. Most importantly, it translates the 8087 $\overline{\text{REQUEST/GRANT}}$ protocol to the HOLD/HLDA protocol required by the 80186. The 82188 reconstructs the $\overline{\text{RD}}$ and $\overline{\text{WR}}$ signals sacrificed by the 80186/80188 to provide queue status signals. The 82188 also furnishes $\overline{\text{DEN}}$, DT/$\overline{\text{R}}$, and auxiliary bus arbitration signals to integrate the 80186/8087 into a larger microprocessor system.

The coprocessor must examine all instructions executed by the host to recognize ESC instructions. When the host fetches an instruction byte from its internal queue, the coprocessor must also fetch an instruction byte.

The queue status state, fetch opcode byte, identifies when an opcode byte is being examined by the host. At the same time, the coprocessor will check if the byte fetched from its internal instruction queue is an ESC opcode. If the instruction is not an ESC, the coprocessor will ignore it. The queue status signals for fetch subsequent byte and flush queue let the coprocessor track the host's queue without knowledge of the length and function of host instructions and addressing modes.

A numeric instruction for the 8087 appears as an ESC instruction to the 80186 or 80188 CPU; both the CPU and the NPX decode and execute the ESC instruction together. Only the 8087, however, recognizes the numeric instructions. The start of a numeric operation begins when the CPU executes the ESC instruction (the instruction may or may not identify a memory operand).

The CPU does, however, distinguish between ESC instructions that refer to memory operands and those that do not. If the instructions refers to a memory operand, the CPU calculates the operand's address using any one of its available addressing modes, and then performs a "dummy read" of the word at that location. The address may fall anywhere within the 1 Mbyte adddress space. This read cycle is normal except that the CPU ignores the data it receives. If the ESC instruction does not contain a memory reference (e.g., an 8087 stack operation), the CPU simply proceeds to the next instruction.

An 8087 instruction has one of three memory reference options:

- To not reference memory.
- To load an operand from memory into the 8087.
- To store an operand from the 8087 into memory.

If the 8087 requires no memory reference, the Numeric Execution Unit simply executes its instruction. If the 8087 does require a memory reference, the control unit uses the "dummy read" cycle initiated by the host CPU to capture and save the address that the CPU places on the bus. If the instruction specifies a register load, the Control Unit also captures the data word when it becomes available on the local data bus. If the 8087 requires data longer than one word, the Control Unit immediately obtains the bus from the CPU using the $\overline{\text{REQUEST/GRANT}}$ protocol and reads in the rest of the information in consecutive bus cycles. In a store operation, the Control Unit captures and saves the store address as in a register load operation, and ignores the data word that follows in the "dummy read" cycle. When the 8087 is ready to perform the store, the Control Unit obtains the bus from the CPU and writes the operand starting at the specified address.

This parallel operation of the host and coprocessor is called concurrent execution. Concurrent execution of instructions requires less total time than strictly sequential execution. System performance will be higher with concurrent execution of instructions between the host and coprocessor.

12.2 USING THE 80C186 WITH THE 80C187 NUMERICS PROCESSOR EXTENSION

The 80C186 supports floating point calculations by providing the necessary hardware interface to the 80C187 numerics processor extension.

12.2.1 OVERVIEW OF THE 80C187 NUMERICS PROCESSOR EXTENSION

The 80C187 numerics processor extension provides a number of new or improved transcendental instructions and refinements above and beyond the capabilities of the 8087. The 80C187 conforms to the most recent revision of IEEE standard 754.

The 80C186 interfaces directly to the 80C187 (see Figure 122). The 80C186 and 80C187 operate asynchronously, each up to its maximum rated clock speed. CLKOUT from the 80C186 may be used as the 80C187 clock input up to 12.5 MHz. The 80C188 cannot be used because the flow of opcodes, instruction pointers, and data passes through 16-bit I/O ports. The 80C186 must be in Enhanced Mode to communicate with the 80C187.

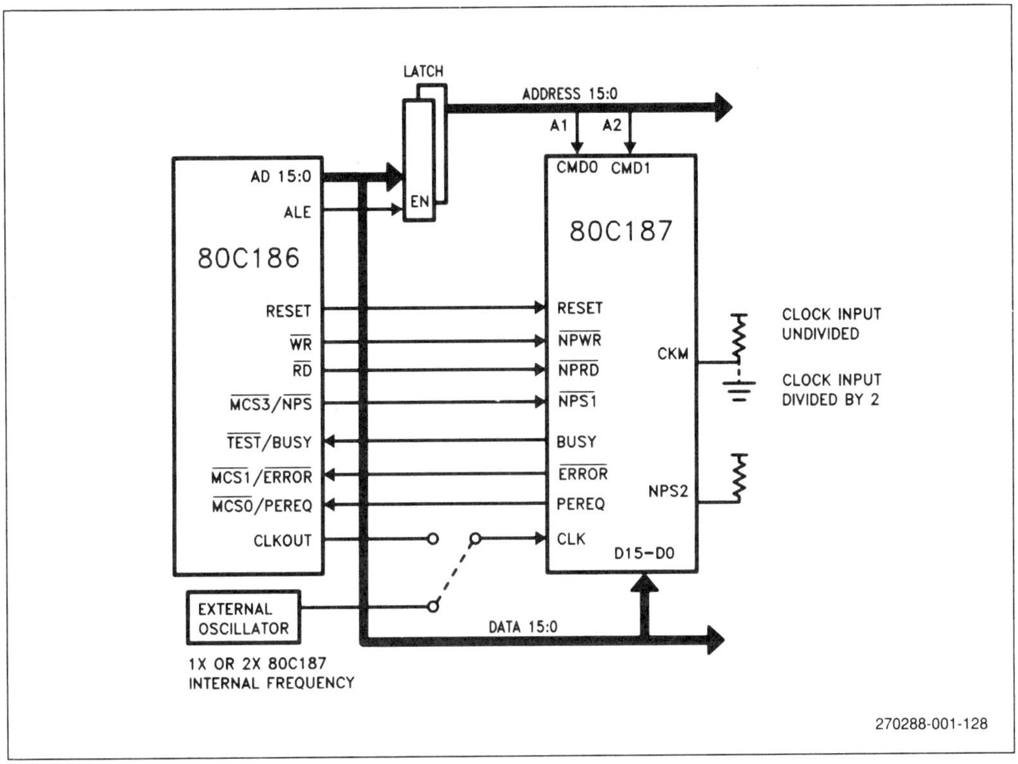

Figure 122.80C186/80C187 System Configuration

12.2.2 80C187 ADDITIONS TO INSTRUCTION SET

The 80C187 adds several new instructions to the 8087 (see Table 28). Other instructions allow operands over an extended range, and a few instructions behave slightly differently in conformance with the IEEE standard.

Of particular interest are the new trigonometric instructions which provide sine or cosine in one operation.

12.2.3 80C186/80C187 INTERFACE

In similar fashion to the 8087, the 80C187 is comprised of three units: a Floating Point Unit, a Data Interface and Control Unit, and a Bus Control Logic Unit. The Floating Point Unit executes all numerics instructions under supervision of the Data Interface and Control Unit, while the Bus Control Logic Unit maintains handshaking and communications with the host 80C186.

Table 28. 80C187 Additions to Instruction Set

Instruction Type	Mnemonic	Description
Arithmetic	FPREM1	Partial Remainder (IEEE)
Comparison	FUCOM FUCOMP FUCOMPP	Unordered Compare Unordered Compare and Pop Unordered Compare and Pop Twice
Transcendental	FCOS FSIN FSINCOS	Cosine Sine Sine and Cosine

The 80C187 is referred to as a numerics processor extension because it operates as a slave device to the host 80C186. All communication between the 80C186 and 80C187 occurs through the dedicated I/O ports shown in Table 29. When the 80C186 encounters a numerics opcode, it writes the opcode to the 80C187, which decodes the instruction and passes elementary instruction information (Opcode Status) back to the 80C186. Since the 80C187 is a slave processor, all loads and stores to memory are performed by the 80C186.

Please note that the 80C186 cannot process any numerics (ESC) opcodes alone. If the 80C186 encounters a numerics instruction (including the FINIT/FNINIT initialization instruction) and the 80C187 is not present, the operation of the 80C186 is indeterminate. In those applications where the 80C187 is offered as an option, problems can be prevented in three ways:

- Remove all numerics (ESC) instructions, including any code which checks for the presence of the NPX.
- Use a jumper or switch setting to indicate the presence of the 80C187, and have the software branch away from numerics instructions when the 80C187 socket is empty.
- Add pull-up and pull-down resistors to various data and control lines to force the 80C186 into predictable operation when the 80C187 socket is empty.

In Enhanced Mode, three of the mid-range memory chip selects are redefined as handshaking pins for the 80C186/80C187 interface. Handshaking is managed by 80C186 microcode. $\overline{\text{MCS2}}$ retains its same function as in Compatible Mode. Additionally, the processor retains the wait state and READY logic programmability for the entire mid-range block, even though $\overline{\text{MCS0}}$, $\overline{\text{MCS1}}$, and $\overline{\text{MCS3}}$ are no longer available as outputs.

Table 29. Numerics Coprocessor I/O Port Assignments

I/O Address	Read Definition	Write Definition
00F8H	Status/Control	Opcode
00FAH	Data	Data
00FCH	reserved	CS:IP, DS:EA
00FEH	Opcode Status	reserved

12.2.4 80C186 BUS CYCLES WITH THE 80C187 NUMERICS PROCESSOR EXTENSION

The 80C186 performs bus cycles to the 80C187 numerics processor extension (NPX) exactly like other I/O bus cycles. This fact has important implications:

- Operations to the 80C187 require external READY to be provided via the SRDY or ARDY pins.
- If the $\overline{\text{PCS}}$ address range is programmed to cover the NPX port addresses, a $\overline{\text{PCS}}$ line goes active during each read or write from the 80C186 to the 80C187. However, ordinary reads and writes to those addresses do not activate $\overline{\text{NPS}}$ on the 80C186.
- DT/$\overline{\text{R}}$ and $\overline{\text{DEN}}$ function normally during $\overline{\text{NPX}}$ transfers. In a buffered system with the 80C187 residing on the local bus, use $\overline{\text{NPS}}$ to qualify $\overline{\text{DEN}}$ to the bus transceivers. Otherwise, contention between the NPX and the transceivers occurs on read cycles.
- The 80C186 local bus is available to the integrated peripherals during execution of numerics instructions when it is not needed by the CPU. This means that DRAM refresh cycles and DMA cycles may be interspersed with accesses to the 80C187.
- The 80C186 local bus is available to alternate bus masters during execution of numerics instructions when it is not needed by the CPU. This means that bus cycles originating from alternate masters (via the HOLD/HLDA protocol) can suspend numerics bus cycles for an indefinite period.
- The $\overline{\text{LOCK}}$ pin functions normally during numerics operations. This means that LOCKed numerics instructions can monopolize the bus for a very long time.

Appendix A

Difference Between the 80186 Family and the 8086/8088

APPENDIX A
DIFFERENCES BETWEEN THE 80186 FAMILY AND THE 8086/8088

A.1 CPU PERFORMANCE

Because of 80186 family hardware enhancements in both the Bus Interface Unit and the Execution Unit, most instructions require fewer clock cycles to execute than on the 8086/8088. Execution speed is gained by performing the effective address calculations (base + displacement + index) with a dedicated hardware adder, which takes only four clock cycles in the 80186 family Bus Interface Unit, rather than with a microcode routine. These calculations are three to six times faster than the 8086/8088 at the same frequency.

In addition, the execution speed of specific instructions was improved. All multiple-bit shift and rotate instructions execute 1.5 to 2.5 times faster than the (same speed) 8086/8088. Multiply and divide instructions execute three times faster. String move instructions run at bus bandwidth, about twice the speed of the 8086/8088. Overall, the 80186 family processors run benchmark programs 1.2 - 2.6 times the performance level of the (same speed) 8086/8088.

A.2 CLOCKING

The 80186 family employs an integrated clock generator which provides a 50 percent duty cycle CPU clock. This is different from the 8086 which utilizes an external clock generator to provide a 33 percent (1/3 HIGH, 2/3 LOW) duty cycle CPU clock. The following points relate to 80186 clock generation:

- The 80186 family uses a crystal or external frequency input that is twice the desired processor clock frequency.
- No oscillator output is available from an 80186 family processor internal oscillator.
- An 80186 family processor does not provide a clock output at reduced frequency. However, a timer output may be easily programmed for this purpose.
- Interfacing the 80186 family to devices needing a 33 percent duty cycle clock (for example, the 8087) is possible, but requires careful timing analysis.

A.3 LOCAL BUS CONTROLLER AND CONTROL SIGNALS

In general, the output drivers on 80186 family products are much larger than those of the 8086. This leads to larger systems without as much need for bus buffering. It also means that the designer should be more careful to provide adequate grounding and bypassing, since large drivers are more apt to cause current transients. In the 68-pin package, an 80186 family device has only two ground pins.

A.4 HOLD/HLDA VS. $\overline{\text{REQUEST}}/\overline{\text{GRANT}}$

The 80186 family uses a HOLD/HLDA protocol for bus arbitration rather than the $\overline{\text{REQUEST}}/\overline{\text{GRANT}}$ protocol used by the 8086 in max mode. This allows compatibility with newer generation Intel bus master peripheral devices.

A.5 STATUS INFORMATION

Three status signals are available on the 8086 but not on the 80186 family. They are S3, S4, and S5. Taken together, S3 and S4 indicate the segment register from which the current physical address has been derived. S5 indicates the state of the interrupt flip-flop. On 80186 family processors, these signals will always be LOW.

Status signal S6 indicates whether the current bus cycle is initiated by either the CPU or a DMA device. Subsequently, it is always LOW on the 8086. On the 80186 family, it is LOW whenever the current bus cycle is initiated by the CPU, and is HIGH when the current bus cycle is initiated by the integrated DMA Unit.

An 80186 family processor simultaneously provides both local bus control outputs and status outputs for use with external Bus Controllers. This is different from the 8086 where the local bus control outputs are sacrificed if status outputs are desired. These differences will manifest themselves in 8086 systems and 80186 family systems as follows:

- Many systems supporting both a system bus and a local bus will not require two separate external bus controllers. The bus control signals may be used to control the local bus while the status signals are concurrently connected to the 82C88 Bus Controller to drive the control signals of the system bus.
- The ALE signal goes active a clock phase earlier on the 80186 family than on the 8086 or 82C88. This minimizes address propagation time through the address latches, since typically the delay time through these latches from valid inputs is less than the propagation delay from the strobe input active.

- The $\overline{RD}$ input must be tied LOW to provide queue status outputs from the 80186 family processor (see Figure A-1). When so strapped into Queue Status Mode, the ALE and $\overline{WR}$ outputs provide queue status information. Notice that queue status information is available one clock phase earlier than from the 8086 (see Figure A-2).

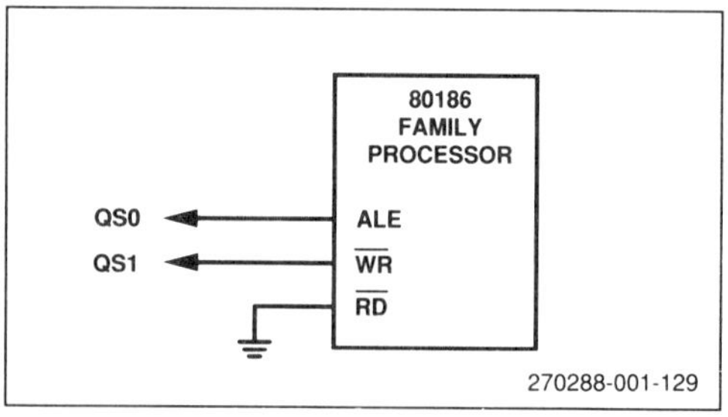

Figure A-1. Generating Queue Status Information

ADDED INSTRUCTIONS:

The 80186 family executes PUSHA, POPA, INS, OUTS, BOUND, ENTER, and LEAVE.

IMPROVED INSTRUCTIONS:

PUSH, IMUL, and SHIFTS/ROTATES may use immediate operands on the 80186 family.

UNDEFINED OPCODES:

When the opcodes 63H, 64H, 65H, 66H, 67H, F1H, FEH XX111XXXB and FFH XX111XXXB are executed, the 80186 family executes an illegal instruction exception, interrupt Type 6. The 8086 will ignore the opcode.

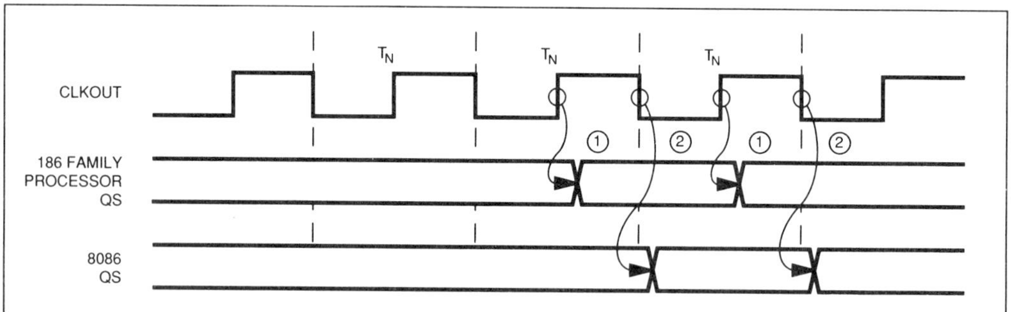

NOTES: 1. 80186 family processor changes queue status off falling edge of CLKOUT.
2. 8086 changes queue status off rising edge of CLK.

Figure A-2. 80186 Family and 8086 Queue Status Generation

A.6 BUS UTILIZATION

A typical instruction mix will require greater bus utilization on the 80186 family than on the 8086. The 80186 family executes most instructions in fewer clock cycles, requiring instructions from the queue at a faster rate. This also means that the effect of wait states is more pronounced in an 80186 family microprocessor system than in an 8086 system.

A.7 INSTRUCTION EXECUTION

The following paragraphs explain the instruction execution differences between the 8086 and the 80186.

0FH OPCODE:

When the opcode 0FH is encountered, the 8086 will execute a POP CS, while the 80186 family will execute an illegal instruction exception, interrupt Type 6.

WORD WRITE AT OFFSET FFFFH:

When a word write is performed at offset FFFFH in a segment, the 8086 will write one byte at offset FFFFH, and the other at offset 0, while an 80186 family processor will write one byte at offset FFFFH, and the other at offset 10000H (one byte beyond the end of the segment). One byte segment underflow will also occur if a stack PUSH is executed and the stack pointer contains the value 1.

SHIFT/ROTATE BY VALUE GREATER THAN 31:

Before the 80186 family performs a shift or rotate by a value (either in the CL register, or an immediate value) it ANDs the value with 1FH, limiting the number of bits rotated to less than 32. The 8086 does not limit the rotation count.

LOCK PREFIX:

The 8086 activates its $\overline{\text{LOCK}}$ signal immediately upon executing the LOCK prefix. An 80186 family processor does not activate the $\overline{\text{LOCK}}$ signal until the processor is ready to begin the data cycles associated with the LOCKed instruction.

On the 80186 or the 80188, back-to-back LOCKed instructions are not allowed. Insert at least six bytes of code (four bytes for the 80188) between the end of the first LOCKed instruction and the beginning of the second LOCKed instruction. This restriction does not apply to the 80C186/80C188. However, between the bus cycles for the first instruction and the bus cycles for the second instruction, $\overline{\text{LOCK}}$ will not remain active, and the processor can perform other bus activities.

INTERRUPTED STRING MOVE INSTRUCTIONS:

If an 8086 is interrupted during the execution of a repeated string move instruction, the return value it will push on the stack will point to the last prefix instruction before the string move instruction. If the instruction has more than one prefix (e.g., a segment override prefix in addition to the repeat prefix), the other prefixes will not be reexecuted upon returning from the interrupt. An 80186 family processor will push an IP value pointing to the first prefix of the repeated instruction (as long as prefixes are not repeated), allowing the string instruction to properly resume.

CONDITIONS CAUSING DIVIDE ERROR WITH AN INTEGER DIVIDE:

The 8086 will cause a divide error whenever the absolute value of the quotient is greater than 7FFFH (for word operations) or if the absolute value of the quotient is greater than 7FH (for byte operations). The 80186 family expanded the range of negative numbers allowed as a quotient by 1 to include 8000H and 80H. These numbers represent the most negative numbers representable using 2's complement arithmetic (equaling -32768 and -128 in decimal, respectively).

ESC OPCODES:

An 80186 family microprocessor has a bit (the ET bit) in the relocation register which can be programmed to cause a Type 7 interrupt upon attempted execution of a coprocessor (ESCape) instruction. The 8086 has no such provision.

On the 80186 and 80188, the initial state of the ET bit is cleared, disabling the trap. On the 80C186, the initial state of the ET bit is cleared in Enhanced Mode or set in Compatible Mode. On the 80C188, the ET bit is not accessible to the user and the ESCape Trap is always enabled, regardless of operating mode.

Execution of numerics opcodes proceeds differently in the 80C186 than in the 8086/8088 or 80186/80188. See Chapter 12 for details. The 80C188 cannot utilize a numerics processor extension at all. When migrating from the 8086/8088 or 80186/80188 to the 80C186/80C188, the user should be aware of these differences. In particular, it may be necessary to check software for unexpected numerics (ESCape) opcodes.

Synchronization of External Inputs

Appendix B

APPENDIX B
SYNCHRONIZATION OF EXTERNAL INPUTS

Many input signals to an 80186 family processor are asynchronous, that is, a specified set up or hold time is not required to ensure proper functioning of the device. Associated with each of these inputs is a synchronizer which samples this external asynchronous signal, and synchronizes it to the internal clock.

B.1 WHY SYNCHRONIZERS ARE REQUIRED

Every data latch requires a certain set up and hold time in order to operate properly. At a certain window within the specified set up and hold time, the part will actually try to latch the data. If the input makes a transition within this window, the output will not attain a stable state within the given output delay time. The actual size of this sampling window is typically much smaller than the window specified by the data sheet; however, part to part variation could move the actual window around within the specified window.

Even if the input to a data latch makes a transition while a data latch is attempting to latch this input, the output of the latch will attain a stable state after a certain amount of time, typically much longer than the normal strobe to output delay time. Figure B-1 shows a normal input to output strobed transition and one in which the input signal makes a transition during the latch's sample window. To synchronize an asynchronous signal, all one needs to do is to sample the signal into one data latch long enough for the output to stabilize, then latch it into a second data latch. The time between the first latch strobe and the second latch strobe allows the first latch to attain a steady state. With the asynchronous signal resolved in this way, the input signal at the second latch satisfies its setup and hold requirements.

Thus, the output of this second latch is a synchronous signal with respect to its strobe input.

A synchronization failure can occur if the synchronizer fails to resolve the asynchronous transition within the time between the strobes of the two latches. The rate of failure is determined by the actual size of the sampling window of the data latch, and by the amount of time between the strobe signals of the two latches. Obviously, as the sampling window gets smaller, the number of times an asynchronous transition will occur during the sampling window will drop. In addition, however, a smaller sampling window is also indicative of a faster resolution time for an input transition which manages to fall within the sampling window.

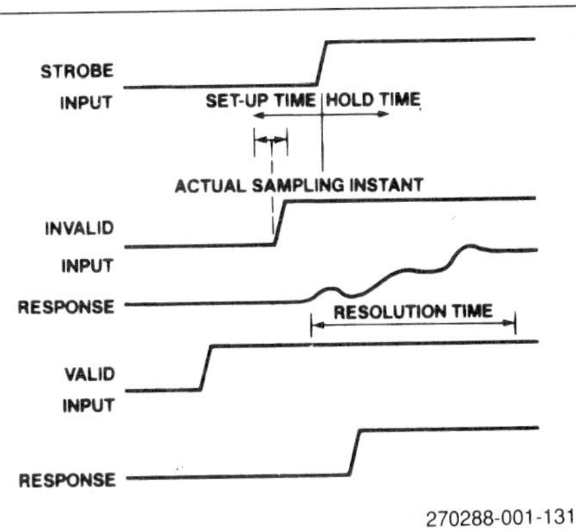

Figure B-1. Valid and Invalid Latch Input Transitions and Response

B.2 80186 FAMILY SYNCHRONIZERS

The 80186 family uses the two stage synchronization technique on TMR IN0-1, DRQ0-1, NMI, INT0-3, and HOLD input lines. ARDY uses a slight modification (see Section 3.6). For the NMOS 80186, the sampling window of the latches was designed to be in the tens of picoseconds, and should allow operation of the synchronizers with a mean time between failures of over 30 years, assuming continuous operation.

Appendix C

Summary of Differences Among Family Members

APPENDIX C
SUMMARY OF DIFFERENCES AMONG 80186 FAMILY MEMBERS

C.1 DIFFERENCES DUE TO DATA BUS WIDTH

The 80188/80C188 is like the 80186/80C186 except it has an 8-bit external bus. It shares the same Execution Unit, timers, peripheral control block, Interrupt Control Unit, Chip Select Unit, and DMA Control Logic Unit. The differences between the two caused by the narrower data bus are:

- The 80188/80C188 has a four byte prefetch queue, rather than the six byte prefetch queue present on the 80186/80C186. The reason is that the 80188/80C188 fetches opcodes one byte at a time, requiring more bus cycles to fill the queue. A smaller queue is required to prevent an inordinate number of bus cycles being wasted by prefetching opcodes to be discarded during a jump.

- AD8-AD15 on the 80186/80C186 are transformed to A8-A15 on the 80188/80C188. Valid address information is present on these lines throughout the bus cycle of the 80188/80C188. Valid address information is not guaranteed on these lines during idle T-states.

- $\overline{\text{BHE}}$/S7 is always defined HIGH by the 80188/80C188 since the upper half of the data bus is non-existent.

- The DMA Control Unit on the 80188/80C188 only performs byte transfers. The B/W bit in the DMA control word is ignored.

- Execution times for most data transfer instructions increases because the BIU funnels the accesses through a narrower data bus. The narrower bus also means that the prefetch queue will run empty more often, causing the Execution Unit itself to be bus-limited. The execution time within the processor, however, is not changed between the 80186/80C186 and 80188/80C188.

Another important point is that the 80188/80C188 is internally a 16-bit machine. This means that access to the integrated peripheral registers of the 80188/80C188 will be done in 16-bit pieces, not in 8-bit pieces. All internal peripheral registers are still 16-bits wide, and only a single read or write is required to access the registers. When a word access is made to the internal registers, the BIU will run two bus cycles externally.

Access to the control block may also be done with byte operations. Internally the full 16 bits of the AX register will be written, while only one bus cycle will be executed externally.

C.2 DIFFERENCES BETWEEN NMOS AND CMOS DEVICES

There are two operating modes of the 80C186 and 80C188, Compatible Mode and Enhanced Mode. In Compatible Mode, the 80C186/80C188 will function identically to the 80186/80188 with the following exceptions:

- All non-initialized registers in the peripheral control block will reset to a random value during power-up on the 80C186/80C188. Non-initialized registers consist of those registers which are not used for control, i.e., address pointers, max count, etc. For compatibility, all registers should be programmed before being used on existing 80186/80188 applications as well as on new 80C186/80C188 applications.

- The ET (ESC Trap) bit in the relocation register has no effect in Compatible Mode. If an ESCape opcode is executed, the 80C186/80C188 will always trap to an interrupt vector Type 7. The 80C186/80C188 does not support any numerics operations when in Compatible Mode.

In Enhanced Mode, the 80C186/80C188 provides two additional features not found on the 80186/80188: power-save operation, and the DRAM Refresh Unit.

Enhanced Mode is selected during RESET. The timing diagram in Figure C-1 shows how the 80C186/80C188 samples the $\overline{\text{TEST}}$ pin ($\overline{\text{TEST}}$/BUSY in the 80C186) before and just after $\overline{\text{RES}}$ input is removed to determine if the device will enter Enhanced Mode. Tying the RESET output pin back to the $\overline{\text{TEST}}$ input pin will automatically force the processor into Enhanced Mode.

When the 80C186 (but not the 80C188) is in Enhanced Mode, three of the $\overline{\text{MCS}}$ chip select lines change functionality to support the 80C187 Numerics Coprocessor Extension. The remaining $\overline{\text{MCS}}$ functionality is illustrated in Figure C-2.

The 80C188 in Enhanced Mode functions similarly to the 80C186 except for numerics operation. It is not possible to

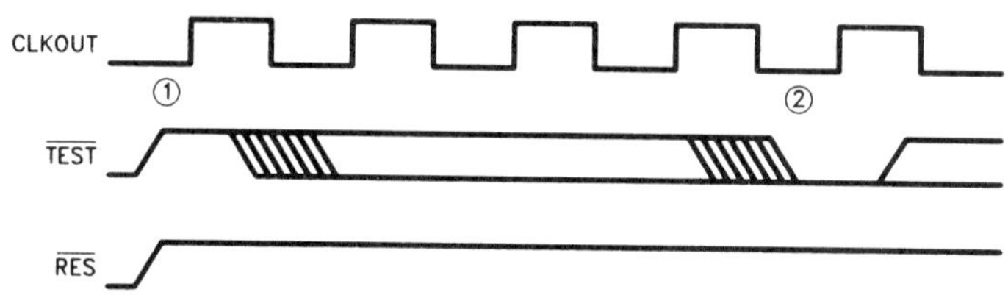

NOTES:
1. TEST maust be high T_{INVCH} when RES transitions high.
2. TEST must be low T_{INVCH} four clocks later.

270288-001-132

Figure C-1. Enhanced Mode Enable Pin Timing

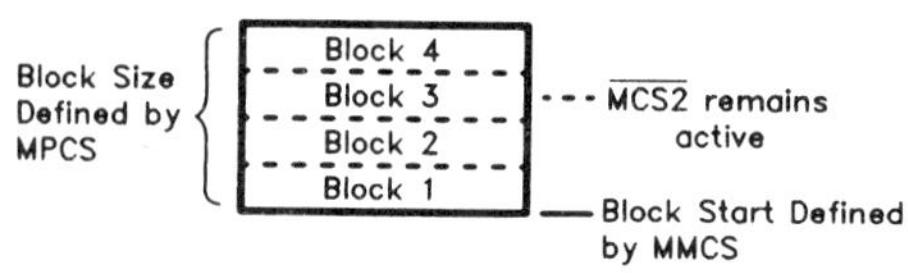

270288-001-133

Figure C-2. MCS2 Functionality During Enhanced Mode

interface a numerics coprocessor with the 80C188. Therefore, none of the MCS pins change functionality when invoking Enhanced Mode. Further, any attempted execution of an ESCape opcode will result in a trap to interrupt vector Type 7.

The external frequency input (EFI) requirements differ somewhat between the NMOS 80186/80188 and the CMOS 80C186/80C188. On the NMOS processors, it is possible to drive either X1 (with X2 unconnected) or X2 (with X1 grounded). Since the internal oscillator consists of an inverter from the X1 pin to the X2 pin, overdriving the X2 pin on the CMOS devices would result in excessive current draw. The correct configuration for the CMOS processors is to drive X1 and leave X2 unconnected.

intel®

DOMESTIC SALES OFFICES

ALABAMA

†Intel Corp.
5015 Bradford Dr., #2
Huntsville 35805
Tel: (205) 830-4010
FAX: (205) 837-2640

ARIZONA

†Intel Corp.
11225 N. 28th Dr.
Suite D-214
Phoenix 85029
Tel: (602) 869-4980
FAX: (602) 869-4294

Intel Corp.
1161 N. El Dorado Place
Suite 301
Tucson 85715
Tel: (602) 299-6815
FAX: (602) 296-8234

CALIFORNIA

†Intel Corp.
21515 Vanowen Street
Suite 116
Canoga Park 91303
Tel: (818) 704-8500
FAX: (818) 340-1144

†Intel Corp.
2250 E. Imperial Highway
Suite 218
El Segundo 90245
Tel: (213) 640-6040
FAX: (213) 640-7133

Intel Corp.
1510 Arden Way
Suite 101
Sacramento 95815
Tel: (916) 920-8096
FAX: (916) 920-8253

†Intel Corp.
9665 Chesapeake Dr.
Suite 325
San Diego 95123
Tel: (619) 292-8086
FAX: (619) 292-0628

†Intel Corp.*
400 N. Tustin Avenue
Suite 450
Santa Ana 92705
Tel: (714) 835-9642
TWX: 910-595-1114
FAX: (714) 541-9157

†Intel Corp.*
San Tomas 4
2700 San Tomas Expressway
2nd Floor
Santa Clara 95051
Tel: (408) 986-8086
TWX: 910-338-0255
FAX: (408) 727-2620

COLORADO

Intel Corp.
4445 Northpark Drive
Suite 100
Colorado Springs 80907
Tel: (719) 594-6622
FAX: (303) 594-0720

†Intel Corp.*
650 S. Cherry St.
Suite 915
Denver 80222
Tel: (303) 321-8086
TWX: 910-931-2289
FAX: (303) 322-8670

CONNECTICUT

†Intel Corp.
301 Lee Farm Corporate Park
83 Wooster Heights Rd.
Danbury 06810
Tel: (203) 748-3130
FAX: (203) 794-0339

FLORIDA

†Intel Corp.
6363 N.W. 6th Way
Suite 100
Ft. Lauderdale 33309
Tel: (305) 771-0600
TWX: 510-956-9407
FAX: (305) 772-8193

†Intel Corp.
5850 T.G. Lee Blvd.
Suite 340
Orlando 32822
Tel: (407) 240-8000
FAX: (407) 240-8097

Intel Corp.
11300 4th Street North
Suite 170
St. Petersburg 33716
Tel: (813) 577-2413
FAX: (813) 578-1607

GEORGIA

Intel Corp.
20 Technology Parkway, N.W.
Suite 150
Norcross 30092
Tel: (404) 449-0541
FAX: (404) 605-9762

ILLINOIS

†Intel Corp.*
300 N. Martingale Road
Suite 400
Schaumburg 60173
Tel: (312) 605-8031
FAX: (312) 706-9762

INDIANA

†Intel Corp.
8777 Purdue Road
Suite 125
Indianapolis 46268
Tel: (317) 875-0623
FAX: (317) 875-8938

IOWA

Intel Corp.
1930 St. Andrews Drive N.E.
2nd Floor
Cedar Rapids 52402
Tel: (319) 393-1294

KANSAS

†Intel Corp.
10985 Cody St.
Suite 140, Bldg. D
Overland Park 66210
Tel: (913) 345-2727
FAX: (913) 345-2076

MARYLAND

†Intel Corp.*
10010 Junction Dr.
Suite 200
Annapolis Junction 20701
Tel: (301) 206-2860
FAX: (301) 206-3677
(301) 206-3678

MASSACHUSETTS

†Intel Corp.*
Westford Corp. Center
3 Carlisle Road
2nd Floor
Westford 01886
Tel: (508) 692-3222
TWX: 710-343-6333
FAX: (508) 692-7867

MICHIGAN

†Intel Corp.
7071 Orchard Lake Road
Suite 100
West Bloomfield 48322
Tel: (313) 851-8096
FAX: (313) 851-8770

MINNESOTA

†Intel Corp.
3500 W. 80th St.
Suite 360
Bloomington 55431
Tel: (612) 835-6722
TWX: 910-576-2867
FAX: (612) 831-6497

MISSOURI

†Intel Corp.
4203 Earth City Expressway
Suite 131
Earth City 63045
Tel: (314) 291-1990
FAX: (314) 291-4341

NEW JERSEY

†Intel Corp.*
Parkway 109 Office Center
328 Newman Springs Road
Red Bank 07701
Tel: (201) 747-2233
FAX: (201) 747-0983

†Intel Corp.
280 Corporate Center
75 Livingston Avenue
First Floor
Roseland 07068
Tel: (201) 740-0111
FAX: (201) 740-0626

NEW YORK

Intel Corp.*
850 Cross Keys Office Park
Fairport 14450
Tel: (716) 425-2750
TWX: 510-253-7391
FAX: (716) 223-2561

†Intel Corp.*
2950 Expressway Dr. South
Suite 130
Islandia 11722
Tel: (516) 231-3300
TWX: 510-227-6236
FAX: (516) 348-7939

†Intel Corp.
Westage Business Center
Bldg. 300, Route 9
Fishkill 12524
Tel: (914) 897-3860
FAX: (914) 897-3125

NORTH CAROLINA

†Intel Corp.
5800 Executive Center Dr.
Suite 105
Charlotte 28212
Tel: (704) 568-8966
FAX: (704) 535-2236

Intel Corp.
5540 Centerview Dr.
Suite 215
Raleigh 27606
Tel: (919) 851-9537
FAX: (919) 851-8974

OHIO

†Intel Corp.*
3401 Park Center Drive
Suite 220
Dayton 45414
Tel: (513) 890-5350
TWX: 810-450-2528
FAX: (513) 890-8658

†Intel Corp.*
25700 Science Park Dr.
Suite 100
Beachwood 44122
Tel: (216) 464-2736
TWX: 810-427-9298
FAX: (804) 282-0673

OKLAHOMA

Intel Corp.
6801 N. Broadway
Suite 115
Oklahoma City 73162
Tel: (405) 848-8086
FAX: (405) 840-9819

OREGON

†Intel Corp.
15254 N.W. Greenbrier Parkway
Building B
Beaverton 97005
Tel: (503) 645-8051
TWX: 910-467-8741
FAX: (503) 645-8181

PENNSYLVANIA

†Intel Corp.*
455 Pennsylvania Avenue
Suite 230
Fort Washington 19034
Tel: (215) 641-1000
TWX: 510-661-2077
FAX: (215) 641-0785

†Intel Corp.*
400 Penn Center Blvd.
Suite 610
Pittsburgh 15235
Tel: (412) 823-4970
FAX: (412) 829-7578

PUERTO RICO

†Intel Corp.
South Industrial Park
P.O. Box 910
Las Piedras 00671
Tel: (809) 733-8616

TEXAS

Intel Corp.
8911 Capital of Texas Hwy.
Austin 78759
Tel: (512) 794-8086
FAX: (512) 338-9335

†Intel Corp.*
12000 Ford Road
Suite 400
Dallas 75234
Tel: (214) 241-8087
FAX: (214) 484-1180

†Intel Corp.*
7322 S.W. Freeway
Suite 1490
Houston 77074
Tel: (713) 988-8086
TWX: 910-881-2490
FAX: (713) 988-3660

UTAH

†Intel Corp.
428 East 6400 South
Suite 104
Murray 84107
Tel: (801) 263-8051
FAX: (801) 268-1457

VIRGINIA

†Intel Corp.
1504 Santa Rosa Road
Suite 108
Richmond 23288
Tel: (804) 282-5668
FAX: (216) 464-2270

WASHINGTON

†Intel Corp.
155 108th Avenue N.E.
Suite 386
Bellevue 98004
Tel: (206) 453-8086
TWX: 910-443-3002
FAX: (206) 451-9556

Intel Corp.
408 N. Mullan Road
Suite 102
Spokane 99206
Tel: (509) 928-8086
FAX: (509) 928-9467

WISCONSIN

Intel Corp.
330 S. Executive Dr.
Suite 102
Brookfield 53005
Tel: (414) 784-8087
FAX: (414) 796-2115

CANADA

BRITISH COLUMBIA

Intel Semiconductor of
Canada, Ltd.
4585 Canada Way
Suite 202
Burnaby V5G 4L6
Tel: (604) 298-0387
FAX: (604) 298-8234

ONTARIO

†Intel Semiconductor of
Canada, Ltd.
2650 Queensview Drive
Suite 250
Ottawa K2B 8H6
Tel: (613) 829-9714
FAX: (613) 820-5936

†Intel Semiconductor of
Canada, Ltd.
190 Attwell Drive
Suite 500
Rexdale M9W 6H8
Tel: (416) 675-2105
FAX: (416) 675-2438

QUEBEC

Intel Semiconductor of
Canada, Ltd.
620 St. Jean Boulevard
Pointe Claire H9R 3K2
Tel: (514) 694-9130
FAX: 514-694-0064

†Sales and Service Office
*Field Application Location

intel®

DOMESTIC DISTRIBUTORS

ALABAMA

Arrow Electronics, Inc.
1015 Henderson Road
Huntsville 35805
Tel: (205) 837-6955

†Hamilton/Avnet Electronics
4940 Research Drive
Huntsville 35805
Tel: (205) 837-7210
TWX: 810-726-2162

Pioneer/Technologies Group, Inc.
4825 University Square
Huntsville 35805
Tel: (205) 837-9300
TWX: 810-726-2197

ARIZONA

†Hamilton/Avnet Electronics
505 S. Madison Drive
Tempe 85281
Tel: (602) 231-5140
TWX: 910-950-0077

Hamilton/Avnet Electronics
30 South McKiemy
Chandler 85226
Tel: (602) 961-6669
TWX: 910-950-0077

Arrow Electronics, Inc.
4134 E. Wood Street
Phoenix 85040
Tel: (602) 437-0750
TWX: 910-951-1550

Wyle Distribution Group
17855 N. Black Canyon Hwy.
Phoenix 85023
Tel: (602) 249-2232
TWX: 910-951-4282

CALIFORNIA

Arrow Electronics, Inc.
10824 Hope Street
Cypress 90630
Tel: (714) 220-6300

Arrow Electronics, Inc.
19748 Dearborn Street
Chatsworth 91311
Tel: (213) 701-7500
TWX: 910-493-2086

†Arow Electronics, Inc.
521 Weddell Drive
Sunnyvale 94086
Tel: (408) 745-6600
TWX: 910-339-9371

Arrow Electronics, Inc.
9511 Ridgehaven Court
San Diego 92123
Tel: (619) 565-4800
TWX: 888-064

†Arrow Electronics, Inc.
2961 Dow Avenue
Tustin 92680
Tel: (714) 838-5422
TWX: 910-595-2860

†Avnet Electronics
350 McCormick Avenue
Costa Mesa 92626
Tel: (714) 754-6071
TWX: 910-595-1928

†Hamilton/Avnet Electronics
1175 Bordeaux Drive
Sunnyvale 94086
Tel: (408) 743-3300
TWX: 910-339-9332

†Hamilton/Avnet Electronics
4545 Ridgeview Avenue
San Diego 92123
Tel: (619) 571-7500
TWX: 910-595-2638

†Hamilton/Avnet Electronics
9650 Desoto Avenue
Chatsworth 91311
Tel: (818) 700-1161

†Hamilton Electro Sales
10950 W. Washington Blvd.
Culver City 20230
Tel: (213) 558-2458
TWX: 910-340-6364

Hamilton Electro Sales
1361B West 190th Street
Gardena 90248
Tel: (213) 217-6700

†Hamilton/Avnet Electronics
3002 'G' Street
Ontario 91761
Tel: (714) 989-9411

†Avnet Electronics
20501 Plummer
Chatsworth 91351
Tel: (213) 700-6271
TWX: 910-494-2207

†Hamilton Electro Sales
3170 Pullman Street
Costa Mesa 92626
Tel: (714) 641-4150
TWX: 910-595-2638

†Hamilton/Avnet Electronics
4103 Northgate Blvd.
Sacramento 95834
Tel: (916) 920-3150

Wyle Distribution Group
124 Maryland Street
El Segundo 90254
Tel: (213) 322-8100

Wyle Distribution Group
7382 Lampson Ave.
Garden Grove 92641
Tel: (714) 891-1717
TWX: 910-348-7140 or 7111

Wyle Distribution Group
11151 Sun Center Drive
Rancho Cordova 95670
Tel: (916) 638-5282

†Wyle Distribution Group
9525 Chesapeake Drive
San Diego 92123
Tel: (619) 565-9171
TWX: 910-335-1590

†Wyle Distribution Group
3000 Bowers Avenue
Santa Clara 95051
Tel: (408) 727-2500
TWX: 910-338-0296

†Wyle Distribution Group
17872 Cowan Avenue
Irvine 92714
Tel: (714) 863-9953
TWX: 910-595-1572

Wyle Distribution Group
26677 W. Agoura Rd.
Calabasas 91302
Tel: (818) 880-9000
TWX: 372-0232

COLORADO

Arrow Electronics, Inc.
7060 South Tucson Way
Englewood 80112
Tel: (303) 790-4444

†Hamilton/Avnet Electronics
8765 E. Orchard Road
Suite 708
Englewood 80111
Tel: (303) 740-1017
TWX: 910-935-0787

†Wyle Distribution Group
451 E. 124th Avenue
Thornton 80241
Tel: (303) 457-9953
TWX: 910-936-0770

CONNECTICUT

†Arrow Electronics, Inc.
12 Beaumont Road
Wallingford 06492
Tel: (203) 265-7741
TWX: 710-476-0162

Hamilton/Avnet Electronics
Commerce Industrial Park
Commerce Drive
Danbury 06810
Tel: (203) 797-2800
TWX: 710-456-9974

†Pioneer Electronics
112 Main Street
Norwalk 06851
Tel: (203) 853-1515
TWX: 710-468-3373

FLORIDA

†Arrow Electronics, Inc.
400 Fairway Drive
Suite 102
Deerfield Beach 33441
Tel: (305) 429-8200
TWX: 510-955-9456

Arrow Electronics, Inc.
37 Skyline Drive
Suite 3101
Lake Marv 32746
Tel: (407) 323-0252
TWX: 510-959-6337

†Hamilton/Avnet Electronics
6801 N.W. 15th Way
Ft. Lauderdale 33309
Tel: (305) 971-2900
TWX: 510-956-3097

†Hamilton/Avnet Electronics
3197 Tech Drive North
St. Petersburg 33702
Tel: (813) 576-3930
TWX: 810-863-0374

†Hamilton/Avnet Electronics
6947 University Boulevard
Winter Park 32792
Tel: (305) 628-3888
TWX: 810-853-0322

†Pioneer/Technologies Group, Inc.
337 S. Lake Blvd.
Alta Monte Springs 32701
Tel: (407) 834-9090
TWX: 810-853-0284

Pioneer/Technologies Group, Inc.
674 S. Military Trail
Deerfield Beach 33442
Tel: (305) 428-8877
TWX: 510-955-9653

GEORGIA

†Arrow Electronics, Inc.
3155 Northwoods Parkway
Suite A
Norcross 30071
Tel: (404) 449-8252
TWX: 810-766-0439

†Hamilton/Avnet Electronics
5825 D Peachtree Corners
Norcross 30092
Tel: (404) 447-7500
TWX: 810-766-0432

Pioneer/Technologies Group, Inc.
3100 F Northwoods Place
Norcross 30071
Tel: (404) 448-1711
TWX: 810-766-4515

ILLINOIS

Arrow Electronics, Inc.
1140 W. Thorndale
Itasca 60143
Tel: (312) 250-0500
TWX: 312-250-0916

†Hamilton/Avnet Electronics
1130 Thorndale Avenue
Bensenville 60106
Tel: (312) 860-7780
TWX: 910-227-0060

MTI Systems Sales
1100 W. Thorndale
Itasca 60143
Tel: (312) 773-2300

†Pioneer Electronics
1551 Carmen Drive
Elk Grove Village 60007
Tel: (312) 437-9680
TWX: 910-222-1834

INDIANA

†Arrow Electronics, Inc.
2495 Directors Row, Suite H
Indianapolis 46241
Tel: (317) 243-9353
TWX: 810-341-3119

Hamilton/Avnet Electronics
485 Gradle Drive
Carmel 46032
Tel: (317) 844-9333
TWX: 810-260-3966

†Pioneer Electronics
6408 Castleplace Drive
Indianapolis 46250
Tel: (317) 849-7300
TWX: 810-260-1794

IOWA

Hamilton/Avnet Electronics
915 33rd Avenue, S.W.
Cedar Rapids 52404
Tel: (319) 362-4757

KANSAS

Arrow Electronics
8208 Melrose Dr., Suite 210
Lenexa 66214
Tel: (913) 541-9542

†Hamilton/Avnet Electronics
9219 Quivera Road
Overland Park 66215
Tel: (913) 888-8900
TWX: 910-743-0005

Pioneer/Tec Gr.
10551 Lockman Rd.
Lenexa 66215
Tel: (913) 492-0500

KENTUCKY

Hamilton/Avnet Electronics
1051 D. Newton Park
Lexington 40511
Tel: (606) 259-1475

MARYLAND

Arrow Electronics, Inc.
8300 Guilford Drive
Suite H, River Center
Columbia 21046
Tel: (301) 995-0003
TWX: 710-236-9005

Hamilton/Avnet Electronics
6822 Oak Hall Lane
Columbia 21045
Tel: (301) 995-3500
TWX: 710-862-1861

†Mesa Technology Corp.
9720 Patuxent Woods Dr.
Columbia 21046
Tel: (301) 290-8150
TWX: 710-828-9702

†Pioneer/Technologies Group, Inc.
9100 Gaither Road
Gaithersburg 20877
Tel: (301) 921-0660
TWX: 710-828-0545

Arrow Electronics, Inc.
7524 Standish Place
Rockville 20855
Tel: 301-424-0244

MASSACHUSETTS

Arrow Electronics, Inc.
25 Upton Dr.
Wilmington 01887
Tel: (617) 935-5134

†Hamilton/Avnet Electronics
10D Centennial Drive
Peabody 01960
Tel: (617) 531-7430
TWX: 710-393-0382

MTI Systems Sales
83 Cambridge St.
Burlington 01813

Pioneer Electronics
44 Hartwell Avenue
Lexington 02173
Tel: (617) 861-9200
TWX: 710-326-6617

MICHIGAN

Arrow Electronics, Inc.
755 Phoenix Drive
Ann Arbor 48104
Tel: (313) 971-8220
TWX: 810-223-6020

Hamilton/Avnet Electronics
2215 29th Street S.E.
Space A5
Grand Rapids 49508
Tel: (616) 243-8805
TWX: 810-274-6921

Pioneer Electronics
4504 Broadmoor S.E.
Grand Rapids 49508
FAX: 616-698-1831

†Hamilton/Avnet Electronics
32487 Schoolcraft Road
Livonia 48150
Tel: (313) 522-4700
TWX: 810-282-8775

†Pioneer/Michigan
13485 Stamford
Livonia 48150
Tel: (313) 525-1800
TWX: 810-242-3271

MINNESOTA

†Arrow Electronics, Inc.
5230 W. 73rd Street
Edina 55435
Tel: (612) 830-1800
TWX: 910-576-3125

†Hamilton/Avnet Electronics
12400 Whitewater Drive
Minnetonka 55434
Tel: (612) 932-0600

†Pioneer Electronics
7625 Golden Triange Dr.
Suite G
Eden Prairi 55343
Tel: (612) 944-3355

MISSOURI

†Arrow Electronics, Inc.
2380 Schuetz
St. Louis 63141
Tel: (314) 567-6888
TWX: 910-764-0882

†Hamilton/Avnet Electronics
13743 Shoreline Court
Earth City 63045
Tel: (314) 344-1200
TWX: 910-762-0684

NEW HAMPSHIRE

†Arrow Electronics, Inc.
3 Perimeter Road
Manchester 03103
Tel: (603) 668-6968
TWX: 710-220-1684

†Hamilton/Avnet Electronics
444 E. Industrial Drive
Manchester 03103
Tel: (603) 624-9400

†Microcomputer System Technical Distributor Center

DOMESTIC DISTRIBUTORS (Contd.)

NEW JERSEY

†Arrow Electronics, Inc.
Four East Stow Road
Unit 11
Marlton 08053
Tel: (609) 596-8000
TWX: 710-897-0829

†Arrow Electronics
6 Century Drive
Parsipanny 07054
Tel: (201) 538-0900

†Hamilton/Avnet Electronics
1 Keystone Ave., Bldg. 36
Cherry Hill 08003
Tel: (609) 424-0110
TWX: 710-940-0262

†Hamilton/Avnet Electronics
10 Industrial
Fairfield 07006
Tel: (201) 575-5300
TWX: 710-734-4388

†MTI Systems Sales
37 Kulick Rd.
Fairfield 07006
Tel: (201) 227-5552

†Pioneer Electronics
45 Route 46
Pinebrook 07058
Tel: (201) 575-3510
TWX: 710-734-4382

NEW MEXICO

Alliance Electronics Inc.
11030 Cochiti S.E.
Albuquerque 87123
Tel: (505) 292-3360
TWX: 910-989-1151

Hamilton/Avnet Electronics
2524 Baylor Drive S.E.
Albuquerque 87106
Tel: (505) 765-1500
TWX: 910-989-0614

NEW YORK

†Arrow Electronics, Inc.
3375 Brighton Henrietta
Townline Rd.
Rochester 14623
Tel: (716) 275-0300
TWX: 510-253-4766

Arrow Electronics, Inc.
20 Oser Avenue
Hauppauge 11788
Tel: (516) 231-1000
TWX: 510-227-6623

Hamilton/Avnet
933 Motor Parkway
Hauppauge 11788
Tel: (516) 231-9800
TWX: 510-224-6166

†Hamilton/Avnet Electronics
333 Metro Park
Rochester 14623
Tel: (716) 475-9130
TWX: 510-253-5470

†Hamilton/Avnet Electronics
103 Twin Oaks Drive
Syracuse 13206
Tel: (315) 437-0288
TWX: 710-541-1560

†MTI Systems Sales
38 Harbor Park Drive
Port Washington 11050
Tel: (516) 621-6200

†Pioneer Electronics
68 Corporate Drive
Binghamton 13904
Tel: (607) 722-9300
TWX: 510-252-0893

Pioneer Electronics
40 Oser Avenue
Hauppauge 11787
Tel: (516) 231-9200

†Pioneer Electronics
60 Crossway Park West
Woodbury, Long Island 11797
Tel: (516) 921-8700
TWX: 510-221-2184

†Pioneer Electronics
840 Fairport Park
Fairport 14450
Tel: (716) 381-7070
TWX: 510-253-7001

NORTH CAROLINA

†Arrow Electronics, Inc.
5240 Greensdairy Road
Raleigh 27604
Tel: (919) 876-3132
TWX: 510-928-1856

†Hamilton/Avnet Electronics
3510 Spring Forest Drive
Raleigh 27604
Tel: (919) 878-0819
TWX: 510-928-1836

Pioneer/Technologies Group, Inc.
9801 A-Southern Pine Blvd.
Charlotte 28210
Tel: (919) 527-8188
TWX: 810-621-0366

OHIO

Arrow Electronics, Inc.
7620 McEwen Road
Centerville 45459
Tel: (513) 435-5563
TWX: 810-459-1611

†Arrow Electronics, Inc.
6238 Cochran Road
Solon 44139
Tel: (216) 248-3990
TWX: 810-427-9409

†Hamilton/Avnet Electronics
954 Senate Drive
Dayton 45459
Tel: (513) 439-6733
TWX: 810-450-2531

Hamilton/Avnet Electronics
1600 Emory Industrial Pkwy
Warrensville Heights 44128
Tel: (216) 349-5100
TWX: 810-427-9452

†Hamilton/Avnet Electronics
777 Brooksedge Blvd.
Westerville 43081
Tel: (614) 882-7004

†Pioneer Electronics
4433 Interpoint Boulevard
Dayton 45424
Tel: (513) 236-9900
TWX: 810-459-1622

†Pioneer Electronics
4800 E. 131st Street
Cleveland 44105
Tel: (216) 587-3600
TWX: 810-422-2211

OKLAHOMA

Arrow Electronics, Inc.
1211 E. 51st St., Suite 101
Tulsa 74146
Tel: (918) 252-7537

†Hamilton/Avnet Electronics
12121 E. 51st St., Suite 102A
Tulsa 74146
Tel: (918) 252-7297

OREGON

†Almac Electronics Corp.
1885 N.W. 169th Place
Beaverton 97005
Tel: (503) 629-8090
TWX: 910-467-8746

†Hamilton/Avnet Electronics
6024 S.W. Jean Road
Bldg. C, Suite 10
Lake Oswego 97034
Tel: (503) 635-7848
TWX: 910-455-8179

Wyle Distribution Group
5250 N.E. Elam Young Parkway
Suite 600
Hillsboro 97124
Tel: (503) 640-6000
TWX: 910-460-2203

PENNSYLVANIA

Arrow Electronics, Inc.
650 Seco Road
Monroeville 15146
Tel: (412) 856-7000

Hamilton/Avnet Electronics
2800 Liberty Ave.
Pittsburgh 15238
Tel: (412) 281-4150

Pioneer Electronics
259 Kappa Drive
Pittsburgh 15238
Tel: (412) 782-2300
TWX: 710-795-3122

†Pioneer/Technologies Group, Inc.
Delaware Valley
261 Gibralter Road
Horsham 19044
Tel: (215) 674-4000
TWX: 510-665-6778

TEXAS

†Arrow Electronics, Inc.
3220 Commander Drive
Carrollton 75006
Tel: (214) 380-6464
TWX: 910-860-5377

†Arrow Electronics, Inc.
10899 Kinghurst
Suite 100
Houston 77099
Tel: (713) 530-4700
TWX: 910-880-4439

†Arrow Electronics, Inc.
2227 W. Braker Lane
Austin 78758
Tel: (512) 835-4180
TWX: 910-874-1348

†Hamilton/Avnet Electronics
1807 W. Braker Lane
Austin 78758
Tel: (512) 837-8911
TWX: 910-874-1319

†Hamilton/Avnet Electronics
2111 W. Walnut Hill Lane
Irving 75038
Tel: (214) 550-6111
TWX: 910-860-5929

†Hamilton/Avnet Electronics
4850 Wright Rd., Suite 190
Stafford 77477
Tel: (713) 240-7733
TWX: 910-881-5523

†Pioneer Electronics
18260 Kramer
Austin 78758
Tel: (512) 835-4000
TWX: 910-874-1323

†Pioneer Electronics
13710 Omega Road
Dallas 75234
Tel: (214) 386-7300
TWX: 910-850-5563

†Pioneer Electronics
5853 Point West Drive
Houston 77036
Tel: (713) 988-5555
TWX: 910-881-1606

Wyle Distribution Group
1810 Greenville Avenue
Richardson 75081
Tel: (214) 235-9953

UTAH

Arrow Electronics
1946 Parkway Blvd.
Salt Lake City 84119
Tel: (801) 973-6913

†Hamilton/Avnet Electronics
1585 West 2100 South
Salt Lake City 84119
Tel: (801) 972-2800
TWX: 910-925-4018

Wyle Distribution Group
1325 West 2200 South
Suite E
West Valley 84119
Tel: (801) 974-9953

WASHINGTON

†Almac Electronics Corp.
14360 S.E. Eastgate Way
Bellevue 98007
Tel: (206) 643-9992
TWX: 910-444-2067

Arrow Electronics, Inc.
19540 68th Ave. South
Kent 98032
Tel: (206) 575-4420

†Hamilton/Avnet Electronics
14212 N.E. 21st Street
Bellevue 98005
Tel: (206) 643-3950
TWX: 910-443-2469

Wyle Distribution Group
15385 N.E. 90th Street
Redmond 98052
Tel: (206) 881-1150

WISCONSIN

Arrow Electronics, Inc.
200 N. Patrick Blvd., Ste. 100
Brookfield 53005
Tel: (414) 767-6600
TWX: 910-262-1193

Hamilton/Avnet Electronics
2975 Moorland Road
New Berlin 53151
Tel: (414) 784-4510
TWX: 910-262-1182

CANADA

ALBERTA

Hamilton/Avnet Electronics
2816 21st Street N.E.
Calgary T2E 6Z3
Tel: (403) 230-3586
TWX: 03-827-642

Zentronics
Bay No. 1
3300 14th Avenue N.E.
Calgary T2A 6J4
Tel: (403) 272-1021

BRITISH COLUMBIA

†Hamilton/Avnet Electronics
105-2550 Boundary
Burmalay V5M 3Z3
Tel: (604) 437-6667

Zentronics
108-11400 Bridgeport Road
Richmond V6X 1T2
Tel: (604) 273-5575
TWX: 04-5077-89

MANITOBA

Zentronics
60-1313 Border Unit 60
Winnipeg R3H 0X4
Tel: (204) 694-1957

ONTARIO

Arrow Electronics, Inc.
36 Antares Dr.
Nepean K2E 7W5
Tel: (613) 226-6903

Arrow Electronics, Inc.
1093 Meyerside
Mississauga L5T 1M4
Tel: (416) 673-7769
TWX: 06-218213

†Hamilton/Avnet Electronics
6845 Rexwood Road
Units 3-4-5
Mississauga L4T 1R2
Tel: (416) 677-7432
TWX: 610-492-8867

Hamilton/Avnet Electronics
6845 Rexwood Rd., Unit 6
Mississauga L4T 1R2
Tel: (416) 277-0484

†Hamilton/Avnet Electronics
190 Colonnade Road South
Nepean K2E 7L5
Tel: (613) 226-1700
TWX: 05-349-71

†Zentronics
8 Tilbury Court
Brampton L6T 3T4
Tel: (416) 451-9600
TWX: 06-976-78

†Zentronics
155 Colonnade Road
Unit 17
Nepean K2E 7K1
Tel: (613) 226-8840

Zentronics
60-1313 Border St.
Winnipeg R3H 0I4
Tel: (204) 694-7957

QUEBEC

†Arrow Electronics Inc.
4050 Jean Talon Quest
Montreal H4P 1W1
Tel: (514) 735-5511
TWX: 05-25590

Arrow Electronics, Inc.
500 Avenue St-Jean Baptiste
Suite 280
Quebec G2E 5R9
Tel: (418) 871-7500
FAX: 418-871-6816

Hamilton/Avnet Electronics
2795 Halpern
St. Laurent H2E 7K1
Tel: (514) 335-1000
TWX: 610-421-3731

Zentronics
817 McCaffrey
St. Laurent H4T 1M3
Tel: (514) 737-9700
TWX: 05-827-535

†Microcomputer System Technical Distributor Center

intel®

EUROPEAN SALES OFFICES

DENMARK

Intel Denmark A/S
Glentevej 61, 3rd Floor
2400 Copenhagen NV
Tel: (45) (31) 19 80 33
TLX: 19567

FINLAND

Intel Finland OY
Ruosilantie 2
00390 Helsinki
Tel: (358) 0 544 644
TLX: 123332

FRANCE

Intel Corporation S.A.R.L.
1, Rue Edison-BP 303
78054 St. Quentin-en-Yvelines
Cedex
Tel: (33) (1) 30 57 70 00
TLX: 699016

WEST GERMANY

Intel Semiconductor GmbH*
Dornacher Strasse 1
8016 Feldkirchen bei Muenchen
Tel: (49) 089/90992-0
TLX: 5-23177

Intel Semiconductor GmbH
Hohenzollern Strasse 5
3000 Hannover 1
Tel: (49) 0511/344081
TLX: 9-23625

Intel Semiconductor GmbH
Abraham Lincoln Strasse 16-18
6200 Wiesbaden
Tel: (49) 06121/7605-0
TLX: 4-186183

Intel Semiconductor GmbH
Zettachring 10A
7000 Stuttgart 80
Tel: (49) 0711/7287-280
TLX: 7-254826

ISRAEL

Intel Semiconductor Ltd.*
Atidim Industrial Park-Neve Sharet
P.O. Box 43202
Tel-Aviv 61430
Tel: (972) 03-498080
TLX: 371215

ITALY

Intel Corporation Italia S.p.A.*
Milanofiori Palazzo E
20090 Assago
Milano
Tel: (39) (02) 89200950
TLX: 341286

NETHERLANDS

Intel Semiconductor B.V.*
Postbus 84130
3099 CC Rotterdam
Tel: (31) 10.407.11.11
TLX: 22283

NORWAY

Intel Norway A/S
Hvamveien 4-PO Box 92
2013 Skjetten
Tel: (47) (6) 842 420
TLX: 78018

SPAIN

Intel Iberia S.A.
Zurbaran, 28
28010 Madrid
Tel: (34) (1) 308.25.52
TLX: 46880

SWEDEN

Intel Sweden A.B.*
Dalvagen 24
171 36 Solna
Tel: (46) 8 734 01 00
TLX: 12261

SWITZERLAND

Intel Semiconductor A.G.
Zuerichstrasse
8185 Winkel-Rueti bei Zuerich
Tel: (41) 01/860 62 62
TLX: 825977

UNITED KINGDOM

Intel Corporation (U.K.) Ltd.*
Pipers Way
Swindon, Wiltshire SN3 1RJ
Tel: (44) (0793) 696000
TLX: 444447/8

EUROPEAN DISTRIBUTORS/REPRESENTATIVES

AUSTRIA

Bacher Electronics G.m.b.H.
Rotenmuehlgasse 26
1120 Wien
Tel: (43) (0222) 83 56 46
TLX: 31532

BELGIUM

Inelco Belgium S.A.
Av. des Croix de Guerre 94
1120 Bruxelles
Oorlogskruisenlaan, 94
1120 Brussel
Tel: (32) (02) 216 01 60
TLX: 64475 or 22090

DENMARK

ITT-Multikomponent
Naverland 29
2600 Glostrup
Tel: (45) (0) 2 45 66 45
TLX: 33 355

FINLAND

OY Fintronic AB
Melkonkatu 24A
00210 Helsinki
Tel: (358) (0) 6926022
TLX: 124224

FRANCE

Almex
Zone industrielle d'Antony
48, rue de l'Aubepine
BP 102
92164 Antony cedex
Tel: (33) (1) 46 66 21 12
TLX: 250067

Jermyn-Generim
60, rue des Gemeaux
Silic 580
94653 Rungis cedex
Tel: (33) (1) 49 78 49 78
TLX: 261585

Metrologie
Tour d'Asnieres
4, av. Laurent-Cely
92606 Asnieres Cedex
Tel: (33) (1) 47 90 62 40
TLX: 611448

Tekelec-Airtronic
Cite des Bruyeres
Rue Carle Vernet - BP 2
92310 Sevres
Tel: (33) (1) 45 34 75 35
TLX: 204552

WEST GERMANY

Electronic 2000 AG
Stahlgruberring 12
8000 Muenchen 82
Tel: (49) 089/42001-0
TLX: 522561

ITT Multikomponent GmbH
Postfach 1265
Bahnhofstrasse 44
7141 Moeglingen
Tel: (49) 07141/4879
TLX: 7264472

Jermyn GmbH
Im Dachsstueck 9
6250 Limburg
Tel: (49) 06431/508-0
TLX: 415257-0

Metrologie GmbH
Meglingerstrasse 49
8000 Muenchen 71
Tel: (49) 089/78042-0
TLX: 5213189

Proelectron Vertriebs GmbH
Max Planck Strasse 1-3
6072 Dreieich
Tel: (49) 06103/30434-3
TLX: 417903

IRELAND

Micro Marketing Ltd.
Glenageary Office Park
Glenageary
Co. Dublin
Tel: (21) (353) (01) 85 63 25
TLX: 31584

ISRAEL

Eastronics Ltd.
11 Rozanis Street
P.O.B. 39300
Tel-Aviv 61392
Tel: (972) 03-475151
TLX: 33638

ITALY

Intesi
Divisione ITT Industries GmbH
Viale Milanofiori
Palazzo E/5
20090 Assago (MI)
Tel: (39) 02/824701
TLX: 311351

Lasi Elettronica S.p.A.
V. le Fulvio Testi, 126
20092 Cinisello Balsamo (MI)
Tel: (39) 02/2440012
TLX: 352040

Telcom S.r.l.
Via M. Civitali 75
20148 Milano
Tel: (39) 02/4049046
TLX: 335654

ITT Multicomponents
Viale Milanofiori E/5
20090 Assago (MI)
Tel: (39) 02/824701
TLX: 311351

Silverstar
Via Dei Gracchi 20
20146 Milano
Tel: (39) 02/49961
TLX: 332189

NETHERLANDS

Koning en Hartman Elektrotechniek
B.V.
Energieweg 1
2627 AP Delft
Tel: (31) (0) 15/609906
TLX: 38250

NORWAY

Nordisk Elektronikk (Norge) A/S
Postboks 123
Smedsvingen 4
1364 Hvalstad
Tel: (47) (02) 84 62 10
TLX: 77546

PORTUGAL

ATD Portugal LDA
Rua Dos Lusiados, 5 Sala B
1300 Lisboa
Tel: (35) (1) 64 80 91
TLX: 61562

Ditram
Avenida Miguel Bombarda, 133
1000 Lisboa
Tel: (35) (1) 54 53 13
TLX: 14182

SPAIN

ATD Electronica, S.A.
Plaza Ciudad de Viena, 6
28040 Madrid
Tel: (34) (1) 234 40 00
TLX: 42477

ITT-SESA
Calle Miguel Angel, 21-3
28010 Madrid
Tel: (34) (1) 419 09 57
TLX: 27461

Metrologia Iberica, S.A.
Ctra. de Fuencarral, n.80
28100 Alcobendas (Madrid)
Tel: (34) (1) 653 86 11

SWEDEN

Nordisk Elektronik AB
Torshamnsgatan 39
Box 36
164 93 Kista
Tel: (46) 08-03 46 30
TLX: 105 47

SWITZERLAND

Industrade A.G.
Hertistrasse 31
8304 Wallisellen
Tel: (41) (01) 8328111
TLX: 56788

TURKEY

EMPA Electronic
Lindwurmstrasse 95A
8000 Muenchen 2
Tel: (49) 089/53 80 570
TLX: 528573

UNITED KINGDOM

Accent Electronic Components Ltd.
Jubilee House, Jubilee Road
Letchworth, Herts SG6 1TL
Tel: (44) (0462) 686666
TLX: 826293

Bytech-Comway Systems
3 The Western Centre
Western Road
Bracknell RG12 1RW
Tel: (44) (0344) 55333
TLX: 847201

Jermyn
Vestry Estate
Otford Road
Sevenoaks
Kent TN14 5EU
Tel: (44) (0732) 450144
TLX: 95142

MMD
Unit 8 Southview Park
Caversham
Reading
Berkshire RG4 0AF
Tel: (44) (0734) 481666
TLX: 846669

Rapid Silicon
Rapid House
Denmark Street
High Wycombe
Buckinghamshire HP11 2ER
Tel: (44) (0494) 442266
TLX: 837931

Rapid Systems
Rapid House
Denmark Street
High Wycombe
Buckinghamshire HP11 2ER
Tel: (44) (0494) 450244
TLX: 837931

YUGOSLAVIA

H.R. Microelectronics Corp.
2005 de la Cruz Blvd., Ste. 223
Santa Clara, CA 95050
U.S.A.
Tel: (1) (408) 988-0286
TLX: 387452

Rapido Electronic Components
S.p.a.
Via C. Beccaria, 8
34133 Trieste
Italia
Tel: (39) 040/360555
TLX: 460461

*Field Application Location

INTERNATIONAL SALES OFFICES

AUSTRALIA

Intel Australia Pty. Ltd.*
Spectrum Building
200 Pacific Hwy., Level 6
Crows Nest, NSE, 2065
Tel: 612-957-2744
FAX: 612-923-2632

BRAZIL

Intel Semicondutores do Brazil LTDA
Av. Paulista, 1159-CJS 404/405
01311 - Sao Paulo - S.P.
Tel: 55-11-287-5899
TLX: 3911153146 ISDB
FAX: 55-11-287-5119

CHINA/HONG KONG

Intel PRC Corporation
15/F, Office 1, Citic Bldg.
Jian Guo Men Wai Street
Beijing, PRC
Tel: (1) 500-4850
TLX: 22947 INTEL CN
FAX: (1) 500-2953

Intel Semiconductor Ltd.*
10/F East Tower
Bond Center
Queensway, Central
Hong Kong
Tel: (5) 8444-555
TLX: 63869 ISHLHK HX
FAX: (5) 8681-989

INDIA

Intel Asia Electronics, Inc.
4/2, Samrah Plaza
St. Mark's Road
Bangalore 560001
Tel: 011-91-812-215065
TLX: 9538452875 DCBY
FAX: 091-812-215067

JAPAN

Intel Japan K.K.
5-6 Tokodai, Tsukuba-shi
Ibaraki, 300-26
Tel: 0298-47-8511
TLX: 3656-160
FAX: 029747-8450

Intel Japan K.K.*
Daiichi Mitsugi Bldg.
1-8889 Fuchu-cho
Fuchu-shi, Tokyo 183
Tel: 0423-60-7871
FAX: 0423-60-0315

Intel Japan K.K.*
Bldg. Kumagaya
2-69 Hon-cho
Kumagaya-shi, Saitama 360
Tel: 0485-24-6871
FAX: 0485-24-7518

Intel Japan K.K.*
Mitsui-Seimei Musashi-kosugi Bldg.
915 Shinmaruko, Nakahara-ku
Kawasaki-shi, Kanagawa 211
Tel: 044-733-7011
FAX: 044-733-7010

Intel Japan K.K.
Nihon Seimei Atsugi Bldg.
1-2-1 Asahi-machi
Atsugi-shi, Kanagawa 243
Tel: 0462-29-3731
FAX: 0462-29-3781

Intel Japan K.K.*
Ryokuchi-Eki Bldg.
2-4-1 Terauchi
Toyonaka-shi, Osaka 560
Tel: 06-863-1091
FAX: 06-863-1084

Intel Japan K.K.
Shinmaru Bldg.
1-5-1 Marunouchi
Chiyoda-ku, Tokyo 100
Tel: 03-201-3621
FAX: 03-201-6850

Intel Japan K.K.
Green Bldg.
1-16-20 Nishiki
Naka-ku, Nagoya-shi
Aichi 450
Tel: 052-204-1261
FAX: 052-204-1285

KOREA

Intel Technology Asia, Ltd.
16th Floor, Life Bldg.
61 Yoido-dong, Youngdeungpo-Ku
Seoul 150-010
Tel: (2) 784-8186, 3286, 8386
TLX: K29312 INTELKO
FAX: (2) 784-8096

SINGAPORE

Intel Singapore Technology, Ltd.
101 Thomson Road #21-05/06
United Square
Singapore 1130
Tel: 250-7811
TLX: 39921 INTEL
FAX: 250-9256

TAIWAN

Intel Technology Far East Ltd.
8th Floor, No. 205
Bank Tower Bldg.
Tung Hua N. Road
Taipei
Tel: 886-2-716-9660
FAX: 886-2-717-2455

INTERNATIONAL DISTRIBUTORS/REPRESENTATIVES

ARGENTINA

DAFSYS S.R.L.
Chacabuco, 90-6 PISO
1069-Buenos Aires
Tel: 54-1-334-7726
FAX: 54-1-334-1871

AUSTRALIA

Email Electronics
15-17 Hume Street
Huntingdale, 3166
Tel: 011-61-3-544-8244
TLX: AA 30895
FAX: 011-61-3-543-8179

NSD-Australia
205 Middleborough Rd.
Box Hill, Victoria 3128
Tel: 03 8000070
FAX: 03 8990819

BRAZIL

Elebra Microelectronica S.A.
Rua Geraldo Flausina Gomes, 78
10th Floor
04575 - Sao Paulo - S.P.
Tel: 55-11-534-9641
TLX: 55-11-54593/54591
FAX: 55-11-534-9424

CHILE

DIN Instruments
Suecia 2323
Casilla 6055, Correo 22
Santiago
Tel: 56-2-225-8139
TLX: 240.846 RUD

CHINA/HONG KONG

Novel Precision Machinery Co., Ltd.
Flat D, 20 Kingsford Ind. Bldg.
Phase 1, 26 Kwai Hei Street
N.T., Kowloon
Hong Kong
Tel: 852-0-4223222
TWX: 39114 JINMI HX
FAX: 852-0-4261602

INDIA

Micronic Devices
Arun Complex
No. 65 D.V.G. Road
Basavanagudi
Bangalore 560 004
Tel: 011-91-812-600-631
011-91-812-611-365
TLX: 9538458332 MDBG

Micronic Devices
No. 516 5th Floor
Swastik Chambers
Sion, Trombay Road
Chembur
Bombay 400 071
TLX: 9531 171447 MDEV

Micronic Devices
25/8, 1st Floor
Bada Bazaar Marg
Old Rajinder Nagar
New Delhi 110 060
Tel: 011-91-11-5723509
011-91-11-589771
TLX: 031 63263 MDND IN

Micronic Devices
6-3-348/12A Dwarakapuri Colony
Hyderabad 500 482
Tel: 011-91-842-226748

S&S Corporation
1587 Kooser Road
San Jose, CA 95118
Tel: (408) 978-6216
TLX: 820281
FAX: (408) 978-8635

JAPAN

Asahi Electronics Co. Ltd.
KMM Bldg. 2-14-1 Asano
Kokurakita-ku
Kitakyushu-shi 802
Tel: 093-511-6471
FAX: 093-551-7861

C. Itoh Techno-Science Co., Ltd.
4-8-1 Dobashi, Miyamae-ku
Kawasaki-shi, Kanagawa 213
Tel: 044-852-5121
FAX: 044-877-4268

Dia Semicon Systems, Inc.
Flower Hill Shinmachi Higashi-kan
1-23-9 Shinmachi, Setagaya-ku
Tokyo 154
Tel: 03-439-1600
FAX: 03-439-1601

Okaya Koki
2-4-18 Sakae
Naka-ku, Nagoya-shi 460
Tel: 052-204-2916
FAX: 052-204-2901

Ryoyo Electro Corp.
Konwa Bldg.
1-12-22 Tsukiji
Chuo-ku, Tokyo 104
Tel: 03-546-5011
FAX: 03-546-5044

KOREA

J-Tek Corporation
6th Floor, Government Pension Bldg.
24-3 Yoido-dong
Youngdeungpo-ku
Seoul 150-010
Tel: 82-2-780-8039
TLX: 25299 KODIGIT
FAX: 82-2-784-8391

Samsung Electronics
150 Taepyungro-2 KA
Chungku, Seoul 100-102
Tel: 82-2-751-3985
TLX: 27970 KORSST
FAX: 82-2-753-0967

MEXICO

SSB Electronics, Inc.
675 Palomar Street, Bldg. 4, Suite A
Chula Vista, CA 92011
Tel: (619) 585-3253
TLX: 287751 CBALL UR
FAX: (619) 585-8322

Dicopel S.A.
Tochtli 368 Fracc. Ind. San Antonio
Azcapotzalco
C.P. 02760-Mexico, D.F.
Tel: 52-5-561-3211
TLX: 177 3790 Dicome
FAX: 52-5-561-1279

PSI de Mexico
Francisco Villas Esq. Ajusto
Cuernavaca – Morelos – CEP 62130
Tel: 52-73-13-9412
FAX: 52-73-17-5333

NEW ZEALAND

Email Electronics
36 Olive Road
Penrose, Auckland
Tel: 011-64-9-591-155
FAX: 011-64-9-592-681

SINGAPORE

Electronic Resources Pte, Ltd.
17 Harvey Road #04-01
Singapore 1336
Tel: 283-0888
TWX: 56541 ERS
FAX: 2895327

SOUTH AFRICA

Electronic Building Elements
178 Erasmus Street (off Watermeyet Street)
Meyerspark, Pretoria, 0184
Tel: 011-2712-803-7680
FAX: 011-2712-803-8294

TAIWAN

Micro Electronics Corporation
5/F 587, Ming Shen East Rd.
Taipei, R.O.C.
Tel: 886-2-501-8231
FAX: 886-2-505-6609

Sertek
15/F 135, Section 2
Chien Juo North Rd.
Taipei 10479, R.O.C.
Tel: (02) 5010055
FAX: (02) 5012521
(02) 5058414

VENEZUELA

P. Benavides S.A.
Avilanes a Rio
Residencia Kamarata
Locales 4 AL 7
La Candelaria, Caracas
Tel: 58-2-574-6338
TLX: 28450
FAX: 58-2-572-3321

*Field Application Location

DOMESTIC SERVICE OFFICES

ALABAMA

*Intel Corp.
5015 Bradford Dr., Suite 2
Huntsville 35805
Tel: (205) 830-4010

ALASKA

Intel Corp.
c/o TransAlaska Data Systems
300 Old Steese Hwy.
Fairbanks 99701-3120
Tel: (907) 452-4401

Intel Corp.
c/o TransAlaska Data Systems
1551 Lore Road
Anchorage 99507
Tel: (907) 522-1776

ARIZONA

*Intel Corp.
11225 N. 28th Dr.
Suite D-214
Phoenix 85029
Tel: (602) 869-4980

*Intel Corp.
500 E. Fry Blvd., Suite M-15
Sierra Vista 85635
Tel: (602) 459-5010

CALIFORNIA

†Intel Corp.
21515 Vanowen St., Ste. 116
Canoga Park 91303
Tel: (818) 704-8500

*Intel Corp.
2250 E. Imperial Hwy., Ste. 218
El Segundo 90245
Tel: (213) 640-6040

*Intel Corp.
1900 Prairie City Rd.
Folsom 95630-9597
Tel: (916) 351-6143
1-800-468-3548

Intel Corp.
9665 Cheasapeake Dr., Suite 325
San Diego 92123-1326
Tel: (619) 292-8086

**Intel Corp.
400 N. Tustin Avenue
Suite 450
Santa Ana 92705
Tel: (714) 835-9642

**†Intel Corp.
San Tomas 4
2700 San Tomas Exp., 2nd Floor
Santa Clara 95051
Tel: (408) 986-8086

COLORADO

*Intel Corp.
650 S. Cherry St., Suite 915
Denver 80222
Tel: (303) 321-8086

CONNECTICUT

*Intel Corp.
301 Lee Farm Corporate Park
83 Wooster Heights Rd.
Danbury 06810
Tel: (203) 748-3130

FLORIDA

**Intel Corp.
6363 N.W. 6th Way, Ste. 100
Ft. Lauderdale 33309
Tel: (305) 771-0600

*Intel Corp.
5850 T.G. Lee Blvd., Ste. 340
Orlando 32822
Tel: (407) 240-8000

GEORGIA

*Intel Corp.
3280 Pointe Pkwy., Ste. 200
Norcross 30092
Tel: (404) 449-0541

HAWAII

*Intel Corp.
U.S.I.S.C. Signal Batt.
Building T-1521
Shafter Plats
Shafter 96856

ILLINOIS

**†Intel Corp.
300 N. Martingale Rd., Ste. 400
Schaumburg 60173
Tel: (312) 605-8031

INDIANA

*Intel Corp.
8777 Purdue Rd., Ste. 125
Indianapolis 46268
Tel: (317) 875-0623

KANSAS

*Intel Corp.
10985 Cody, Suite 140
Overland Park 66210
Tel: (913) 345-2727

MARYLAND

**†Intel Corp.
10010 Junction Dr., Suite 200
Annapolis Junction 20701
Tel: (301) 206-2860
FAX: 301-206-3677

MASSACHUSETTS

**†Intel Corp.
3 Carlisle Rd., 2nd Floor
Westford 01886
Tel: (508) 692-1060

MICHIGAN

*†Intel Corp.
7071 Orchard Lake Rd., Ste. 100
West Bloomfield 48322
Tel: (313) 851-8905

MINNESOTA

*†Intel Corp.
3500 W. 80th St., Suite 360
Bloomington 55431
Tel: (612) 835-6722

MISSOURI

*Intel Corp.
4203 Earth City Exp., Ste. 131
Earth City 63045
Tel: (314) 291-1990

NEW JERSEY

**Intel Corp.
300 Sylvan Avenue
Englewood Cliffs 07632
Tel: (201) 567-0821

*Intel Corp.
Parkway 109 Office Center
328 Newman Springs Road
Red Bank 07701
Tel: (201) 747-2233

*Intel Corp.
280 Corporate Center
75 Livingston Ave., 1st Floor
Roseland 07068
Tel: (201) 740-0111

NEW YORK

*†Intel Corp.
2950 Expressway Dr. South
Islandia 11722
Tel: (516) 231-3300

*Intel Corp.
Westage Business Center
Bldg. 300, Route 9
Fishkill 12524
Tel: (914) 897-3860

NORTH CAROLINA

*Intel Corp.
5800 Executive Dr., Ste. 105
Charlotte 28212
Tel: (704) 568-8966

**Intel Corp.
2700 Wycliff Road
Suite 102
Raleigh 27607
Tel: (919) 781-8022

OHIO

**†Intel Corp.
3401 Park Center Dr., Ste. 220
Dayton 45414
Tel: (513) 890-5350

*†Intel Corp.
25700 Science Park Dr., Ste. 100
Beachwood 44122
Tel: (216) 464-2736

OREGON

Intel Corp.
15254 N.W. Greenbrier Parkway
Building B
Beaverton 97005
Tel: (503) 645-8051

*Intel Corp.
5200 N.E. Elam Young Parkway
Hillsboro 97123
Tel: (503) 681-8080

PENNSYLVANIA

*†Intel Corp.
455 Pennsylvania Ave., Ste. 230
Fort Washington 19034
Tel: (215) 641-1000

†Intel Corp.
400 Penn Center Blvd., Ste. 610
Pittsburgh 15235
Tel: (412) 823-4970

Intel Corp.
1513 Cedar Cliff Dr.
Camp Hill 17011
Tel: (717) 761-0860

PUERTO RICO

Intel Corp.
South Industrial Park
P.O. Box 910
Las Piedras 00671
Tel: (809) 733-8616

TEXAS

Intel Corp.
8815 Dyer St., Suite 225
El Paso 79904
Tel: (915) 751-0186

*Intel Corp.
313 E. Anderson Lane, Suite 314
Austin 78752
Tel: (512) 454-3628

**†Intel Corp.
12000 Ford Rd., Suite 401
Dallas 75234
Tel: (214) 241-8087

*Intel Corp.
7322 S.W. Freeway, Ste. 1490
Houston 77074
Tel: (713) 988-8086

UTAH

Intel Corp.
428 East 6400 South, Ste. 104
Murray 84107
Tel: (801) 263-8051

VIRGINIA

*Intel Corp.
1504 Santa Rosa Rd., Ste. 108
Richmond 23288
Tel: (804) 282-5668

WASHINGTON

*Intel Corp.
155 108th Avenue N.E., Ste. 386
Bellevue 98004
Tel: (206) 453-8086

CANADA

ONTARIO

Intel Semiconductor of
Canada, Ltd.
2650 Queensview Dr., Ste. 250
Ottawa K2B 8H6
Tel: (613) 829-9714
FAX: 613-820-5936

Intel Semiconductor of
Canada, Ltd.
190 Attwell Dr., Ste. 102
Rexdale M9W 6H8
Tel: (416) 675-2105
FAX: 416-675-2438

CUSTOMER TRAINING CENTERS

CALIFORNIA

2700 San Tomas Expressway
Santa Clara 95051
Tel: (408) 970-1700
1-800-421-0386

ILLINOIS

300 N. Martingale Road
Suite 300
Schaumburg 60173
Tel: (708) 706-5700
1-800-421-0386

MASSACHUSETTS

3 Carlisle Road, First Floor
Westford 01886
Tel: (301) 220-3380
1-800-328-0386

MARYLAND

10010 Junction Dr.
Suite 200
Annapolis Junction 20701
Tel: (301) 206-2860
1-800-328-0386

SYSTEMS ENGINEERING MANAGERS OFFICES

MINNESOTA

3500 W. 80th Street
Suite 360
Bloomington 55431
Tel: (612) 835-6722

NEW YORK

2950 Expressway Dr., South
Islandia 11722
Tel: (506) 231-3300

†System Engineering locations
*Carry-in locations
**Carry-in/mail-in locations